Sermons On The First Readings

Series III

Cycle C

Derl G. Keefer
David J. Kalas
Stephen P. McCutchan
Chrysanne Timm
R. Kevin Mohr

CSS Publishing Company, Inc., Lima, Ohio

SERMONS ON THE FIRST READINGS, SERIES III, CYCLE C

Some scripture quotations are from the New Revised Standard Version of the Bible, copyright 1989 by the Division of Christian Education of the National Council of the Churches of Christ in the USA. Used by permission.

Some scripture quotations are from the Revised Standard Version of the Bible, copyrighted 1946, 1952 ©, 1971, 1973, by the Division of Christian Education of the National Council of the Churches of Christ in the USA. Used by permission.

Some scripture quotations are from the Holy Bible, New Living Translation, copyright © 1996. Used by permission of Tyndale House Publishers, Inc., Wheaton, Illinois 60189. All rights reserved.

Some scripture quotations are from the New American Standard Bible, © 1960, 1962, 1963, 1968, 1971, 1972, 1973, 1975, 1977 by The Lockman Foundation. Used by permission.

Some scripture quotations are from the Holy Bible, New International Version. Copyright © 1973, 1978, 1984, International Bible Society. Used by permission of Zondervan Bible Publishers. All rights reserved.

Some scripture quotations are from the Holy Bible, Today's New International Version. Copyright © 2001, 2005 by International Bible Society. Used by permission of Zondervan. All rights reserved.

For more information about CSS Publishing Company resources, visit our website at www.csspub.com or email us at csr@csspub.com or call (800) 241-4056.

Cover design by Barbara Spencer

ISSN: 1937-1446

ISBN-13: 978-0-7880-2619-5
ISBN-10: 0-7880-2619-4

PRINTED IN USA

Table Of Contents

Sermons For Sundays
In Advent, Christmas, And Epiphany
From Tragedy To Redemption
by Derl G. Keefer

Advent 1   **15**
God's Gift
Jeremiah 33:14-16

Advent 2   **21**
Finding Redemption In The Midst Of Judgment
Malachi 3:1-4

Advent 3   **29**
Hope Again!
Zephaniah 3:14-20

Advent 4   **35**
Born At Bethlehem — Hope
Micah 5:2-5a

Christmas Eve/Christmas Day   **41**
Born In Bethlehem — Light
Isaiah 9:2-7

Christmas 1   **47**
Hidden Potential
1 Samuel 2:18-20, 26

Christmas 2   **53**
From Tragedy To Salvation
Jeremiah 31:7-14

The Epiphany Of Our Lord   59
To God Be The Glory!
Isaiah 60:1-6

The Baptism Of Our Lord   65
Epiphany 1
Ordinary Time 1
A New Life
Isaiah 43:1-7

Epiphany 2   71
Ordinary Time 2
A New Name
Isaiah 62:1-5

Epiphany 3   79
Ordinary Time 3
The Winning Word
Nehemiah 8:1-3, 5-6, 8-10

Epiphany 4   87
Ordinary Time 4
The Call Of God
Jeremiah 1:4-10

Epiphany 5   93
Ordinary Time 5
The Call Of Holiness
Isaiah 6:1-8 (9-13)

Epiphany 6   99
Ordinary Time 6
Lessons From A Hurricane
Jeremiah 17:5-10

Epiphany 7   105
Ordinary Time 7
Breaking The Cycle — God's Answer In Forgiveness
Genesis 45:3-11, 15

Epiphany 8   **111**
Ordinary Time 8
    Restarting Joy — Rejoice
    Isaiah 55:10-13

Epiphany 9   **117**
Ordinary Time 9
    Strengthening Your Grip On Prayer
    1 Kings 8:22-23, 41-43

The Transfiguration Of Our Lord   **123**
(Last Sunday After Epiphany)
    The Radiant Life
    Exodus 34:29-35

                    Sermons For Sundays
                    In Lent And Easter
                    God All Along
                    by David J. Kalas
Ash Wednesday   **131**
    Trumpet Medley
    Joel 2:1-2, 12-17

Lent 1   **137**
    Anatomy Of A Testimony
    Deuteronomy 26:1-11

Lent 2   **143**
    A Resume Of Righteousness
    Genesis 15:1-12, 17-18

Lent 3   **149**
    RSVP
    Isaiah 55:1-9

Lent 4   **155**
    Joshua's New Diet
    Joshua 5:9-12

Lent 5   **161**
   Heisman In The Hudson
   Isaiah 43:16-21

Passion/Palm Sunday   **167**
   Profile Of A Savior
   Isaiah 50:4-9a

Maundy Thursday   **173**
   Prelude To A Sacrament
   Exodus 12:1-4 (5-10) 11-14

Good Friday   **179**
   That's Why We Call It Good
   Isaiah 52:13—53:12

Easter Day   **185**
   The Gospel According To Pronouns
   Acts 10:34-43

Easter 2   **191**
   A Tale Of Two Peters
   Acts 5:27-32

Easter 3   **197**
   God All Along
   Acts 9:1-6 (7-20)

Easter 4   **203**
   The Good Works We Leave Behind
   Acts 9:36-43

Easter 5   **209**
   Look Who's Talking
   Acts 11:1-18

Easter 6   **215**
    The Man Who Wasn't There
    Acts 16:9-15

The Ascension Of Our Lord   **221**
    A Stupid Question
    Acts 1:1-11

Easter 7   **227**
    The Place Of Prayer
    Acts 16:16-34

**Sermons For Sundays
After Pentecost (First Third)**
God's Playful Wisdom
by Stephen P. McCutchan
The Day Of Pentecost   **235**
    Birthdays And Marriages
    Acts 2:1-21

The Holy Trinity   **241**
    God's Playful Wisdom
    Proverbs 8:1-4, 22-31

Proper 4   **245**
Pentecost 2
Ordinary Time 9
    Mugwumpers
    1 Kings 18:20-21 (22-29) 30-39

Proper 5   **251**
Pentecost 3
Ordinary Time 10
    The Sinner And The Sinned Against
    1 Kings 17:1-24

Proper 6   **255**
Pentecost 4
Ordinary Time 11
  On Loan From God
  1 Kings 21:1-10 (11-14) 15-21a

Proper 7   **259**
Pentecost 5
Ordinary Time 12
  At Points Of Despair
  1 Kings 19:1-4 (5-7) 8-15a

Proper 8   **263**
Pentecost 6
Ordinary Time 13
  Seeing A Chariot Of Fire
  2 Kings 2:1-2, 6-14

Proper 9   **267**
Pentecost 7
Ordinary Time 14
  The Naaman Syndrome
  2 Kings 4:1-14

Proper 10   **271**
Pentecost 8
Ordinary Time 15
  When God Measures The Church
  Amos 7:7-17

Proper 11   **275**
Pentecost 9
Ordinary Time 16
  When The Fruit Is Spoiled
  Amos 8:1-12

**Sermons For Sundays
After Pentecost (Middle Third)**
When God Calls
by Chrysanne Timm

Proper 12   283
Pentecost 10
Ordinary Time 17
   A Marriage Made In Heaven
   Hosea 1:2-10

Proper 13   291
Pentecost 11
Ordinary Time 18
   Parenting — Not For The Faint Of Heart
   Hosea 11:1-11

Proper 14   299
Pentecost 12
Ordinary Time 19
   What God Expects From Worship
   Isaiah 1:1, 10-20

Proper 15   305
Pentecost 13
Ordinary Time 20
   Garden Gone Bad
   Isaiah 5:1-7

Proper 16   311
Pentecost 14
Ordinary Time 21
   When God Calls
   Jeremiah 1:4-10

Proper 17   **319**
Pentecost 15
Ordinary Time 22
    Finding Fault With God
    Jeremiah 2:4-13

Proper 18   **325**
Pentecost 16
Ordinary Time 23
    In The Potter's Hands
    Jeremiah 18:1-11

Proper 19   **333**
Pentecost 17
Ordinary Time 24
    From Life To Death To ...
    Jeremiah 4:11-12, 22-28

Proper 20   **339**
Pentecost 18
Ordinary Time 25
    When There's Nothing Left To Do But Mourn
    Jeremiah 8:18—9:1

Proper 21   **347**
Pentecost 19
Ordinary Time 26
    Sold!
    Jeremiah 32:1-3a, 6-15

Proper 22   **353**
Pentecost 20
Ordinary Time 27
    The ABC's Of Grief
    Lamentations 1:1-6

Sermons For Sundays
After Pentecost (Last Third)
Restoring God's Activity
by R. Kevin Mohr

Introduction 361

Proper 23 363
Pentecost 21
Ordinary Time 28
Making Ourselves At Home
Jeremiah 29:1, 4-7

Proper 24 369
Pentecost 22
Ordinary Time 29
Not Another Rerun!
Jeremiah 31:27-34

Proper 25 375
Pentecost 23
Ordinary Time 30
Earth, Wind, And Fire
Joel 2:23-32

Reformation Day 381
Put Within Us
Jeremiah 31:31-34

All Saints 387
Oh, By The Way ...
Daniel 7:1-3, 15-18

Proper 26 391
Pentecost 24
Ordinary Time 31
Help From Habakkuk?
Habakkuk 1:1-4; 2:1-4

Proper 27   **397**
Pentecost 25
Ordinary Time 32
  Making Something Out Of Nothing
  Haggai 1:15b—2:9

Proper 28   **403**
Pentecost 26
Ordinary Time 33
  A New Beginning
  Isaiah 65:17-25

Christ The King   **409**
Proper 29
  Shepherds Who Will Shepherd
  Jeremiah 23:1-6

Thanksgiving Day   **413**
  Thanksgiving Is Nine-Tenths Of Possession
  Deuteronomy 26:1-11

Lectionary Preaching After Pentecost   **417**

US/Canadian Lectionary Comparison   **419**

About The Authors   **421**

Sermons On The First Readings

For Sundays In Advent, Christmas, And Epiphany

From Tragedy To Redemption

Derl G. Keefer

God's Gift

Margery Tallcott relates that during the Depression she and her husband were barely making the money stretch from week to week. It was particularly tight during the weeks leading up to Christmas. Their finances would not allow for purchasing gifts for each other or for their son, Pete.

With Christmas a week away, they told Pete there would be no store-bought presents for any of them. "But I'll tell you what we can do," said his father with an inspiration born of heartbreak. "We can make pictures of the presents we'd like to give each other."

For the next few days each of the family members worked secretly with some laughs and giggles along the way. They were able to scrape together enough to purchase a small, straggly tree and trimmed it with pitiful-looking decorations. It still seemed beautiful to them. Tallcott writes, "Yet, on Christmas morning, never was a tree heaped with such riches! The gifts were only pictures of gifts, to be sure, cut out or drawn and colored and painted, nailed and hammered, and pasted and sewed. But they were presents, luxurious beyond our dreams...."

Peter's gift to his parents was a crayon drawing of flashy colors in the most modernistic style of the Depression era. It was the picture of three people laughing — a man, a woman, and a little boy. They had their arms around one another and were, in a sense, one person. Under the picture Pete had printed one word: US.[1]

The prophet Jeremiah looks down the corridor of time to see that God has given us a gift. It is the gift of his one and only son,

15

Jesus, who has come to put his arms around us and share the Father's love!

God's Gift Includes His Faithful Promises (Jeremiah 33:14)

A promise is a pledge from one person to another. God has pledged to restore Israel and in a limited sense that occurs in a nationalistic setting. The completeness of their return hinges on the coming of David's Son, the Messiah. For centuries the Jews looked forward to the coming of the Messianic redeemer who would free them from bondage. As invaders came and raped the nation their only hope lay in a nationalistic redeemer, a Savior, a Messiah who would bring them freedom from the invading armies. As God's time came for the Messiah to be born in Israel, the people were waiting and expecting him to release them from the overlords of Rome. God's promise was not for political release, but spiritual release. Their sins held them in bondage more than any invading army ... they just didn't seem to understand that fact.

Many seek God to release them from their bondage to some exterior enemy ... when their real enemy lies inside of them. People think if only God would release them from their illnesses, inferior jobs, bad marriages, financial difficulties, dependencies on alcohol or drugs, or whatever demon holds them they would be free. But God has promised to enter our lives and live inside of us where he can rid our sinful lifestyle by releasing us of our sins that have captured and enslaved us. Then and only then will we be free and his promise be realized!

Booker T. Washington describes meeting an ex-slave from Virginia in his book, *Up from Slavery*. He writes that the slave had made a contract with his master, prior to the Emancipation Proclamation, to the effect that the slave was permitted to buy his own freedom, by paying so much per year for his body; and while he was paying for his freedom, he was permitted to labor where and for whom he pleased.

He discovered that Ohio paid better wages so he decided to travel there for work. When the Emancipation Proclamation became law he was freed from any obligation to his master. But this man continued to work until he had enough money to pay the full

16

price of his freedom. He walked the greater portion of the distance back to where his old master lived in Virginia and placed the last dollar, with interest, in his hands.

Washington said that in talking to the man about this event, he was told that he knew that he did not have to pay his debt, but that he had given his word to his master, and his word he had never broken![2]

God has given his promise of restoration and he has never broken his promise.

God's Gift Includes His Righteousness (Jeremiah 33:15)

The concept of righteousness carries with it the connotation of fairness, justice, and honesty. Righteousness is applied to someone who is right in character and action, equally in what is said and what is done.

God is righteous and possesses righteousness. Because of who God is he is under obligation to do right in whatever action he takes. (See Genesis 18:25; Romans 9:14.)

Donald Metz wrote about the concept of righteousness as the conformity of God to the moral and spiritual law, which he has revealed. Metz writes, "Righteousness is the consistent and unvarying expression of God's nature in complete harmony with his holiness. To Brunner, the righteousness of God means, 'the constancy of God's will in view of his purpose and plan for Israel ...' thus righteousness 'is simply the holiness of God as it is expressed when confronted with the created world.' To Barth, the righteousness of God means that in founding and maintaining the fellowship with his creation God 'wills and expresses and establishes what corresponds to his own worth.' "[3]

We need a God who is fair. He will be impartial, non-discriminatory, non-biased, just, and reasonable. All people will be judged with his open-mindedness.

We need a God who understands justice. He will deal with us impartially on culture, race, sex, social or financial status, age, or any other label humans like to use.

We need a God who tells us the honest truth. God stands as the ultimate truth even if our age does not believe in ultimate truth.

Leo Cox said that our righteousness is conforming to the image of God by his grace and in childlike innocence and simplicity. When we are converted and become a child of God we have a positive inclination to do good deeds. It is more than just wanting to do good things. It is an inward righteousness by the grace of God on the inside manifesting itself outwardly in action toward others. We must be honest in our lifestyle. George Washington said, "I hope I shall always possess firmness and virtue enough to maintain what I consider the most enviable of all titles, the character of an honest man."[4]

The basis of this is found in Matthew 23 when a Pharisaical lawyer asked Jesus a question to test him. He asked, "Teacher, which is the great commandment in the law?" (Matthew 22:36 RSV) and Jesus answered him with the twin commandments:

> You shall love the Lord your God with all your heart, and with all your soul, and with all your mind. This is the great and first command. And a second is like it. You shall love your neighbor as yourself.
> — Matthew 22:37-39 (RSV)

As the old song says, "You can't have the one without the other."

God's Gift Includes A Messiah (Jeremiah 33:15-16)

The ultimate gift and proof of his faithfulness and love would be the Messiah. Both the Messiah and the city of Jerusalem are to have the same name, which indicates the unity that will be established between God and his people. Christ is the righteous descendent sprouting from David, the man after God's own heart. The Messiah, unlike any previous Davidic descendent, would be the ideal king. He would sum up in himself all the finest qualities of the best rulers and more!

The Messiah brings hope to a lost people. Our world has sunk its hope in a variety of messiahs ... political regimes, financial institutions, scientific endeavors, immoral leaders, and religious dogmas only to find emptiness and loneliness. Jesus, the Messiah, doesn't promise to give us something to handle life's vacant moments. He promises us himself! That is all, and he is enough!

The Messiah brings mercy to a lost people. Mercy denotes a combination of righteousness and love. Stephen Gunter, in *Beacon Dictionary of Theology*, writes that many Bible scholars are inclined to translate the word "mercy" as "steadfast love," implying that God has entered into a covenant relationship with anyone who accepts his offer of acceptance and pardon. It is in this context that God's righteous love becomes mercy. Mercy is compassion in action redeeming the lost.

The Messiah brings salvation to a lost people. The true Messiah that Jeremiah saw would become Jesus. He came into the world as a baby, grew to manhood, and is the God-Man who can take away the sins of the lost people of the world.

> *At Calvary sin received its mortal wound. There the victim became the victor. He fell but crushed the enemy in the fall. He died, but sin was nailed to the cross. His cross becomes the fountain of our life; His tomb, the birthplace of our immortality.*
> — Sim A. Wilson[5]

We must praise God's gift of the Messiah, Jesus. Any language is appropriate! Amen.

Doxologia
A Dios, el Padre celestial,
Al Hijo, nuestro Redentor,
Y al Eternal Consolador,
Unidos, todos alabad.

---

1. James S. Hewett, *Illustrations Unlimited* (Wheaton: Tyndale House Publishers, 1988), p. 234.

2. Craig Brian Larson, editor, *Illustrations for Preaching and Teaching* (Grand Rapids: Baker Books, 1993), p. 190.

3. J. Kenneth Grider and Willard H. Taylor, *Beacon Dictionary of Theology* (Kansas City: Beacon Hill Press of Kansas City, 1983), p. 57.

4. Jan Karon, *Patches of Godlight* (New York: Penguin Books, 2001), npn.

5. Albert M. Wells Jr., compiler, *Inspiring Quotations* (Nashville: Thomas Nelson Publishers, 1988), p. 174.

Finding Redemption
In The Midst Of Judgment

*A vase shatters, brushed by a careless elbow; a toy
breaks, handled roughly by young fingers; and fabric
rips, pulled by strong angry hands. Spills and rips take
time to clean up, effort to repair, and money to replace,
but far more costly are shattered relationships. Unfaithfulness, untruths, hateful words, and forsaken vows tear
delicate personal bonds and inflict wounds not easily
healed. Most tragic, however, is a broken relationship
with God.*[1]

Malachi understood all too well the tragedy of a broken relationship with God. He saw it in his congregation, his fellow Jews.
They had been in Babylonian exile. After years of deportation, the
exiles returned under the leadership of their governor, Zerubbabel,
they finished the temple in 516 BC. Forty-eight years later in 458
BC, the community was encouraged as several thousand more Jews
and the priest, Ezra, marched back into the city.

Thirteen years later in 445 BC, King Artaxerxes permitted his
cupbearer Nehemiah, to return to Jerusalem and rebuild the walls.
As newly appointed governor he reformed the city and nation by
helping the poor, encouraged the people to have a pure race by
discouraging intermarriage with other nationalities, and taught them
to keep the sabbath as a holy day and to bring their tithes and offerings faithfully to the temple of God.

True to human nature, once Nehemiah returned as he had
promised King Artaxerxes in 433 BC, the people fell back into

21

their sinful lifestyles. They claimed pessimism and discouragement was their excuse to sin! Their discouragement centered on several issues.

- Their glorious future announced by their prophets hadn't come to fruition (Malachi 3:1).
- Their God hadn't come to his temple in all his majesty and glory as they expected.
- Their exalted kingdom still wasn't exalted.
- Their trust in God's covenant love now wavered (Malachi 1:2).
- Their understanding of God's justice sank like a rock (Malachi 2:17; 3:14-15).

Malachi understands their frustration and discouragement, but he certainly condemns their sin.

The people lay at the feet of God the charge that he is unjust because he has failed to come in judgment of the Gentiles and has failed to exalt his people the Jews. Malachi answers with an announcement and a warning ringing in their ears. He will come to judge, "like a refiner's fire" (Malachi 3:1-2 RSV) and they will be the first in line (Malachi 3:5). Their anticipation of that day will burn like a furnace (Malachi 4:1-6) because of their sin.

We also live in a day where sin dominates the lives of people of all races, cultures, gender, and age. There is no one who escapes its ugliness. The Bible says, "All have sinned and fall short of the glory of God" (Romans 3:23 NIV). So what are we to do? Are we destined for the fires of eternal hell without hope? Is that what Malachi's message was to the people of Israel? No! Malachi predicts that the Lord's coming will fulfill God's work in human history. The fulfillment will be accomplished in the Messiah who God will bring to his people. So in the midst of judgment, salvation can be found only in the Messiah, Jesus Christ.

Redemption Comes In The Midst Of Worship (Malachi 3:1)
Worship is the acknowledgment of my deepest heart need. The psalmist wrote, "My heart says to you 'Seek his face!' Your face,

Lord, I will seek" (Psalm 27:8 NIV). I long for him. I hope for him. I seek for him. The inner part of my life craves to be filled with the Spirit of God. That's the essence of worship!

> *To worship is to quicken the conscience by the holiness of God, to feed the mind with the truth of God, to purge the imagination by the beauty of God, to open the heart to the love of God, to devote the will to the purpose of God.*[2]

Worship is a heart-to-heart communication between the holy God and me! He speaks and my job is to listen and respond to his Spirit. C. S. Lewis said, "In the process of worshiping God he communicates his Spirit to us." That requires focus and time. Community worship experiences bring the corporate body into concentrating on God. The same principle holds true in individual worship as our center of attention is spotlighted on the living God and nothing should divert that focal point!

At the heart of Christian worship are awe, praise, reverence, and adoration. Worship enflames the human spirit as the spark of God touches the embers of the human spirit. That flame will inspire, sustain, and encourage the life of the believer. Exodus 25:22 says, "And I will meet with you there and talk to you...."

The story is told of a young climber to the Alps who was making his first climb. He hired two experienced guides. It was a steep, hazardous ascent to the top. But he felt secure with one guide ahead and the other following. Hours passed as they climbed the rocky side of the mountain. The summit was in sight and breathlessly they reached for those rocks protruding through the snow above them.

The lead guide wanted to let the young climber have the first glorious view of the incredible sight and moved aside to let him go first. Forgetting the gales that would blow across those summit rocks, the young man leaped to his feet. But the lead guide dragged him down. "On your knees, sir!" he shouted. "You are never safe here except on your knees."

If we are to worship our God, it is on our knees in humility and reverence. It is on our knees that we find redemption from our haughtiness and sin.

Redemption Comes In The Midst Of Love (Malachi 3:1a)

God is sending his messenger. Why would he do that? After all it is the Israelites who have rebelled and been unfaithful. The messenger comes from a heart of love. Love tempers judgment. The Old and New Testaments are filled with stories, illustrations, quotes, and messages of God's eternal love. The one verse that clings to the mind and typifies the essence of redemption is the classic, John 3:16: "For God so loved the world that he gave his one and only Son, that whoever believes in him shall not perish but have eternal life" (NIV). The writer, John, goes further as he pens, "For God did not send his Son into the world to condemn the world, but to save the world through him" (John 3:17 NIV). What great and glorious news for the people of a fallen world who stand under eternal condemnation!

> *Nothing that is worth doing can be achieved in our lifetime; therefore we must be saved by hope. Nothing which is true or beautiful or good makes complete sense in any immediate context of history; therefore we must be saved by faith. Nothing we do, however virtuous, can be accomplished alone; therefore, we must be saved by love.*[3]

> *A Christian is sure to grow lovely — by just loving — by just going on in love for Christ ... The soul grows wondrously lovely just by loving, by pouring out its faithful affection; and all the more so when the object of its affection is the Lord Jesus Christ, the one altogether lovely. We behold his face, Jesus' face, as in a glass, and are changed into the same image, from glory to glory, even as by the Spirit of the Lord. But the result is permanent.*[4]

Have you accepted this love that God offers? The offer is free, but it has come with a price. The price paid is the death of Jesus on the cross for your eternal redemption. Reach out today and accept that offer of love by loving him back.

Redemption Comes In The Midst Of Relationship (Malachi 3:2, 4)

Relationships mean that we are intertwined with people. There is a natural association between two people. It connects us with others.

A meaningful relationship comes when God is connected with us. Though the Christian faith is listed as a religion in textbooks, it is not just a religion. It is a relationship with God for a world that is lost and lonely. Redemption is much more than signing on a dotted line, or raising a hand, or bowing at an altar. It is saying, "Yes" to a God who seeks to flood our lives with his love. His desire is to latch on and never let us go. Someone once said that religion is not worth your time or mine. But a relationship with God, a relationship in which you give love and receive love is worth Christ's life.

A God/human relationship is a must, but God also wants us to be caring about others who are our neighbors.

Dr. Ward Williams tells about a man named George Mason who didn't care much for people. He was a bachelor and spent evenings and weekends alone at home in a comfortable apartment. He was absorbed in his business and turned down invitations for social outings.

Late one Christmas Eve, after his employees had left, George Mason went into the office vault to get a little extra cash. Soundlessly, on newly oiled hinges, the heavy vault door swung shut behind him. Sudden darkness and the final click of the automatic lock startled him. He began to panic. George did everything he could from yelling to pounding on the door for someone to help him, but everyone including the cleaning lady was gone! He consoled himself with the thought that he would be released from his "prison" the next morning and he could survive. Then he remembered that the next day was not a working day, it was Christmas!

His heart pounded and he became very much afraid. His mind began the checklist ... would he have enough air ... what would happen if the automatic lock froze ... all of those things that play a trick with your mind when you are in the dark and afraid. Trying to calm himself, he remembered that when the new vault was installed they had told him something about a "safety hole." Feeling around in the darkness he located it at the top of the back wall ... too small for burglars, but large enough so that he could breathe.

Christmas Eve and Christmas Day passed. He was alone, as he usually was. But there was a huge difference. He was uncomfortable, hungry, and thirsty in the deepest darkness he had ever experienced.

The morning after Christmas finally came and the chief cashier arrived and unlocked the vault but didn't open it. Without anyone seeing him, George Mason staggered out of his prison and tottered to the water cooler. After a long drink of cold water, he took a taxi to his solitary apartment and freshened himself.

In a short time he was back at the office in his usual role and desk. Nobody asked him how he had spent Christmas. Not one person missed him. No one seemed to care. After all, he never asked about them, never showed an interest in their lives and seemed to not care about them.

After that experience George Mason was a changed man. In an obscure place on the back wall of the vault Mason put a sign to remind him of those desperate hours. It read, "To be indispensable somewhere, is the secret of happiness. To love people, is the purpose of life."[5]

It may not have been a heart-changing experience where George discovered his dependence on God, but he certainly discovered his dependence on other people. We need both a relationship with God and others. Relationship will change us ... period.

People who have discovered the transforming power of redemption through worship, love, and relationship will have a wonderful day at his coming. What better time to remember than at this Christmas season? Amen.

1. *Life Application Study Bible New Living Translation* (Wheaton: Tyndale House Publishers, 1996), p. 1385.

2. Albert M. Wells Jr., compiler, *Inspiring Quotations* (Nashville: Thomas Nelson Publishers, 1988), p. 221.

3. Jan Karon, *Patches of Godlight* (New York: Penguin Publishers, 2001), npn.

4. G. B. F. Hallock, *Five Thousand Best Modern Illustrations* (New York: George H. Doran Company, 1927), p. 460.

5. King Duncan, editor, *Dynamic Preaching* magazine, December 1994, Volume IX, No. 12. Published by Seven Worlds, Knoxville, Tennessee, pp. 5-6.

Hope Again!

Charles Swindoll wrote a book titled *Hope Again*, with the subtitle "When Life Hurts and Dreams Fade." On the back cover describing the contents of the book the publisher entices the reader with the following words:

> *Hope is more than mere wishful thinking. Hope is a vital necessity of life — a gift that God wants to give to you. And in a world that regularly writes dreams off as foolish and drains the hope from the heart with dark pessimism,* Hope Again *is a voice crying in the wilderness ... a word of enthusiasm for life in the midst of any difficult situation you are in.*

Zephaniah's audience could identify with that need for hope! They were overwhelmed with grief and prolonged distress, along with a history of defiance of God's commands and demands dating back to their two previous kings, Manasseh and Amon. The prophet's purpose was to shake the people of Judah out of their doldrums and complacency and return to God.

Zephaniah's main theme is the coming of the day of the Lord, when God will severely punish the nations. It will not be a day of rejoicing and celebration in which the enemies of God's people will be destroyed and the people of Judah exalted. According to the prophet there is coming a time of accountability and judgment.

You can catch the progression of Zephaniah's thinking in his short book. Chapter 1 includes God's thunderous judgment and punishment for all who defy him. There is wrath and pronouncement of destruction. "I will sweep away the birds of the air and the fish of the sea. The wicked will have only heaps of rubble when I cut off man from the face of the earth, declares the Lord" (Zephaniah 1:3 NIV). As the *Life Application Bible* introduction to Zephaniah says, "We can sense the oppression and depression his listeners must have felt. They were judged guilty and they were doomed" (p. 1366).

In chapter 2 there is a whisper from the prophet of hope. He calls on the people to beg the Lord to save them and perhaps he will listen and respond (2:3). Later Zephaniah writes that there will be a remnant of survivors from the judgment and calamity that will fall on them as a people. "Restoration" is a hopeful word! (2:7).

The hope rises to an increasing surge of passionate care and love from God who will bring salvation and forgiveness to those who are faithful to him. There is almost a lilt, a rhythm, as the prophet writes,

> *Sing, O daughter of Zion; shout aloud, O Israel! Be glad and rejoice with all your heart, O daughter of Jerusalem! For the Lord will remove his hand of judgment and will disperse the armies of your enemy. And the Lord himself, the King of Israel, will live among you! At last your troubles will be over, and you will fear disaster no more.*
> — Zephaniah 3:14-15 (NLT)

Hope to press on ... hope to endure ... hope to stay focused ... hope to see dreams fulfilled ... that is what God is giving them in the midst of judgment and despair!

That need still exists! In a world filled with hopelessness and abandonment, we need to hear the voice of God saying that he will live among us! He will bring hope in the midst of fear. He has brought that hope in the being of the Messiah, Jesus!

Zephaniah has two themes in his prophecy ... one is negative and the other positive.

First Is A Negative Theme (Zephaniah 1—3:13)

As you browse through Zephaniah's message to Judah you begin to feel a deep dark dread. It begins as he delivers God's message, "I will sweep away everything from the face of the earth, declares the Lord" (1:2 NIV). These words have all the earmarks of catastrophe written! This negative theme includes:

Fear. One day in hot July, a farmer sat on the porch of his shack, smoking his corncob pipe. Along came a stranger from the city who asked, "How's your cotton coming?"

"Ain't got none," he replied. "Didn't plant none. 'Fraid of the boll weevil."

"Well, how's your corn?"

"Didn't plant none. 'Fraid o' drought."

"How about your potato garden?"

"Ain't got none. Scairt o' tater bugs."

The city stranger finally asked, "Well, what did you plant?"

The farmer answered, "Nothin', I just played it safe."[1]

Some of us are fearful of action because there may be something out there in life that we are not prepared to meet, so we play it safe and do nothing. Paralysis grips us.

Despair. This is a horrible feeling of being overcome by the sense of futility and defeat. We have the feeling that we are alone and no one cares about us.

"I am now the most miserable man living," wrote a famous American leader. "If what I feel were equally distributed to the whole human family, there would not be one cheerful face on earth. To remain as I am is impossible. I must die or be better." Who was that famous leader? Abraham Lincoln.

In his book, *The Collected Works of Abraham Lincoln*, Ray Basler comments that in the darkest days of the Civil War, Lincoln constantly wrestled with unrelenting depression and despair. Basler writes about those twin feelings ...

> *It can strike anyone. No one is immune. Not even a nation's president. Here is this marvelous man with magnificent character, feeling absolutely alone ... Surely, the president ought to sleep well because of his*

protection, because of his wise counsel, to say nothing
of his financial security. Yet there he was, tossing and
turning through the night, haunted by dark and debili-
tating thoughts.[2]

The people of Judah were haunted by those feelings as they tossed and turned at night. Do you?

Sorrows. Webster defines sorrow as "Mental anguish or pain caused by injury, loss or despair."[3] Because of Judah's unfaithful behavior and action, they brought on themselves as a nation and as individuals more sorrow than they could stand. Add in natural calamities and you have a recipe for sorrow.

Today we also have sorrows that come as a result of our own foolish decisions plus experiences we have no control over ... illness, death, financial reverses on Wall Street, war, and hatred that come to our street. Is it any wonder that we are filled with negative feelings in life?

Other negatives in the lives of Zephaniah's readers included burdens, homelessness, war, injury, and family disputes. Situations have not changed over the millenniums, have they?

Second, A Positive Theme (Zephaniah 3:14-20)

In the last section of his prophecy, Zephaniah loudly exclaims that all is not lost! The day of judgment has turned to the day of hope! The prophet warned the people of Judah that if they refused to repent, the entire nation, including the holy city of Jerusalem, would be lost. Zephaniah held out hope and blessing for the people of Judah telling them their punishment for sin would be a means of their purification. God sends words of encouragement to them.

Fear Not! Fear is dispelled because God will bring us strength. John Ogilvie calls strength an "inside secret." The innermost being of God is his Holy Spirit. He supplies limitless power, strength, fortitude, and help, and his well never runs dry! When we need strength to overcome fear, he dips his hand into the well and brings up a bucketful for us to drink.

Note the glorious progression ... the Lord takes great
delight in you. In spite of all our failures, he chose to

> *be our God and to cherish us ... next the Lord quiets us*
> *with his love. The unqualified, indefatigable love of the*
> *Lord gives us silent confidence, security, and peace.*
> *There's no need to prove ourselves or blow our own*
> *horns.*

He sets us free from overwhelming fear.

Salvation has come! When God comes, he brings salvation from destruction ... hope for the future ... forgiveness for the penitent ... presence with his people. God says to the people of Judah that he has come to bring them life. Reverend Barbara Brown Taylor wrote:

> *What God cares about, with all the power of God's holy*
> *being, is the quality of my life ... not just the continua-*
> *tion of my breath and the health of my cells ... but the*
> *quality of my life, the scope of my life, the heft and zest*
> *of my life ... fear of death turns life into a stingy, cau-*
> *tious way of living that is not really living at all ... to*
> *follow Jesus means going beyond the limits of our own*
> *comfort and safety. It means receiving our lives as gifts*
> *instead of guarding them as possessions.*[4]

God told the inhabitants of Judah that he had come to bring them meaningful life and to get up from their degradation and follow his leadership. It started from the top down. King Josiah caught the vision. Reforms swept away the idols and unfaithfulness and the people agreed. Salvation was the result!

Rejoicing results. The positive attitudes continue as we fear not and receive salvation from the heart of God and with that we experience rejoicing results! It is knowing that God is happy to see us!

The story is told of Brennan Manning who met his spiritual director at a retreat center at a secluded destination several years ago. Manning's usual habit was to park a mile from the meeting location. He would leave his car to begin the one-mile walk toward the center's entrance where his mentor would be waiting for him. The highlight of the whole week for Manning was the greeting from his mentor. As Brennan came into sight from his trek up the side of the mountain path, his mentor would begin jumping and shouting "Brennan, Brennan it is so good to see you!" He would continue to shout and jump until they finally came together in a spiritual embrace. God is with us on the journey and aware of our coming to him as he is jumping, shouting, dancing, and calling our personal name in anticipation because of his great love! We cannot help but rejoice at our homecoming, knowing that we will be greeted with such exuberance by God himself.

As Swindoll said on the back cover of his book, "If you want to smile through your tears, if you want to rejoice through times of suffering, just keep reminding yourself that what you're going through isn't the end of the story ... it's simply the rough journey that leads to the right destination." Amen.

---

1. James S. Hewett, editor, *Illustrations Unlimited* (Wheaton: Tyndale House, 1988), pp. 204-205.

2. Charles Swindoll, *The Tale of the Tardy Oxcart* (Nashville: Word Publishing, 1998), p. 160.

3. Senior Devotional Bible NIV (Grand Rapids: Zondervan Publishing House, 1996), p. 1172.

4. Jan Karon, *Patches of Godlight* (New York: Penguin Books, 2002), npn.

Born At Bethlehem — Hope

Ellyn Sanna was twelve years old when she went on a camping trip to New England with her family. Four children and two parents were packed inside the family car. The tent was stowed away on top of the vehicle traveling from site to site. Each night they set up camp as the light faded. She tells that there were many happy memories from that vacation, but there was also the deep feeling of loneliness and being misunderstood.

She was the youngest of the four children and too young to go on the long hiking trips with the other siblings, yet too old to be happy staying behind with her mom and dad. It was an awkward age and she felt painfully aware of her physical appearance. At night she would huddle alone at the picnic table resentful and miserable as she watched groups of teenagers walk by her at the camping sites. She relates how she desperately wished that she were older and less shy; wishing that she was anyone but herself.

One of those bright, beautiful, sunny days, her parents decided to take their family to a lighthouse on a rocky point reaching far out into the Atlantic Ocean. As they pulled into the parking lot and made their way to the entrance, they discovered that the fee for going to the top of the lighthouse was ten cents per person. The price was too steep for the family to pay even for such a scenic view.

A sister pointed to the sign that stated, "Children twelve and under free." Then she said, "Ellyn could go up."

Her parents agreed that she could come back and tell them all about the beautiful scenery from atop the lighthouse. So all alone she climbed to the top. She said, "For once I was just the right age: old enough to be allowed out of my mother's sight, young enough to pay no fee. Panting after the long, winding climb, I emerged into the wind and light at the top."

She relates how breathtaking the view was from her vantage point. The ocean stretched out before her, and she could see the waves rolling to the shore. The wind tore at her clothes and the sun warmed her head and filled her with wild, joyful singing! "I felt as though I could fly, as though the Holy Spirit were in the strong gusts, ready to lift me off my feet into heaven."

Ellyn continues, "I stayed there as long as I dared. Knowing that my family would be waiting impatiently, I went down the spiral stairs at last. But inside my heart, I felt as though I carried a promise from God. At twelve, I didn't know what to call the feeling inside of me. But I know now it was hope."[1]

Many people in our world have lost hope through the ravages of poverty, hatred, terrorism, natural disasters, and a host of other things that have taken the wind out of their sails. You and I have the opportunity to share with them the greatest news available that can lift their spirits and their very lives. They can put their hope not in a thing, but a person ... Jesus!

Edward Mote wrote the words to one of my favorite songs, "The Solid Rock," in 1834.

> *My hope is built on nothing less*
> *Than Jesus' blood and righteousness.*
> *I dare not trust the sweetest frame,*
> *But wholly lean on Jesus name.*
>
> *When darkness seems to hide his face,*
> *I rest on his unchanging grace.*
> *In every high and stormy gale,*
> *My anchor holds within the veil.*
>
> *When he shall come with trumpet sound,*
> *O may I then in him be found!*
> *Dressed in his righteousness alone,*
> *Faultless to stand before the throne!*

On Christ, the solid rock, I stand;
All other ground is sinking sand;
All other ground is sinking sand.

Micah had a breathtaking view atop his prophetic vantage point. The ocean of time stretched out before him with the waves of centuries rolling in front of him. He saw one star studded night that in Bethlehem Ephrathah, hope would be born. And he was right!

Hope In The Ruler Of The Ages (Micah 5:2)

Like his fellow prophets, Micah denounces the sins of the people and the sins of the nobility. The people of Judah and Samaria have prostituted themselves to idols. The people have become spiritually unfaithful to their one and only God, Jehovah. Their sin is the misplaced loyalty to the only God who truly loves and cares deeply for them. The leaders of the nation hated justice and perverted all that is righteous and holy. They are building Zion with blood and Jerusalem with iniquity. The judges, priests, and false prophets cared only for themselves, and they would achieve their success at any cost whether through extortion, robbery, or human misery.

The judges were taking bribes so impartially and blind justice was impossible.

The priests were to teach the people about God, but they would only if the price was right. They had exchanged their caring for greediness.

The prophets, too, like the judges and priests would only give their divine predictions for money. It tainted the truth and they only gave favorable prophecies to people who could pay the price.

Leaders and followers alike were proud and offensive to God. Their cup of wickedness was full and running over, so God would pour out his wrath and judgment upon all of them. Micah predicts that because of their sins, Zion would be plowed as a field and Jerusalem would become a heap of dirt. The invasion and destruction by Nebuchadnezzar fulfilled the prophecy with agonizing accuracy. Truly the wages of sin is death and death in every realm and sphere of life.

The Babylonians take Jerusalem's king, kill his sons before his eyes, and then blind him, put him in shackles, and haul him away to Babylon where he is imprisoned.

Micah shifts to a positive ruler that will be born and become the shepherd-king to his people. It is a prophecy that will have future ramifications. This shepherd-king who will bring hope to the people will be born in the smallest of areas. Christians assert and believe that it is none other than Jesus Christ who Micah writes and speaks about! He is not only the fulfillment of prophecy, but the fulfillment of hope! His rule is a kingship of care, love, and direction in a world that lost its hope.

Hope In The Strength Of The Lord (Micah 5:4)

His strength comes from surrender, service, and sacrifice. Hope is born to that end. Tom Barnard wrote, "In the spiritual life, there are things that belong together, like perfectly matched oars. Two of the more important ones are *surrender* and *service*. They go together. Surrender without service is hollow piety. Service without surrender is sterile duty. Try activating one without the other, and the spiritual cruise will result in circle making. No significant gain will result from such foolish exercise.

"All true Christian service begins with personal surrender to God. Call it what you want — consecration, yielding, commitment — it is a prerequisite to authentic service. One cannot know Christ personally and deeply without catching the winsome contagion of his caring Spirit for others. Yielding to his Spirit calls for the response of one's heart in meaningful service to others. As someone said, 'Wherever the Spirit of the Lord controls the heart, there is a passion to serve.' "[2]

God authored surrender and service at a specific time and place ... Bethlehem, Christmas night. Christ would grow into adulthood and model surrender and service to a motley group of disciples. He took off his robe, picked up a pitcher of water used for ceremonial cleansing, wrapped a towel around his waist, and proceeded to wash the grime off the feet of each of those men. It was a perfect act of love.

38

Then he said to the men, "You call me 'Teacher' and 'Lord,' and you are right, because it is true. And since I, the Lord and Teacher, have washed your feet, you ought to wash each other's feet. I have given you an example to follow. Do as I have done to you."
— John 13:13-15 (NLT)

What have you done lately to birth hope to those mired in sin, loneliness, desperation, despair, and helplessness? Think of people right now who need you to bring them hope. Write down their names and what you can do to bring them an inkling of hope! Remember, you are not going to bring them hope in your own strength but in the strength of the Lord!

Hope In The Peace Of A Savior
When we think of peace normally we view it as a cessation or freedom from war. Peace in the Old Testament also connotes prosperity.

The people in the text are in for big trouble! Their enemy would soon be upon them literally, and they would know the ravages of war. It is spiritual night for them. They have no vision of good and turn to the plans of their fallible leaders who are leading them to destruction. Micah sees beyond the immediate into the future. Humankind is being ravaged by Satan, sin, and evil and needs someone to lead them to victory and peace. Looking down the corridor of time he envisions that God will provide for this very situation. He will graciously send a Messiah, the Lord Jesus, as the light of the world to give light to this people sitting in darkness (Isaiah 9:20). Out of his birth, ministry, death, and resurrection there will come the dispelling of all gloom, darkness, and night from sad hearts.

He will bring peace to a fearful heart! How do we find this peace?

- Draw near to God. "Let us then approach the throne of grace with confidence, so that we may receive mercy and find grace to help us in our time of need" (Hebrews 4:16 NIV).

- Pray to God. "The prayer of a righteous man is powerful and effective" (James 5:16b NIV).
- Live a life of thanksgiving. "Do not be anxious about anything, but in everything, by prayer and petition, with thanksgiving, present your requests to God" (Philippians 4:6 NIV).

The ancient prayer of Francis of Assisi should be our model.

Lord, make me an instrument of your peace!
Where there is hatred, let me sow love;
Where there is injury, pardon;
Where there is doubt, faith;
Where there is despair, hope;
Where there is darkness, light;
Where there is sadness, joy.
Oh, divine master, grant that I may not so much seek
To be consoled, as to console;
To be understood, as to understand;
To be loved, as to love.
For it is in giving that we receive;
It is in pardoning that we are pardoned;
It is in dying that we are born to eternal life!
All of this is found in the Savior ... Christ the Lord.

From the cradle to the cross Jesus brings us hope. Hope to go on, even though we feel that life is scattered. Hope to continue to grow in our faith even if we fail and fall. Hope to endure, even when life falters. Hope to believe, even though dreams fade. Give birth to hope that is found in Christ! Amen.

---

1. Ellyn Sanna, *A Beacon Of Hope* (Uhrichsville, Ohio: Humble Creek Publishing, 2000), pp. 25-26.

2. Tom Barnard, *Tuesday Morning* email devotions, November 15, 2005. Used by permission.

**Christmas Eve/Christmas Day
Isaiah 9:2-7**

Born In Bethlehem — Light

*Have you ever awakened in the early hours before
dawn? Thick darkness covers the earth. Trees, rivers,
and houses obscured. Silence reigns supreme. Chill, as
cool as melting ice, fills the air. Then slowly a faint
flush of gray begins to roll through the blackness, forms
take shape. Hazy colors appear. Suddenly, as a rocket
explodes into space, the sun rises on the horizon. There
is a glow on the hills. The leaves on the tree sparkle as
they flutter in the soft breeze. The birds greet the new
day with their songs. The whole world has changed.
Why? Because* light *has come.*[1]

God's effort to enlighten and redeem people has been a struggle
to penetrate the thick, dense clouds of unfaithfulness, wickedness,
and spiritual ignorance. Though a few rays penetrated and pierced
the gloom through the efforts of the prophets, a day was coming
when that light would burst forth with the brilliance of the sun.
That light would be his one and only Son, Jesus. "For to us a child
is born, to us a son is given ..." (Isaiah 9:6a NIV).

The whole world has changed because of his entrance into the
world!

The Light Has Come To Dispel The Darkness (Isaiah 9:2)

Darkness is the absence of light and is used as a sinister metaphor for light's absence. It conceals reality. It represents evil, wickedness, hatred, gloom, and sin.

41

Light is one of the greatest benefits God has ever given people. These random verses on light may help us in our journey through this dark world we live in today.

- "And God said, 'Let there be light,' and there was light. God saw that the light was good, and he separated the light from the darkness" (Genesis 1:3-4 NIV). Think how life would be if we only lived in darkness. How depressing and awful it would be all of the time. Consider the Egyptians who had to live in thick darkness (Exodus 10:22-23).
- Escaping Egyptian tyranny, the Israelites were led by a pillar of cloud by daylight and a pillar of fire to give them light by night (Exodus 13:21; 14:20; Psalm 78:14). Bruce Kendall Barnard (Lead Pastor, Warwick Valley Church of the Nazarene, New York) wrote: "There was a time when God just traveled with the people in full view as a pillar of fire. That was cool. No matter how incredible a temple is, people might look at it and say, 'Maybe God is in there.' But when you see a pillar of fire, whoa! If I had a pillar of fire behind me and said, 'Believe in God,' you'd say, 'Okay, that's cool.' God wants to lead you in the light right now."
- God is seen as light. An almost-forgotten term from the Old Testament, "Shekinah Glory," appeared at the completion of both the tabernacle (Exodus 40:34-38) and the temple (1 Kings 8:11; 2 Chronicles 5:13-14). Louis Bouck suggests that the term "Shekinah" is the visible manifestation of the presence of God ... it was used in Jewish paraphrases as a synonym for God or his glory. In the Old Testament the Shekinah pointed forward to Christ, the brightness of God's glory. He continues his thought as he writes, "Identified by some with the Holy Spirit, the Shekinah (meaning to dwell) suggests the companionship, purity, and radiance of the comforter abiding in the sanctified heart." It is the "awe" of one who stands in the presence of a holy God.

In *Pulpit Digest*, Bob Woods tells the story of a couple who took their eleven-year-old son and seven-year-old daughter to

Carlsbad Caverns. As always, when the tour reached the deepest and darkest point in the cavern, the guide turned off the lights to dramatize how completely dark and silent it is below the surface of the earth.

The daughter became frightened at the suddenness of the darkness that enveloped her. She began to whimper and cry.

Immediately her brother whispered to her, "Don't cry. Somebody here knows how to turn on the lights."[2]

In a real sense, the message of Christmas is that God knows how to turn on the lights!

The Light Has Come To Bring Us Joy (Isaiah 9:3)

Joy is an exhilarating emotion of happiness or pleasure. It is from a wellspring of emotion that is very human. Something good has happened to us and we have an excited feeling. It may occur with the discovery of a higher motivation or value. It happens when we find that kindness brings more satisfaction than selfishness.

When the light of God develops through an experience with Christ, a deep joy invades us. What moves us to joy?

- freedom from sin that has separated us from God
- reconciliation with God
- recovery from our lost state with God
- adoption into the family of God
- making spiritual progress in our relationship with God
- life's blessings that come from God

All of these areas bring joy to the heart of the person who has discovered the joy of knowing and experiencing God. In God we have found our renewing and dependable resource when life seems shaken to its core.

Some scriptures to remind us of joy are:

> *Surely God is my salvation; I will trust and not be afraid.*
> *The Lord, is my strength and my song; he has become*
> *my salvation. With joy you will draw water from the*
> *wells of salvation.* — Isaiah 12:2-3 (NIV)

Rejoice in the Lord always. I will say it again: Rejoice!
— Philippians 4:4 (NIV)

I have told you this so that my joy may be in you and that your joy may be complete.
— John 15:11 (NIV)

Do not be afraid. I bring you good news of great joy that will be for all the people.
— Luke 2:10 (NIV)

Are you a person of joy? Don't let the temporal afflictions destroy your joy. When we walk with God, "weeping may remain for a night, but rejoicing comes in the morning" (Psalm 30:5b NIV).

The Light Has Come To Bring Us Liberation (Isaiah 9:4)

Oppression brings fear and bondage to human life, but God has come to shatter the yoke of oppression. The bondage that has held humankind is slavery to sin. "Sin brings one under its power and reduces its victim to abject helplessness by the tyranny of its guilt, the irresistibility of its pull, and the grip of its habit"[3] wrote Richard S. Taylor.

As light streams into our lives, it dispels the bondage that has held us captive.

- Light dispels the sin of Pharisaic legalism. Legalism is an excessive bondage to the letter of the law that misses the intent of what the law is to do.
- Light dispels the sin of antinomianism or those who reject moral law as binding in terms of conduct.
- Light dispels the bondage to appetites and vices contrary to God's morality for humans.
- Light dispels the bondage of attitude toward other individuals. We now see them in the light of Jesus.
- Light dispels the fear of Satan and hell. Not to imply that they are not real, but no longer do they have the hold on those who belong to Jesus.

When Christ comes into the heart, there is no more cosmetic cover up. No darkness can hide the light. When the searchlight of God comes into the heart, the awful truth of illicit relationships, uncaring attitudes, lies, cheating, anything unclean is revealed. Our confession has to be made and God's light drives out all that sin from within the heart.

The Light Has Come To Bring Us Experience (Isaiah 9:7b)

> *What I have in Christ is not an impression, but a life change; not an impression of personal influence, which might evaporate, but faith of central personal change. I do not merely feel changes; I am changed. He has possessed me. I am not his loyal subject; but his absolute property.*[4]

P. T. Forsyth grasped the importance of Christ's light in his own heart. He realized that God had given him a new moral self. He found that forgiveness and reconciliation were from the grace that only comes through Christ. Forsyth pens, "He has not merely healed me, in passing of an old problem but he has given me eternal life."

Every person in the world can come to this light. It is shining for all. Philip Bliss wrote about this in 1875 in his hymn "The Light Of The World Is Jesus."

> *The whole world was lost in the darkness of sin;*
> *The Light of the world is Jesus.*
> *Like sunshine at noonday his glory shone in;*
> *The Light of the world is Jesus.*

> **Refrain:**
> *Come to the light; 'tis shining for thee,*
> *Sweetly the light has dawned upon me.*
> *Once I was blind, but now I can see.*
> *The light of the world is Jesus.*

Decades ago near the North Pole, with the night lasting for months and months, when the people expected that day was about to dawn, some messengers got up to the highest point to watch. When they saw the first streaks of day they put on their brightest possible clothing, and embraced each other and cried, "Behold the sun!" and the cry went around all the land, "Behold the sun!"

For centuries the world from Isaiah's day forward had darkness covering the land. The cry from heaven on that first Christmas night was "Behold the Son!" and the Son of righteousness had come. The sun in the material world is what Christ is to us in the spiritual world. He is the author, the source of light. He has visited our darkened world to bring eternal light! Amen.

---

1. Mark McCuistion, *Come Ye Apart* (Kansas City: Nazarene Publishing House), November 7, 1976.

2. Craig Larson, editor, *Illustrations for Preaching and Teaching* (Grand Rapids: Baker Books, 1993), p. 122.

3. Richard S. Taylor, editor, *Beacon Dictionary of Theology* (Kansas City: Beacon Hill Press of Kansas City, 1983), p. 82.

4. P. T. Forsyth, *The Person and Place of Jesus Christ* (London: Haddon and Stoughton, 1909). Author's personal note from a sermon titled, "Jesus the Great Light."

Hidden Potential

Home and Garden television produces a program titled *Hidden Potential* hosted by Brandie Malay and architect/designer Barry Wood. Homebuyers are looking for a new home in a certain price range in their city. They are taken to three different homes that are not ready-to-move-in quality. The premise of the show is that the architect/designer will renovate the room by computer-generated graphic designing through his own personal redesign of that house. These computer-generated graphics will showcase the home's "hidden potential" by knocking out a wall, enlarging the space, renovating a disastrous bathroom, putting new cabinets in a dilapidated kitchen or enhancing the front entrance. All of this will make a dramatic difference. At the end of each episode the homebuyer must choose one of the three "hidden potential" houses to turn into their dream home.

The scripture text takes us to a time period in Israel's history (1050-1000 BC) when Israel went through a series of ugly house destroying problems, including a series of national, cultural, and religious crises, and a total breakdown of law and order within its society. Compounded problems shattered much of the external beauty of Israel by the threat of enemies like the Philistines who pushed their border in the southwest coastal region into the territories of Israel through raids, torture, and murder. Israel's house structure was also shattered by charges that the priestly family in charge of the Tabernacle at Shiloh was corrupt and abusive in their dealings with the worshipers. This is the context in which God calls a spiritual and national architect/designer to bring a new design of the hidden potential for Israel's house. This architect/designer's name is Samuel.

The circumstance of Samuel's birth begins like other key biblical figures, such as Isaac, Jacob, Samson, and John the Baptist. In this case, a desperate barren woman named Hannah was pleading with God for a child. During an annual pilgrimage to the tabernacle at Shiloh, she strikes a bargain with God. If God would grant her a son, she would consecrate him as a Nazirite and give him back to God for his service at the tabernacle. Hannah returned home with an assurance from the priest, Eli, that God would answer her petition. As Paul Harvey would say, "And here is the rest of the story." Hannah conceives and gives birth to a son whom she called Samuel. True to her word and as an act of worship she gives Samuel to Eli to raise and to serve at God's discretion.

The Bible declares, "... the boy Samuel grew up in the presence of the Lord" (1 Samuel 2:21) and "... the boy Samuel continued to grow in stature and in favor with the Lord and with men" (1 Samuel 2:26).

Samuel was to become a man who would bring needed renovations. "Like his predecessors, Moses and Joshua, he called the people to return to God with all their heart, to put away the foreign gods that were among them and to serve him alone (8:3). Samuel faithfully served the nation as a charismatic military leader, priest, prophet, circuit judge, and wise counselor."[1]

How did he serve his people so faithfully? There are three characteristics that produce a man who could bring out Israel's hidden potential.

Samuel Was Available To God

Samuel wanted to be available to God for his use, his purpose, his goals, his aims! A prayer from an unknown author echoes Samuel's heart.

> *Almighty and eternal God, so guide my mind, so fill my imagination so control my will, that I may be wholly yours, utterly dedicated unto you; and then use me, I pray, as you will, and always to your glory, and the*

welfare of your people; through our Lord and Savior
Jesus Christ. Amen.[2]

That should also be our prayer! We are offering ourselves to God to do as he pleases. God would not abandon his people without proper leadership. He wanted to provide a leader to guide them through the dark dreary days of their existence. God would not force a "yes" out of Samuel, but offered him an opportunity to respond. Samuel had to first make himself available. Making ourselves available for the vision God has for us is accomplished by:

- waiting for the vision God has for us,
- acting on the vision God has for us,
- becoming energized by the vision God has for us,
- loyalty to the vision God has for us,
- liberty in the vision God has for us, and
- living the vision God has for us.

Samuel Was Attentive To God

The priest, Eli, was faithful in transmitting the faith of his generation to the next through Samuel. When God was calling Samuel, the boy thought it was the voice of Eli. Samuel ran to where Eli was sleeping and said, "Here am I." Three times Samuel appears before Eli. Finally Eli realizes that it is God who is speaking to the child and tells him to be attentive to God's voice.

We need to be attentive to God's voice in our day. God speaks to us through our prayer and meditation. Prayer is not a platform to impress others. It is not a show of piety but a sincere desire to listen to God. It is a place we retreat to get direction, guidance, encouragement, help, strength, and courage. It is not a place to plead or beg or hammer away at God. It is a place where we can connect with him in specific ways. We need to talk with God like he is our friend ... because he is our friend! God knows exactly what we think and how we feel. We do not need to hide anything from him but rather listen to what he wants.

Charles Swindoll relates that the late Dr. Donald Barnhouse of a generation ago once came to his congregation and made a bold statement, "Prayer changes nothing!" There was hushed silence throughout the church. Swindoll writes that Barnhouse's statement "was designed to make Christians realize that God is sovereignly in charge of everything. Our times are literally in his hands. No puny human being by uttering a few words in prayer takes charge of events and changes them. God does the shaping, the changing, it is he who is in control ... except in one minor detail. Prayer changes me."[3]

So in prayer, as you become attentive, follow these guidelines:

- Tell God all that is on your heart.
- Tell God your troubles and let him bring comfort and advice.
- Tell God the joys of your life that he may refine them.
- Tell God your longings that he may purify and sanctify them.
- Tell God your fears that he may help you conquer them.
- Tell God your temptations that he may give you strength to endure them.
- Tell God your hurts so that he may heal and bind them.
- Tell God everything and he will be attentive!

> *Prayer is heart desire and all possible effort. Not words, not forms of speech; these may mean much or nothing. God's eyes are on the heart, the longing, struggling desire, with the outstretched thought and hand to utmost tension.* — P. F. Bresee[4]

Samuel's Aim ... Faithfulness

Samuel was faithful to God throughout all of his life. We have the highlights in 1 Samuel, but the one characteristic that we can follow through his life is faithfulness. From the time of his call to his days of retirement, Samuel wanted to be faithful to his God. With Saul as king over Israel, Samuel retired from his office as Israel's judge. In chapter 12, Samuel proclaims the core prophetic conviction that if the people and the king would live in obedience to God things would go well. He challenged the people to reverence God and to serve him faithfully with their whole heart.

As for me, far be it from me that I should sin against the Lord by failing to pray for you. And I will teach you the way that is good and right. But be sure to fear the Lord and serve him faithfully with all your heart; consider what great things he has done for you. Yet if you persist in doing evil, both you and your king will be swept away.
— Samuel 12:23-24 (NIV)

Help me this day to live a simple, sincere and serene life, repelling promptly every thought of discontent, anxiety, discouragement, impurity, and self-seeking; cultivating cheerfulness, magnanimity, charity ... in particular I will try to be faithful in those habits of prayer, work, study, physical exercise, eating and sleeping that I believe the Holy Spirit has shown me to be right.
— Author unknown[5]

We cannot be faithful on our own strength or by our own works. Faithfulness comes as we are obedient, attentive, and listening for the voice of God. Only then will we have spiritual success.

Your life has such hidden potential, but with God host of your life, it can be a showcase for all to emulate! Be an example to all. "Don't let anyone look down on you because you are young, but set an example for the believers in speech, in life, in love, in faith, and in purity" (1 Timothy 4:12 NIV).

---

1. Alex Varughese, editor, *Discovering the Bible* (Kansas City: Beacon Hill Press of Kansas City, 2006), p. 121.

2. Jan Karon, *Patches of Godlight* (New York: Penguin Books, 2001), npn.

3. Charles Swindoll, *Strengthening Your Grip* (Waco: Word Books, 1982), p. 157.

4. Harold Ivan Smith, compiler, *The Quotable Breese* (Kansas City: Beacon Hill Press of Kansas City, 1983), p. 169.

5. *Op cit*, Karon, npn.

From Tragedy To Salvation

On January 13, 1982, Washington DC and the surrounding area experienced a blizzard that paralyzed everything including the National Airport. Most of the day the airport would not allow any air flight takeoffs or landings. On that fateful day a decision was made to allow Air Florida Flight 90 to attempt a takeoff. The 737 had been delayed for hours. The chain of events that led to the ultimate crash into the 14th Street Bridge that broke the plane into three pieces and eventually caused it to fall into the icy waters of the Potomac River just as darkness approached seem unimaginable. Renda Brumbeloe chronicles those chains of events. He writes that the bad weather conditions led to a string of optional irregular operating procedures and departures from company policy. Regrettably, no one stepped up to the plate to ask the hard question, "What are we doing?" while flight procedures and the operating manual were seriously disregarded. Renda lists six areas that should have been warning signs to cancel the flight.

1. The tug was unable to push the aircraft off the gate in the deep snow, so an irregular engine assisted power back procedure was used. The swirling snow actually froze in the sensor probes of the engine intake.

2. The engine bleed air anti-ice system was purposely turned off to make more takeoff power available. Another bad option, which resulted in iced up sensors and a false high power indication on the EPR gauges during takeoff.

53

3. No one confirmed that the aircraft was free of structural ice before the takeoff.
4. The first officer told the captain that something was not right on the takeoff roll. (The aircraft accelerated too slowly due to improper power setting and runway conditions.)
5. Distraction and tunnel vision ensued full blown at liftoff. The iced up airplane wobbled nose high into the air at an unknown percent of takeoff power and never became a flying machine. According to voice recorder the first officer said to the captain, "Larry, we are going down." The captain replied, "Yes, I know." Bewilderment!
6. The pilots were distracted with control problems and the complicated departure path near the White House. Tragically, had the power levers been pushed up to maximum power, the flight might have been saved.

The flight recorder indicated the pilots unknowingly used only 70% of power on takeoff. The pilots thought they had maximum takeoff power but failed to interpret the other engine gauges. It is incredible that they missed this, but they did.

Brumbeloe writes, "Abnormal operations in extreme conditions are what started the chain of events. There is never a good reason to depart from and ignore the flight manual. Pilots are not invincible. At the end of the day, the question remains: What are we doing?"[1]

Israel is doing incredibly foolish things that are about to bring them into a crash course with God. Jeremiah the prophet urgently warns and pleads with them, as well as giving the Israelites dire announcements of the coming disaster. Gloom and doom dominate his thinking, preaching, and writing for the first thirty chapters, but suddenly, almost without warning, his tune changes. Israel had departed from the normal operational manual of praise to their God and had drifted toward disaster. Now Jeremiah says that salvation from that horrific crash is about to be avoided! How? Because God is alerted to the situation and tells them "I will" be the one who will change your course. God says, "I will be the one who will restore you and your land. Trust me. Tune your instrumental panels into my frequency and see the difference. I will bring you from the brink of disaster to portals of success!" It is time to sing the song of salvation.

The Song Of Salvation Is A Shout Of Joy (Jeremiah 31:7-9)

Elmer Martin writes that Jeremiah sees ahead for Israel's remnant "an anticipation of the reconstruction process, the return of joyful times, uninterrupted economic pursuits and vigorous religious activity ... a united Israel in worship."[2]

Praise is the celebration of God ... the basis for true worship. Sometimes it comes as a quiet inner sound. At other times it comes as a shout of joy from our lips. Both are praises of God. In *Worship: Rediscovering the Missing Jewel*, Ronald Allen reminds his readers that when we worship we extol God, we sound praises and we boast of him and his incredible deeds on our behalf. Allen concludes with these words, "As a thoughtful gift is a celebration of a birthday, as a special evening out is a celebration of an anniversary, as a warm eulogy is a celebration of a life, as a sexual embrace is a celebration of a marriage"[3] — so a shout in worship is a celebration of God. This shout of praise should be:

- praise mixed with joy,
- praise mixed with human emotion,
- praise aimed at the source of salvation — God,
- praise mixed with loud voices,
- praise mixed with inner hope, or
- praise mixed with prayerful communication.

Praise comes by keeping our eyes focused on God as the absolute source of our faith, anticipating life's goodness even when hope looks empty, circumstances seem overwhelming, and temptations and trials assault us.

Augustine wrote, "The Christian should be an alleluia from head to foot."

55

The Song Of Salvation Is A Chorus Of Proclamation (Jeremiah 31:10-13)

Jeremiah proclaims salvation begins in the saving action of the great shepherd. He promises to ransom and redeem the people. To ransom something means that a great price will have to be paid to set it free. The concept is to "buy back." The Hebrew understood this as a rich spiritual word that required a blood offering to avenge bloodshed that was happening in the siege and exile of Israel.

The Christian has the hindsight to know that Christ died on the cross ... he paid a great price for the redemption of humankind. Paul penned to the Corinthian church, "Now, brothers, I want to remind you of the gospel I preached to you, which you received and on which you have taken your stand. By this gospel you are saved, if you hold firmly to the word I preached to you. Otherwise, you have believed in vain. For what I received I passed on to you as of first importance: that Christ died for our sins according to the scriptures ..." (1 Corinthians 15:1-3 NIV).

Working among the poor and neglected of London was a woman who inspired others because of her Christian faith and compassion. A newspaper man observed this Christian in action and asked what led her to work with the underprivileged. She related that as a young Jew, she had fled the German Gestapo in France during World War II. The Gestapo was closing in on her when she found sanctuary in the home of a French Huguenot widow. The young Jew later was told she must flee immediately to a new location, but the distraught girl replied that it was no use as the Gestapo would find her anyway. The widow responded, "Yes, they will find someone here." This Christian lady took her Jewish friend's identification papers and sent her off with other Huguenots escorting Jews to safety.

The young woman understood the plan. The German Gestapo would think that the widow was her and as an escaping Jew would arrest her instead. The Jewish refugee asked, "Why are you doing this?" The widow responded, "It's the least I can do. Christ has already done that and more for me." As predicted the widow was

56

taken and imprisoned in the Jewish girl's place. Six months later she died in the concentration camp.[4]

The Jewish woman was able to outrun the German Gestapo but could never outrun the Christian's personal sacrifice. The Christian Huguenot's sacrifice was for one. Christ's sacrifice was for the entire world for all ages! We must proclaim the redemption of Israel's God and our Savior Jesus Christ. How can we remain silent?

The Song Of Salvation Is A Chorus Of Peace (Jeremiah 31:14)

Omar Nelson Bradley served in the US Army between 1915 and 1953. He achieved the rank of General and served as the Army Chief of Staff and Chairman of the Joint Chiefs of Staff. He served in three major wars — World War I, World War II, and the Korean War. Known as "The G.I.'s General," he was beloved by those who served with him and for him. In an essay he wrote during his years as Chairman of the Joint Chiefs of Staff, titled "On Wishful Thinking," Bradley wrote:

> *We must accept reality and react promptly to all the facts — not only to those we want to hear. And we must fight constantly for the whole truth. For peace can come only from truth, knowledge, and honest understanding. Half the truth will produce only half a peace — and half a peace is no longer enough.*[5]

In a world so out of synch with peace, isn't it good to know we have a Savior who can bring peace to our lives and hearts? Peace of heart does not hinge on the outer circumstances of life, ruffled by adversity, overshadowed by regret, buffeted by guilt, or disturbed by fear. Peace hinges on who I know. Jesus is all truth, all knowledge, and all trustworthiness! When he resides in the heart ... true peace exists.

Don't search in all the wrong places or follow in the wrong direction. It will only lead to a spiritual crash and tragic ending. Search in the right places that leads to salvation and gives us a song to the very end! Amen.

1. Renda Brumbeloe, *Morning Musing*, February 25, 2008 devotional, "What Are We Doing." Website rendabrumbeloe.org. Used by permission. Additional information ... National Transportation Safety Board ... NTSB Number AAR-82/08, NTIS Number PB82-910408.

2. Walter A. Elwell, editor, *Evangelical Commentary* (Grand Rapids: Baker Book House, 1989), p. 541.

3. Ronald Allen, *Worship: Rediscovering The Missing Jewel* (Eugene, Oregon: Wipf and Stock Publishers, 2001).

4. *God's Little Devotional Book for Men* (Tulsa: Honor Books, 1996), p. 35.

5. Tom Barnard, *Tuesday Morning* newsletter, to subscribe, email to barnard22@cox.net.

The Epiphany Of Our Lord
Isaiah 60:1-6

To God Be The Glory!

One of the most prolific songwriters of the nineteenth century was Fanny Crosby. She was the daughter of John and Mercy Crosby from Putnam County, New York. Fanny was born on March 24, 1820. At age six weeks she became ill with a slight cold, causing inflammation of the eyes. Her concerned parents sent for the doctor to come and examine her. The family doctor was out of town and a doctor unfamiliar with the Crosby family came to the home. He recommended the use of hot poultices, which destroyed her sight. Growing up in a sightless world did not deter Fanny Crosby; she would not let anyone feel sorry for her. At the age of fifteen, she entered the New York Institution for the Blind, where she earned an excellent education. She became a teacher in the Institution in 1847 and continued her work until March 1, 1858. She taught English grammar, rhetoric, and Roman and American history. During this period of her life she began to develop a passion for song writing and poetry.

She wrote several secular songs that were very popular in her day. Hymn writing, however, is what the world remembers best about Fanny Crosby. She wrote over 4,000 of them in her lifetime. She had a dynamic relationship with Jesus Christ since childhood, and it inspired her hymn writing. She wrote the songs, "Safe In The Arms Of Jesus," "Rescue The Perishing," "Pass Me Not, O Gentle Saviour," "Jesus Keep Me Near The Cross," "Blessed Assurance," and more. Another of her hymns, "To God Be The Glory" is one that the prophet Isaiah could have related to very well. Sing with her words:

To God be the glory, great things he hath done!
So loved he the world that he gave us His Son,
who yielded his life an atonement for sin,
and opened the lifegate that all may go in.

O perfect redemption, the purchase of blood,
to every believer, the promise of God;
The vilest offender who truly believes,
that moment from Jesus a pardon receives.

Great things he hath taught us, great things he hath done,
and great our rejoicing thru Jesus, the Son;
but purer, and higher, and greater will be
our wonder, our transport when Jesus we see!

Refrain:
Praise the Lord, praise the Lord;
let the earth hear His voice!
Praise the Lord! Praise the Lord;
let the people rejoice!
O come to the Father thru Jesus the Son,
and give him the glory — great things he hath done![1]

Fanny Crosby may not have been able to see the glory of God with her eyes, but she certainly saw him with her heart! Today, we are called to see the glory of God with our heart in a dark, dismal world. He has come to shine on us.

The Old Testament usually translates "glory" with the word *kabod*, which means "importance, weight, or radiance." Isaiah understood the radiance of God when he wrote, "Arise, shine, for your light has come, and the glory (radiance) of the Lord rises upon you" (Isaiah 60:1 NIV). Have you experienced that brilliance, radiance, glory in your life? Without that holy glory, darkness shadows the soul. God's glory doesn't automatically splash on you, it is something that has to be desired, longed after, and asked for by each individual.

God's Glory Dispels Darkness (Isaiah 60:2-3a)

There are many dark spots in the world because of pride, hatred, prejudice, child trafficking, prostitution, pornography, sex tourism, domestic servitude, forced soldiering, slave work, sweat shops, and all colors of sin.

Dr. Hermann Gschwandtner wrote an article titled "The Village without Men: Sharing God's Love" that paints the darkness of sin. He writes about the "paradise island" known for its beautiful, lush green countryside known as Sri Lanka. "But life is no paradise in the small eastern village of Sathurukondan. Although its people are welcoming and friendly, they have suffered great tragedy: Only women and girls reside there." Why only women and girls? Simple. All 800 of the men and boys were murdered by men who came into their village and massacred them. "The attackers' motivation remains unclear, but hundreds lost their lives in the slaughter."

Sathurukondan is caught in the middle of Sri Lanka's civil war. More than 150,000 have fled the area, and most resettle elsewhere. It is difficult to know how to share God's love and his glory with those left behind. How does God display his glory and radiance in the middle of such utter horror and downright despair?[2]

- Through people who care — Christians who will carry out programs of compassion ... nutritional, educational, agricultural, and spiritual.
- Through people who share — they share the promise of God's forgiveness from sin with all of its ugliness.
- Through people who converse — these people will listen and talk through the grief and hurt.
- Through our own experience of discovering God's grace and mercy in all situations of life.
- Through our own experience of exercising faith and realizing that God has faith in us as well.
- Through our own experience of walking daily with Jesus we can see the reminders of his universe, world, and people.

The glory of God must be passed from one generation to another.

God's Glory Shines Inside The Heart (Isaiah 60:5)

Discovering God's glory in and around our earth is great ... the beauty of the earth, the intricacies of our bodies, the sight of a rainbow, the variety of species, the details of a snowflake. It is also discovering God's glory inside our hearts. His glory will bring a distinctiveness or noble character to a life that has been ravaged by sin. Though we were chained like a slave, held by sin's galling fetters in life, God broke those chains apart and now there is a glorious freedom from the dungeon of life. Glorious light! Holy light! Pure sunshine! Jesus incarnated by the Holy Spirit born of a woman — flesh and divinity perfectly matched. As the theologians would say about Jesus, "very God and very man." When he is invited into our hearts he comes to live inside so that we now possess a glorious heart — a redeemed heart — a pure heart — a clean heart!

In 1907, Kate Byron wrote the song, "He's Everything To Me" (sometimes attributed to Kate Ulmer) and the words are so meaningful.

> *In sin I once had wandered, all weary, sad, and lone,*
> *till Jesus through his mercy, adopted me his own.*
> *E'er since I learned to trust him, his grace doth make*
> *   me free,*
> *and now I feel his pardon. He's everything to me.*
>
> ***Refrain:***
> *He's everything to me; from sin he sets me free.*
> *His peace and love my portion through all eternity!*
> *He's everything to me, more than I dreamed could be.*
> *O praise his name forever! He's everything to me.*[3]

We cannot sing that song unless the glory of the Lord shines within us!

God's Glory Radiates Outside (Isaiah 60:6b)

Living near Lake Michigan for nearly a quarter of a century allowed me to observe lighthouses from Chicago's shores to "Big

Red" in Holland, Michigan. No matter the architectural style, shape, color, or design, the purpose of all lighthouses is to send out the light! With our hearts throbbing and swelling with God's glory, we will radiate like lighthouses through the dark waters on which spiritual vessels sail. We will send out the light of God's glory. How?

- Through our attitude of joy.

> *Happiness is caused by things that happen around me, and circumstances will mar it; but joy flows right through trouble; joy flows in the night as well as in the day; joy flows through persecution and opposition. It is an unceasing fountain bubbling up in the heart; secret spring the world can't see and doesn't know anything about.*[4]

- Through our attitude of assurance — we have a confidence that endures because it is in God.

> *Blessed assurance, Jesus is mine!*
> *O what a foretaste of glory divine!*
> *Heir of salvation, purchase of God,*
> *born of his Spirit, washed in his blood.*
> *This is my story, this is my song,*
> *praising my Savior all the day long.*
> *This is my story, this is my song,*
> *praising my Savior all the day long.*[5]

- Through an attitude of hope — the Christian's light brightly shows the attitude of hope to a world that is sickened with the disease of hopelessness. Armies line up on one another's borders and territories. Terrorists have no boundaries. Hatred knows no friendships. Many in the world shake their heads in despair, but God gives a hope and his name is Jesus!

In both the Old and New Testaments the glory of God is an expression of God's inherent majesty that his people recognize and for which they have a passion! Give God glory wherever you are today ... whenever you want to express a "glory to God" ... whatever circumstance you are in, give God praise, honor, and glory! Amen.

---

1. "To God Be The Glory," words by Fanny J. Crosby, 1875. In the public domain.

2. *Nazarene Compassionate Ministries* magazine 2008, Vol. 5, No. 1, p. 7.

3. "He's Everything To Me," words by Kate Byron, also attributed to Kate Ulmer, 1907. In the public domain.

4. Lila Empson, editor, *Soul Retreats for Leaders* (Grand Rapids: Inspirio, 2003), p. 37.

5. "Blessed Assurance," words by Fanny J. Crosby, 1873. In the public domain.

The Baptism Of Our Lord
Epiphany 1
Ordinary Time 1
Isaiah 43:1-7

A New Life

The old traditional idea of camping out under the stars with only a blanket or sleeping bag next to a running river, hauling water from a stream, cooking over the open fire, and hearing the sounds of coyote in the distance has been replaced! Motor homes of all sizes, shapes, and conveniences allow the traveler the comforts of home! Modern campers can now park a fully equipped motor home on a cement pad in the middle of a forest with a lake as a background, but they can hook up to water and a separate sewer line, and an electric outlet to allow them to watch their favorite television program on a flat-screen television in HD! Their cell phone keeps them connected to the family; the computer hookup gives them access to the world through the web. No more inconveniences of dirt roads, no more need for smoke in the eyes with an open fire, no more drudgery of walking to the stream for a bath. One can choose whether to go outside or stay inside looking through their double-size window that brings all outdoors indoors.

People buy motor homes with the hope of seeing new places, getting out into the world and seeing new sites, making new friends, and having new adventures.

"New" is the optimum word in this scripture. We look for new opportunities and new challenges. In his word God is giving Israel a new opportunity. In chapter 42, Isaiah culminates with punishment for the people of Israel for their consistent sinful ways. Chapter 43 takes a new turn. It is a chapter filled with the promise of new adventures if they turn from their evil ways and follow his direction for their lives. God's fury of sin is now replaced with his new desire for their redemption (43:1). But that has always been the way. God absolutely hates sin, but his absolute love and consistent purpose is working for their redemption. The culmination point is the coming of Jesus to redeem not just Israel, but all of human-kind. David McKenna comments, "For a moment at least, we turn the pages from the Old Testament to the New Testament and find in this chapter the theological roots of our Christian faith."[1]

Isaiah is giving rise to the idea of a new creation, a new love story, a new family reunion.

A New Creation (Isaiah 43:1)

Creation deals with the idea of origins. In the physical realm it is the origin of matter, energy, stars, planets, animals, plants, man, and everything from the beginning until now.

> *Creation may be defined as the free act of God by which he brought into existence the universe and all that it contains, without the use of preexistent materials —* creatio ex nihilo.[2]

Isaiah understands that it is this same God who formed the world and all that is in it, who created and formed the people of Israel. It is out of this formation that they become a special people.

> *God's naming of Israel is also a special act of his new creation. Like a father and mother giving their child its name at the time of dedication or baptism, God gives Israel his own name as members of the family.*[3]

God who formed the world and all that is in it has created a special people through the death and resurrection of Jesus. Like Israel they were powerless to save themselves. Good works do not save. Attempts to keep the Ten Commandments or the Mosaic Law do not save them. Wishing does not save. These individuals have come to a point of recognizing their sin, acknowledging their need of turning from their sin while turning to God, and requesting that he forgives them of their sin. These people are called Christians.

What does it mean to be a new creation in Christ? How are we redeemed by God as Israel was redeemed?

- The distinctive element is the fact that these people centered on the person of Jesus Christ (Acts 11:26; Acts 26:28; 1 Peter 4:16).
- There is a fervent commitment to Christ as Savior and Lord of their lives.
- It meant a formal identification with the body of Christ ... the church.
- There is an acceptance of the spiritual principles of the Christian community.
- There is a continuing identification with Christ.

This new creation births Christians all around the globe in all shapes, sizes, races, colors, and ages.

> *Being a Christian means allowing the interpretation of life found in Christ Jesus to shape one's existence. This becomes a unifying center for one's life. It is the context in which all else is seen. It is, of all life's considerations, the most important and it relativizes all else.*[4]

A New Love Story (Isaiah 43:2-4)

I enjoy a good story. Stories can transport me to incredible lands. Whether real or fictional they create characters with unique quirks that demonstrate strengths and weaknesses, or show their high or low motivation to do something in life. Stories can trigger my imagination and unravel any of my preconceived ideas. A rhythm can build to a crescendo like a mountain peak or surprise me with a sudden drop, not unlike that of a roller coaster. A good story triggers more questions than it gives answers. Anticipation should build throughout the story as it creates an "Oh" or "Wow" moment. The depth of the story gives me understanding and background of the events that come with the experiences they reveal. A truly good story calls me back to read it a second time. The end doesn't just summarize, but concludes the story. It climaxes all that has gone before and is satisfying all that I need to know.

Isaiah wrote a love story about God. When life seems unbearable, filled with trials, tragedies, or temptations, God demonstrates his strength of character by coming alongside us. When we pass through the waters and rivers, fires and flames, he enters our troubles and unravels our preconceived ideas by surprising us with his holy presence. When sin wraps itself around our heart, the depth of the story is revealed in the power of God! God sends his Son into the world to break the power of sin, Satan, evil, and hell. At the baptism of Jesus, God speaks, "You are my Son, whom I love; with you I am well pleased" (Luke 3:22 NIV). This is God coming in flesh to make his powerful presence available to people who seek him. What a love story! The champion of the oppressed, bleeding, and dying, God himself becomes our defender. John tells us how much God loves us. Say it aloud, "For God so loved the world that he gave his one and only Son, that whoever believes in him shall not perish but have eternal life. For God did not send his Son into the world to condemn the world, but to save the world through him" (John 3:16-17 NIV). Take time and read the story again!

A New Family Reunion (Isaiah 43:5-7)
These verses are reminders of God's love in relationship to his children ... his family. The people of Israel had lost their identity as a nation. God, through his prophet Isaiah, says he will bring his family home from the east, west, north, and south. No corner of the world will be left untouched.

An even more grandiose family reunion is being planned. God is sending his Son, Jesus, back to the earth and will call all of his children home to a family reunion in the new kingdom! They will come from the east, west, north, and south. No corner of the world will be left untouched. All who are dead and those who are still living will be caught up with him in the sky and transported to their new home ... heaven! It will be an incredible day for those who know him. There will be laughing, shouts of joy, hugging, and loving beyond our wildest imagination. People we have not seen in decades will greet us and those that we have only heard or read about will be at that reunion as they will be our brothers and sisters in the faith.

But there is more! I read about a young boy who had been serving the Lord for a few months who visited a friend who was dying. The youngster offered to read some of the promises from the Bible. He read the first two verses of John 14. "My friend," said the old Christian, "those are great verses, comforting verses, but look at me, my friend; do you think it is a mansion that this old man is longing for, a pearly gate to walk through, or golden streets that my old feet are longing to walk on? No, friend, please read the next verses."

Then the boy read, "Where I am, there you may be also." The aged man said, "Now you have it! It is the master that I want to see and be with forever!"[5]

I have been at many airports and have observed many family reunions. I especially enjoy watching military families. I know that they have kept constant correspondence through letters, emails, and exchange of gifts. But when they see each other at the airport the letters that the postman brought that morning go unnoticed and the packages unopened, but there is a rush to be in one another's arms.

God has sent us letters and gifts over our lifetime, but when Jesus comes, the letters and gifts will be set aside and we will rush into his loving arms — forever!

Are you ready for the greatest of family reunions? Amen.

1. Lloyd J. Ogilvie, editor, *The Communicator's Commentary*, Isaiah 40-66 by David Mckenna (Dallas: Word Books, 1994).

2. J. Kenneth Grider/Willard H. Taylor, *Beacon Dictionary of Theology* (Kansas City: Beacon Hill Press of Kansas City, 1983), p. 139.

3. *Op cit*, Ogilvie, p. 450.

4. Albert M. Wells Jr., compiler, *Inspiring Quotations* (Nashville: Thomas Nelson, 1988), p. 30.

5. G. B. F. Hallock, *Five Thousand Best Modern Illustrations* (New York: George Doran Company, 1927), p. 360.

Epiphany 2
Ordinary Time 2
Isaiah 62:1-5

A New Name

Let's play a game. I am going to say a name and you think about that person. What emotions does the name bring to mind? What nostalgic feature? What accomplishments do you remember about them or what negatives have they produced in your thinking?

- Abraham Lincoln
- Eve
- Tommy Dorsey
- Joan of Arc
- Paul the apostle
- Amelia Earhart
- Mohammad Ali
- Albert Einstein
- Mary the Mother of Jesus
- Osama bin Laden
- Mother Teresa

Now think of the names of people in your life who have influenced you

- parents
- grandparents
- other relatives
- Sunday school teachers
- schoolteachers
- pastors

- friends
- classmates
- coworkers

The first set of names you have read about, and you have formed opinions from someone else's perception. The latter are names that you know or have known personally. They have intersected your life either positively or negatively.

Charles Swindoll reminds us that in *Pilgrim's Progress* the pilgrim's name throughout the book is Christian, but that was not his original name. At the start of the allegory, the scene shows the pilgrim talking with a porter:

Porter: What is your name?

Pilgrim: My name is now *Christian*, but my name at the first was *Graceless*.

"The same could be said for all of us today who claim the glorious name of Jesus Christ as our Lord and Savior. Our name is now Christian, but it has not always been so. That title was given to us the moment we believed, the day we took God at his word and accepted the gift of eternal life he offered us. Prior to the name change, we were Graceless, indeed."[1]

When was your name changed to Christian? Can you reflect on that day? What stands out as you remember when you received a new name? How has the new name affected your outlook? What problems has it caused? What excitement has it brought?

A New Name Denotes A New Identity (Isaiah 62:1)

My identity is the collection of the characteristics by which I am known or recognized by others. I was once known as "sinner" because of how I acted and lived. When I came to know and experience forgiveness from God my name was changed to Christian. C. Austin Miles titled one of his songs, "A New Name In Glory" and penned these words:

> *I was once a sinner, but I came*
> *pardon to receive from my Lord.*
> *This was freely given and I found*
> *that he always kept his word.*

72

God's power of forgiveness allows me to change my identity. He puts me on a new track in life. We can help others in their identity crisis by forgiving them.

Walter Rathenau was Germany's Jewish foreign minister in 1922. He was born in Berlin, the son of Emil and Mathilde Rathenau, a prominent Jewish family in 1867. He became an engineer after studying physics, chemistry, and philosophy in Berlin and Strasbourg. His father founded Allgemeine Elektrizitats-Gesellschaft (AEG) electrical-engineering company, bringing it to the forefront of Germany's economy and amassing a fortune. When Emil Rathenau died in 1915, Walter became the chairman of AEG and prominent in the new industrialization of Germany.

Walter Rathenau was a moderate liberal in politics and was one of the founders of the German Democratic Party. He rejected the tide of socialism that was sweeping through Germany and advocated for privatization of industry and greater worker participation in the management of companies. He greatly influenced the post World War I government of Germany.

In 1921, Rathenau was appointed Minister of Reconstruction and on February 1, 1922, became Foreign Minister of Germany. He insisted that Germany should fulfill its obligations under the Treaty of Versailles, while working for a revision of its terms. He also negotiated the Treaty of Rapallo with the Soviet Union. Both of these items infuriated German nationalists including the (still obscure) Nazi Party and other right wing groups.

On June 24, 1922, he was driving from his house to Wilhelmstrabe, as he routinely did. During the trip his car was passed by another with three machine-gun-armed men who peppered his car with bullets and riddled Rathenau's body. He was killed at the scene.[3]

73

According to Victor M. Parachin's article in the *Standard* the three assassins were captured and two of them ended their lives by suicide. Ernst Werner Techow was the only one who came to trial. According to Parachin, "Mathilde Rathenau, the victim's mother, wrote to the mother of Ernst saying, 'In grief unspeakable, I give you my hand ... Say to your son that, in the name and spirit of him he has murdered, I forgive....' "

Her words were read in an open court as Techow listened. Techow was sentenced to fifteen years for his part in the assassination. Just five years later, in 1927, he was released for good behavior. The impact of Mathilde's words dramatically changed the killer. In prison, he began to seriously study Jewish history, art, literature, religion, and culture. He mastered Hebrew, becoming an erudite scholar of Judaism. Parachin writes that Techow also became highly sensitive to issues concerning the Jews.

Techow wanted to start life over and atone for his murderous act. He changed his name to Ernst Tessier and joined the French Foreign Legion, becoming a highly decorated officer. He became the officer in charge of Fort Flatters, a Legion desert outpost. He met another legionnaire whose name was Rathenau. He asked if he was related to the late Walter Rathenau. The legionnaire stated that he was his nephew. Carefully choosing his words he told the young man his story and pulled the letter from a trunk that Mathilde Rathenau had written. He explained how her forgiveness and compassion changed his life.

When France surrendered to Nazi Germany in 1940 Techow left the Foreign Legion and moved to Marseille and disguised himself as a dock worker. It is there that he began to smuggle Jews out of France to Spain to safety. He enabled over 700 Jews to flee for freedom. Techow's dramatic transformation came on the part of Mathilde Rathenau whose conscious choice was an equally dramatic act of forgiveness.[4]

His new identity made a difference. Since you have taken on a new identity what difference have you made in life? What ways can you influence others? It may not be as dramatic as Techow's, but even the little acts can make a difference.

A New Name Denotes A New Gift From God (Isaiah 62:2)

God offers his gift of righteousness through his grace and manifested in his work and character on our behalf. Just as it is in God, so it should be in the redeemed of Israel of Isaiah's day and so it is in the New Testament believer. God instills within the believer his righteousness as characterized through our life and work by his grace.

What is grace? How would you define it?

> *The most popular two-word definition is "unmerited favor." To amplify that a bit: Grace is what God does for mankind, which we do not deserve, which we cannot earn, and which we will never be able to repay. Awash in our sinfulness, helpless to change on our own, polluted to the core with no possibility of cleaning ourselves up, we cry out for grace. It is our only hope.*[5]

The word "righteous" means "to be right and to be right is to be fair, just, or straight." Since God is righteous, he will deal with each of us in a just manner. Since we are hopelessly lost, we need a redeemer. His name is Jesus who took our sins and punishment upon himself so we could have an eternal hope. This is the meaning and purpose of Christ's death for all people — the righteous one dying to make the sinner righteous.

Cliff Barrows, who for many years was the song leader of the Billy Graham Crusade ministry, had an incident occur in his home when his children were small that illustrates the word "righteousness."

Cliff said, "They had done something I had forbidden them to do. I told them if they did the same thing again I would have to discipline them. When I returned from work and found that they hadn't minded me, the heart went out of me. I just couldn't discipline them."

He wasn't sure what to do. It was just one of those circumstances that made it hard on a dad to know how to handle it. Bobby and Bettie Ruth were very young and Cliff called them into his bedroom. He took off his belt and his shirt. With his bare back exposed, he knelt down beside the bed and made them both strap him ten times each with his belt. Barrows says, "You should have heard the crying! From them, I mean! They didn't want to do it. But I told them the penalty had to be paid and so through their sobs and tears they did what I told them."

He said that it hurt them to do it. But the result was that never again did he have to spank them, because they got the point. They hugged and kissed one another and then prayed together.[6]

Barrows modeled the love of God by taking the penalty for their wrong upon him. God's righteousness, holiness, and justice have been satisfied with the death of Jesus. The power of the resurrection is that gift was given to us so that we would have the strength to live life ... righteously.

A New Name Denotes A Fresh Start (Isaiah 62:3-4)

After living a life full of sin, we all need a new beginning, a fresh start to real life. God offers that freely to each one who asks. This includes:

- Future-positive possibilities — the old lifestyle gave me limited possibilities to make my life choices, but never in the will of God because I didn't ask his direction. My future was self-centered and out of focus because my life was not God centered. With God I have the possibility of making right choices with his direction that gives rise to a positive future.
- A redeemable past — though my life was ruled by sin and my past strewn with wrong decisions, because of the fresh start, God redeemed, forgave, and forgot my past. David wrote, "As far as the east is from the west, so far has he removed our transgressions from us" (Psalm 103:12 NIV).
- A filled heart — Blaise Pascal wrote, "There is a God-shaped vacuum in the heart of every person and it can never be filled by any created thing. It can only be filled by God, made known through Jesus Christ."

This fresh start puts me into a right relationship with God. Oswald Chambers offers the bottom line.

You never can measure what God will do through you if you are rightly related to Jesus Christ. Keep your relationship right with him, then whatever circumstances you are in, and whoever you meet day by day, he is pouring rivers of living water through you ... it is the work that God does through us that counts, not what we do for him.[7]

Remember the song at the beginning of this sermon, "A New Name In Glory" by C. Austin Miles? Do you have a new name? God offers it to you *now*! Amen.

---

1. Charles Swindoll, *The Tale of the Tardy Oxcart* (Nashville: Word Publishing, 1998), p. 409.

2. "A New Name In Glory," words by C. Austin Miles (1910). In the public domain.

3. http://en.wikipedia.org/wiki/Walter_Rathenau.

4. Everett Leadingham, editor, *Standard*, published quarterly by Word Action Publishing Company, 2923 Troost Ave., Kansas City, Missouri.

5. Charles Swindoll, *Growing Deep in the Christian Life* (Portland: Multnomah Press, 1986), p. 215.

6. *Ibid*, pp. 257-258.

7. Jan Karon, *Patches of Godlight* (New York: Penguin Group, 2001), npn.

The Winning Word

Tom Barnard tells of his great love for sports stories, especially where an athlete survives an ugly situation and is honored for his or her lifetime achievements. One of those celebrations occurred on baseball's opening day, 2008. It happened to William Joseph "Bill" Buckner, a former major league baseball player for the Los Angeles Dodgers, Chicago Cubs, California Angels, Kansas City Royals, and the Boston Red Sox.

Accompanied by a loud, standing ovation prior to the start of the Red Sox home opener against the Detroit Tigers, the former first baseman threw out the ceremonial "first pitch" to his former teammate, Dwight Evans. The full house of just under 38,000 fans celebrated as they enjoyed season opener 108 for the Sox.

By anyone's standards, Bill Buckner had an outstanding professional baseball career. In 2,517 games played over a period of 22 years, he accumulated 2,715 hits, averaged .289, and had only 453 strikeouts. Buckner led the National League in batting average in 1980 (.324) and was named an All-Star once (1981).

With all of his success, Bill Buckner is remembered most for *one error* he made while a member of the Red Sox. It happened during the World Series of 1986. Boston led the best-of-seven series against the New York Mets, 3 games to 2, and had a two-run lead with two outs in the bottom of the tenth inning. New York came back to tie the game with three straight singles off Calvin Schiraldi and a wild pitch by Bob Stanley. The next batter was Mookie Wilson, who fouled off several pitches before hitting a routine ground ball to Buckner at first base. The ball rolled under

Buckner's glove, through his legs, allowing the winning run to score and forcing a seventh game, which the Mets won, and along with it a World Series. In July 1987, the Red Sox released Bill. He rejoined the team briefly in 1990 and retired after 22 games.

In an April 9, 2008, *Boston Globe* article titled "Buckner's Appearance Marks the End of an Error," writer Amalie Benjamin wrote:

> *This was not the first time Buckner had faced Fenway and the fans since his infamous 1986 moment ... But since that time, there has been healing in Red Sox Nation. His name might still evoke a picture of the ball heading between his legs in Game 6 of the 1986 World Series, but with two championships in the meantime (2004 and 2007), the hurt has subsided.*

While the Boston media remember the error that lost the team a possible World Series, the fans have put it behind them. And what management did to celebrate a player for what he had accomplished in life was a classy thing.[1]

There is no holiness hall of fame, but if there were, it would include the names of men like Nehemiah and Ezra. These two men made a lasting impression on their nation, the people, and the religious community for centuries. They were not looking for fame, or fortune, or a lasting name, but for something more valuable. Their desire was to spread the word of the Lord. Nehemiah did it as a layperson by physically building the safeguards of the walls of Jerusalem and Ezra did it as a priest by laying the spiritual foundation for the word of God at a time of spiritual ineptness.

The scriptural background finds the walls laid despite the continual interference from those jealous of the Jews, Senballat, Tobiah, and Geshem and the rest of the enemies of God's people. The people numbering approximately 50,000 (Nehemiah 7:66-67) have settled into their homes and a routine of life. Ezra was deeply committed to understanding and obeying God's law and will. He took seriously the job of communicating the laws of God to the people.

Gene Getz calls Ezra the priest a "diligent student" who devoted himself to learning the word of God. Ezra understood that before he could teach God's truth effectively, he had to grasp it himself. By wrestling with the truths he applied them to his own personal life. He was a "faithful practitioner" and did not ask people to do something he was not practicing himself. However, it was not just that Ezra had knowledge of the scriptures, and it wasn't just his innate ability to communicate. He was also an "anointed servant" of the master of the universe according to Ezra 7:6, "for the hand of the Lord his God was on him." Ezra had a dynamic relationship with God! It is no wonder that he was the "one person" who stood in the seventh month of the Jewish calendar on the first day and began reading the Book of the Law (Torah) to a waiting people. What he read was the word of God winning over sin and degradation.

We need to allow the Word of God to win in our lives!

We Need To Allow God To Break Through Our Sin

The books of Ezra and Nehemiah are seamless in the Hebrew tradition. They are considered a unified work. When Ezra arrived in Jerusalem he was greeted with a deplorable situation of moral and spiritual decay. He was so distraught after hearing how unfaithful laity and clergy had been that in his auto-biographical writing he states, "When I heard this, I tore my tunic and cloak, pulled hair from my head and beard and sat down appalled" (Ezra 9:3 NIV).

> How many days and weeks and perhaps months Ezra prayed and wept before God, we're not told ... while he was "praying and making confession, weeping and prostrating himself before the house of God," a large group of people involving whole families gathered one day and joined him in his weeping and confession (Ezra 10:1). This was a breakthrough — the beginning point of revival and renewal in Israel.[2]

Spiritual renewal does not begin unless there is confession, sincerity, and spiritual transparency before God. We cannot possess a spirit of haughtiness, superiority, selfishness, or egotism.

81

God is ready to forgive us. He stands ready by the redeeming work of Jesus Christ. Whatever language you read it in, God loves you and me!

> *Ty så älskade Gud världen, att han utgav sin enfödde Son, på det att var och en som tror på honom skall icke förgås, utan hava evigt liv.* — John 3:16 (Swedish)[3]

> *Car Dieu a tant aimé le monde qu'il a donné son Fils unique, afin que quiconque croit en lui ne périsse point, mais qu'il ait la vie éternelle* — John 3:16 (French)[4]

> *For God so loved the world that he gave his one and only Son, that whoever believes in him shall not perish but have eternal life.* — John 3:16 (NIV)

Every language, culture, nationality, age, or gender needs God's redeeming work! Have you confessed your sins and asked God into your life? John wrote, "If we confess our sins, he is faithful and just and will forgive us our sins and purify us from all unrighteousness" (1 John 1:9 NIV).

After Christ has come into your life you are ready for the journey.

We Need To Worship The Lord On Our Journey Of Life

The word of God began to speak to this holy man of God. Nehemiah 8:6 reveals that as Ezra opens the word of God at daybreak, he becomes overwhelmed with emotion and praises God overtly. The people observing Ezra in his excitement and joyful celebration raise their hands and respond, "Amen! Amen!" The word "amen" translates, "let it be so!" I believe the people were saying, "Let God's word speak to our hearts," and they bow with their faces to the ground in worship to their God. What a sight it must have been. Commentators estimate the crowd to be between 30,000 to 50,000 people. When God's Spirit comes upon a congregation there can be an overwhelming feeling of worship that must be expressed.

The act of divine worship is the inestimable privilege
of man, the only created being who bows in humility
and adoration. — Hosea Ballou[5]

As a congregation are we willing to worship God? Worship includes:

- a willingness to listen to God,
- an offering of ourselves to the glory of Christ,
- a sense of repentance ... a godly sorrow for sin,
- a sacrificial love for the sake of the Savior,
- a spirit of holy living as a community of believers as well as individual holiness,
- an inspirational quality that is the very breath of God, and
- a valuing of the promises that God gives his people as his holy possessions.

We Need To Respond To God With Appropriate Actions

The Israelites worshiped the God of the word, but they also responded with obedience. These worshipers translated their affirmative attitude into positive appropriate actions! We need to make the appropriate actions when God touches our lives.

The appropriate action occurred when Israel's leaders began to assume their God-given responsibilities for spiritual leadership. Gene Getz observed that after Ezra had shared the law of God with the total congregation, a smaller group gathered around Ezra to learn even more of God's law. He continued the point by writing,

This ... was a very important key in sustaining the re-
newal and revival that had begun in Israel. If this kind
of work is to continue in the hearts of people, it must
continue at the leadership level.[6]

The appropriate action occurred when the people remembered their heritage. As Ezra read the passage of the Feast of the Tabernacle, the people learned that God had given their forefathers this special festival. It was a reminder of their temporary wandering in the wilderness and dwelling places after fleeing Egypt and the forty years of displacement. It reminded them that even though they were out of God's will, they were not out of God's heart. All during their wandering experiences God protected them, provided for their needs, and never forsook them!

Now these descendents wanted to celebrate and remember their heritage. Today, we need to remember and celebrate the heritage of our ancestors who have passed the faith to us. We need to remember the God who led, guided, sustained, and nourished them and never forsook them in spite of their misgivings, misalignments, and mistakes will also lead us. Where does your spiritual heritage begin? Maybe you are the first in your family to have a spiritual relationship. Rejoice! You have been found by God. Start your family's spiritual heritage and someday your great-great-grandchildren will remember their legacy and tradition.

The appropriate action occurred when the people separated themselves from their pagan alliances and practices. The out of synch spiritual world will systematically try to draw you into its circle of immoral and illicit involvement. It will try to make you think you are the one out of step with reality. My friend, if you are in step with God, you will be out of step with the sinful side of humanity. We must determine, like the children of Israel on that memorial day thousands of years ago, to separate ourselves from anything that would cause us to sin, separate us from God, or detour our way to heaven. It can only be done as we learn his word and hide it in our hearts. Keep close to God through continual communication through prayer with him. Allow fellow believers to help you in your journey. Keep in step through the correction and guidance of the Holy Spirit who leads us into holy living.

Do your actions match your words?

As we apply this sermon today to our lives, focus on the divine principles that relate to the word of God. Ezra, the priest, laid the foundation through the scriptures that effectively brought renewal and revival to Israel. Without the spiritual foundation laid; Nehemiah could not have successfully rebuilt the walls of Jerusalem in 52 days. Without the winning word of the Lord we cannot live successful holy lives. Be a winner ... let God and his word be the foundation upon which you build! Amen.

1. Dr. Tom Barnard, *Tuesday Morning* email devotional, April 15, 2008. Barnard22@cox.net or www.snu.edu. Used by permission.

2. Gene A. Getz, *Nehemiah-Becoming a Disciplined Leader* (Nashville: Broadman & Holman Publishers, 1995), p. 163.

3. NYA Testamentet och Psaltaren (Stockholm: Aktiebolaget P. Herzog & Soner, 1952).

4. Le Nouveau Testament (New Paris, Indiana: World Missionary Press, Inc.) Used by permission.

5. G. B. F. Hallock, *Five Thousand Best Modern Illustrations* (New York: George H. Doran Company, 1927), pp. 757-758.

6. *Op cit*, Getz, p. 167.

The Call Of God

Jeremiah had a task, a vision, and a promise from God. The prophet Jeremiah had a call from God to preach his word to a people needing to hear from God. His call has been duplicated multiple times over the centuries.

Moses, Samuel, Amos, Isaiah, and Ezekiel could point to a precise moment in their journey when God called them to be prophets ... ones who announced God's actions and words. Preaching, announcing God's presence, word, direction comes first from a person who has a passion for what matters in life spiritually. When God calls a person to preach, he gives them the necessary gifts to preach and expects him/her to prepare as if eternity were at stake ... and it is for the hearers. Jerry Vines wrote, "Men prepare sermons; God prepares men."

The story is told of Saint Francis of Assisi who invited a young monk to accompany him to town to preach. The young friar was excited to be with Francis and wanted to learn as much from him as possible so he watched him closely. He observed his mentor carefully as they strolled along the streets of the community. Saint Francis would often stop to visit with the children and the merchants. After a while they returned to the abbey. The young priest said, "Sir, you have forgotten that we went to town to preach." Wisely Francis replied, "My son, we have preached! We have been seen by many. Our behavior was closely observed. Our attitudes were closely measured. Our words have been overheard. It was by these measures that we preached our morning sermon."

God has called certain people to preach sermons like Jeremiah in a public pulpit; however, he has called all of us to preach sermons in the marketplace of life. The pulpit ministry and the marketplace ministry have similarities.

The Call (Jeremiah 1:4-5)

"The word of the Lord came to me" in verse 4 indicates a very personal call from God. He recognizes our gifts, abilities, talents, attitudes, and personalities because he has made us. God initiates the call. It is his appointment. His loving approval sends us to the lost world to share the kingdom message through our words, actions, and righteousness.

Andrew Blackwood Jr. writes, "God's initiative does not destroy man's responsibility; quite the contrary. God has acted, therefore man is responsible to act."[1]

The call of God stresses several areas:

- a divine compulsion to respond to the call that God lays on the heart,
- a deep compassion that others are in need of the God that they share,
- a directed concern for the lost who are in desperate need of God's redemption,
- a diligence that drives one to understand and study the word, and
- a depth of accountability for their own spiritual well being.

Whether we are pastors or laypersons, we carry the responsibility of listening and responding to the call of God.

God Knows The Person He Has Called (Jeremiah 1:6-9)

God has called all of us, clergy and laity alike, to the essential aspects of ministry. Often both laity and clergy are running in circles trying to do everything and missing the essential!

I heard about the pilot who announced over the intercom, "Ladies and gentlemen, I have good news and bad news. The good news is that we have a tailwind, and we are making excellent time.

The bad news is that our compass is broken, and we have no idea where we are going!"

Many pastors and their congregants have the same problem. They wander aimlessly around not knowing where they are headed and what they are called to do. They see a responsibility that needs to be tackled, but ask, "Who will fulfill the task?" Instead of asking, "Who feels called to undertake this ministry?" The difference is ever so subtle. God is not calling us to take a task but to fulfill ministry. Ministry is with people, not an organizational chart. God knows the person he has called to do the ministry. He has equipped them with his power and purpose. He has done this by giving individuals:

- Expectations — God will give us the power to overcome obstacles that would hinder our vision or expectations. Dr. Charles Spurgeon was talking to a young preacher, "feeling him out," and he said, "Young man, you really don't expect much to happen in your pastorate, do you?" The young fellow replied, "Well ... no ... not really." Spurgeon exploded, "Then you won't see much happen, either!" Ask God to give you a high expectation of what can occur in your local church, whether it is a Sunday school class, preaching, maintenance or janitorial work, music ... whatever expect God to bless your effort for the church and his kingdom!
- Talents — God-given abilities for God's glory. Phillips Brooks told the story of some illiterate tribesmen to whom a sundial was given. They desired to honor it and keep it sacred so they built a roof over it! Do the talents God has given you seem so valuable that you carefully put a roof over them to shelter and honor them instead of using them for God?
- Wisdom

> *Wisdom is the ability to see with discernment, to view life as God perceives it. Understanding is the skill to respond with insight. Knowledge is the rare trait of learning with perception — discovering and growing.*[2]

- Leadership — Fred Smith said that leadership is both something you are and something you do. Clergy and lay leadership need both — character and action.
- Faith — God has given us the power to have faith. Accept it now.

> *Faith is companion to all the ingredients that make for the best things in life — hope, love, joy, to name a few. Fear is stranger to all of these. Thus, fear can only nurture itself on the things that breed the worst in life — despair, misery, and the like.*[3]

God Uses The Person He Has Called (Jeremiah 1:10)

God commissions Jeremiah to share the good news of God with the people in verse 9. God's hand touches Jeremiah and declares that he has put his words into his mouth. He has given him a direction to speak.

> *Jeremiah gives a clearer picture than any other biblical writer of what it means to receive and transmit God's word. Certainly Jeremiah is nothing like a tape-recorder that unthinkingly repeats whatever is spoken into the microphone; he is a man, fully possessed by the Spirit (hand) of God, who believes that he is responsible to use all his God-given intellect to express the divine word in human words.*[4]

We have been called by God through the testimony of our mouths to declare the salvation, righteousness, and holiness of God to a lost and dying world. Jeremiah, as a man, has little authority. However, through the presence of God and as his representative he has full authority.

God tells Jeremiah that he has been appointed his spokesman to express to his society their spiraling downward plunge into the abyss of destruction. God says that Israel will be uprooted, torn down, destroyed, and overthrown. Today's society parallels that ancient society of Jeremiah. Morals, actions, and philosophy are all so anti-Christian that it calls for men and women to stand up and cry out against them. The reason God tells Jeremiah there must be this uprooting is to rebuild or replant a godly society.

In her book, *Gardening Mercies*, Laurie Ostby Kehler writes about a neighbor who came by her house and viewed her garden for the first time. The neighbor told Kehler how hopeless her gardening was because of the soil conditions. "I have cement-hard clay soil, plus oak root fungus disease in my soil." That combination kills things. So her friend said that nothing would grow.

> *Everyone has obstacles to overcome in gardening. If you're looking for a gardening experience without obstacles, forget about gardening ... some gardeners start out with big problems. Steep slopes, high altitude, short growing seasons, heavy wind, diseased soil ... If something isn't happening to challenge you, you're not gardening.*[5]

Just as Jeremiah saw the obstacles he also saw the solution ... it was in God. Today there are many obstacles that come our way, but with God's help we can overcome them. These obstacles become our launching pad to conversation with our neighbors and friends about what Jesus can do in their lives. As we share with others, we will begin to see changes in their hearts and lives as they allow God to do his gardening work and cut out the diseased soil.

Let this prayer soak your soul.

> *Almighty God, in every age you have called out men and women to be your faithful servants. We believe you have now called us to join that great company who seek to follow you. Grant unto us today and always a clear vision of your call and strength to fulfill the ministry assigned to us. We pray in the name of Christ. Amen.*[6]

---

1. Andrew W. Blackwood Jr., *Commentary on Jeremiah* (Waco: Word Books, 1977), p. 37.

2. Charles Swindoll, *The Tale of the Tardy Oxcart* (Nashville: Word Publishing, 1998), p. 613.

3. C. Neil Strait, *Strait Lines* (Kansas City: Beacon Hill Press of Kansas City, 1976), p. 26.

4. *Op cit*, Blackwood, p. 39.

5. Laurie Ostby Kehler, *Gardening Mercies* (Minneapolis: Bethany House, 2001), pp. 178-179.

6. Reuben P. Job, Norman Shawchuck, *A Guide to Prayer* (Nashville: The Upper Room, 1983), p. 65.

The Call Of Holiness

These were not the best of times for Israel. Bleakness, despair, and frustration ruled the day. Israel's King Uzziah died. He started his career as king well. He was a sixteen-year-old boy who succeeded beyond expectation. He was powerful, famous, and rich. His religious reforms were vital to Israel's spiritual life.

Once he was king, Uzziah entered the temple to burn incense on the golden altar, which only the priests were allowed to do and was immediately stricken with leprosy as he lingered there. The Jewish historian, Josephus, tells us that Uzziah was smitten when he threatened to kill the eighty priests, who were already warning him to leave. But, after being stricken with leprosy, he left the temple and moved outside the city, while his son, Jotham, reigned as king. A year later Uzziah died and was "buried by himself in his own gardens." What a tragic ending to an illustrious and spiritually productive life and career!

Not only was that tragic, but Israel's eyes were focused on the mighty Assyrian King, Tiglath-Pileser, who was moving quickly south into Israel, gobbling up one city after another (2 Kings 15:29). Jerusalem was in disarray. The people were frightened and trembled before the bloodthirsty Assyrians. Who would protect them?

> *Isaiah's own visit to the temple was, quite possibly, associated with a national cry for God to intervene and save the city from destruction. The prayers of the day were for God's sovereignty, justice, and faithfulness.*[1]

God's call to Israel was not to panic but to become holy. Not to live in a state of perpetual sin but a state of holy living. His call was not just for that specific time or nation or people; but rather, for all time, all nations, and all people. There is a call to holiness wrapped up in Isaiah's vision.

The Call To Holiness Is A Call To God

A call to God is to all people transcending nations, cultures, people groups, and denominations. God was not just the private property of Israel, but God was the God of all! Nor is God the private possession of America but the God of all nations.

Deneff observed that in contrast to the panic on earth in Isaiah's text, there was something else happening in heaven.

> *In the middle of the crisis, the angels were not throwing lightning to the earth. They were covering their faces and feet, worshiping God — not because nothing else mattered, but because nothing else mattered more. All of heaven was obsessed with the holiness of God.*[2]

Holiness is not just one of God's attributes, it describes his entire being. His attributes would include:

- his eternality ... his timelessness. He exists outside the categories of time and space.
- his immutability or unchanging nature. God neither improves nor deteriorates.
- his omniscience. His knowledge is inclusive of all things and comprehensive. God knows all things as they actually come to pass: past, present, and future.
- his omnipotence.

> *God's perfect power means that by the exercise of his will he can realize whatever is present in his will.... God reveals his power in creation; in works of providence, and in the redemption of sinners. God's absolute power, however, may never be divorced from his perfections.*[3]

94

• his truth. God has perfect knowledge of what we are and what we can be. He is never misleading in his word to us.

God's holiness is his moral and ethical character and that becomes a problem for us. His divine love on one hand, and his divine repudiation of sin that separates itself from the unholy on the other, is defined by his holiness. His holiness either saves us or judges us. We as moral beings have the freedom to determine which it will be for us. His holiness draws us to him, but if we reject him, we reject his holiness; we reject him, and we will be separated from him.

He is a holy God.

The Call Of Holiness Is A Call To Humility

There is a tendency in our era to over-familiarize and patronize God. It is true that God is our friend. We sing hymns extolling that friendship. I am excited to know that I am special to him. But we come to God in worship and in awe of who he is.

Our worship begins in his holy and glorious presence spotlighting him and not us. Each time we enter his presence through meditation or with the community of believers, we should be struck with his greatness and our unworthiness. Our worth lies in him. He reaches down and brings us up.

In his book, *Reality In Worship*, J. P. Allen likens our worship to entering a planetarium from a busy, noisy street.

> *Dimming lights hush the sounds and the universe opens up over our heads. Earth becomes one of the smallest of planets and we become one of its smallest creatures. In that awesome moment, we focus upon the greatness, the goodness, and the grace of God. Our worship should be like that. It should not begin with the focus upon ourselves and our own needs, but upon the character of God; we should not proceed without the expectation of the visitation of his Spirit, but wait in his holy presence until He comes; we should not assume there is nothing new under the sun that we have not seen, but come expecting a glimpse of his glory.*[4]

95

It is in this humbling experience that we begin to realize that we can be imprinted by his holy mark on our lives. There is nothing in all the world that we can do to imprint ourselves when it comes to holiness. If we have been with God, we will bear his holy mark and people will observe his mark upon our lives. They will see his purity, compassion, joy, reverence, justice, and love stamped all over us.

A Call To Holiness Is A Call To All People

A quarter of a century ago, author Keith Drury, from the Wesleyan Church, wrote a book titled, *Holiness For Ordinary People*. What a great title! Often we think that holiness is dressed in long, flowing robes and left to the pious saints of the past. Sometimes we think of powerful communicating preachers, gray-haired grandmas, or dedicated missionaries, but the truth is God has called all of us into a lifestyle of holiness.

> *The work of entire sanctification and a walk in holiness is for every believer. Holiness must not be reserved for a select few of God's people who live above the ordinary humdrum of daily life. It must not be reserved for preachers, missionaries, and retired folk who "have enough time to pray all day." Holiness is for all of us. It is for ordinary people living an ordinary existence on this globe.* [5]

Holiness transcends race, ethnicity, sex, denomination, or any other barrier or excuse that keeps us far away from God. Holiness draws us toward Jesus with a hungering and thirsting after righteousness ... right living. It is sold out obedience to God. Even in human "jars of clay" we are called to be pure, clean, and holy. Holiness is seeking Jesus because I understand I need him. After Pentecost the disciples were transformed from self-seekers to God-seekers. They were empowered by the Holy Spirit to live life to its fullest. Holiness is the fulfillment of fullest! It is not done in our own strength but in God's strength. Holiness unto the Lord truly becomes our watchword and song.

A Call To Holiness Is A Call To Service

After we accept grace, forgiveness, and cleansing, we are ready to truly serve in God's name. God is not recruiting people to service. When they are spiritually ready God is ready to challenge them to serve as disciples. There are definite similarities between humanitarian effort and Christian service.

Each sees people in need. People on this earth have endured tsunamis, tornadoes, earthquakes, diseases, famine, floods, injustices, hatred, and war. Compassionate people care and see the incredible needs of fellow human beings.

Each cares about people in need. People have been touched to their very souls about people in need. This care is genuine and part of the divine residue in spite of the fall of humankind in the Garden of Eden.

Each reaches out to people in need. There are food pantries, compassionate centers, utilities subsidies, elderly or child care, and multitudes of other helpful organizations.

The difference is that one has a caring heart with limits because of its focus. The other has a God heart that sees no limitation. Christ demonstrated how to love, care, and give. Those who are his followers must be the same.

If we are truly Christian, *if* we are called by God, there will be no tasks too small or too large for us. There are no score sheets, no great lists, no tallies of what we have done in the name of Christ. It is simply doing for Jesus.

> *We must realize that the symbol of Christianity is not a beautifully polished cross, but a lopsided, crude, splintery cross over which is draped a towel — not the lush, plush kind of towel we buy for our guest bathroom, but a dirty old rag, wet with the sweat and dirt of men's feet.* — Norman Schouten[6]

Just a year before the death of A.W. Tozer, he was asked to speak at a conference of ministers on any subject he chose. God's holiness was the subject and he is quoted as saying,

*I believe we ought to have again the old biblical con-
cept of God which makes God awful and makes men lie
face down and cry, "Holy, holy, holy, Lord God almighty." That would do more for the church than everything or anything else.*[7]

Tozer was right. Have you heard the call of God to the life of
holiness, purity, and service? More importantly ... have you accepted his call? Amen.

---

1. Steve Deneff, *Whatever Became of Holiness* (Indianapolis: Wesleyan Publishing House, 1996), p. 24.

2. *Ibid*, p. 25.

3. Richard S. Taylor, editor, *Beacon Dictionary of Theology* (Kansas City: Beacon Hill Press of Kansas City, 1983), p. 57.

4. David McKenna, *Communicator's Commentary Isaiah 1-39* (Dallas: Word
Books, 1993), p. 110.

5. Keith Drury, *Holiness for Ordinary People* (Indianapolis: Wesleyan Publishing House, 2004).

6. Albert M. Wells Jr., *Inspiring Quotations* (Nashville: Thomas Nelson, 1988),
p. 184.

7. *Op cit*, Deneff, p. 29.

Epiphany 6
Ordinary Time 6
Jeremiah 17:5-10

Lessons From A Hurricane

It developed as a tropical wave leaving the coast of Africa on September 9, 1989, and within a few days became a Category 5 hurricane. In its path were Guadeloupe, Montserrat, Puerto Rico, St. Croix, South Carolina, and North Carolina. The aftermath of that violent upheaval of nature was 82 dead and 56,000 people homeless.

Mark Lewis and his family were living on the island of St. Croix when Hurricane Hugo struck. He and his wife, Angela, took their two daughters into the shower stall of their bathroom and huddled together while the sounds of fury roared outside.

Lewis comments that he had been through some scary moments in his life when he had experienced intense fear, but they paled in the relentless terror of Hugo. He stated that he prayed repeatedly for wisdom to know what to do and the courage and strength to do it once it was revealed. He envisioned the hands of the protector God holding up the walls around him and his family. He asked God to spare his wife and girls because of his insecurity of his own survival.

Finally, the relentless winds died down, and he risked a one-man reconnaissance trip to inspect the damage. The living room had blown away and all their possessions looked like they had been "blenderized" with equal parts of glass, wood, assorted building materials, and rainwater to create an ugly hurricane stew.

Lewis realized that life is more important than so many of the petty differences and irritations that arise in any relationship. He wrote that there was a new appreciation between him and his wife.[1]

99

Judah had been through some devastating circumstances in Jeremiah's time that resembled a hurricane's force as well. There were Josiah's reforms in 627 BC, Jeremiah's call to prophetic ministry in 626 BC, and then a wholesale upheaval following the death of Josiah at the Battle of Megiddo in 609 BC to the Battle of Carchemish in 605 with Emperor Nebuchadnezzar. The first deportation to Babylon occurred in 597 BC, then the siege of Jerusalem under Pharaoh Hophra (Apreies) in 588 BC, and the fall of Jerusalem in 586 BC. A second deportation in 586 BC and a third deportation to Babylon occur for the inhabitants. Is it any wonder as to a need for divine help and strength?

The text lends itself to help us learn some lessons from hurricane forces that occasionally hit our lives.

Encounter God In Life's Hurricane (Jeremiah 17:5a)

We live in a world of high rise apartments, gated communities, and fenced-in homes designed to keep people out. What a striking contrast that is with our God! He delights in meeting with people. He offers his love and availability at every turn in our lives. His desire is for intimate connection with us. Humanity is his parish! God comes to seek and to save all people who desire his divine love.

> *Some of us are faced with nervousness when we consider the implications of having an encounter with God. The very thought of coming into the presence of a holy God means that there is bound to be power — even radical transformation. As we spend time in the word, we can't help but be surprised by the outcomes of the many encounters between God and his people throughout history.* — Julie Reid[2]

I encounter God by pouring my life into his. My empty container is then filled with his divine presence. I cannot come into the presence of God without being filled with a sense of courage and hope that radiates from him.

Another hurricane disaster forms the backdrop for a story of courage and hope. This account comes from the city of New Orleans after the devastation of Hurricane Katrina in 2005. Hy and Libba McEnery worked as missionaries with child evangelism in New Orleans' inner city. Thousands of children had put their faith in Jesus Christ during Hy and Libba's nine-year ministry. One of those was a young man by the name of Herbert. Starting at age nine, Herbert was faithfully taught the Bible and its promises. Herbert had a personal encounter with God and began to develop a love for Jesus as a child. He was filled with courage and hope that reached out to others in his community.

When Herbert was fourteen, he started a little church in the small kitchen of his house. He preached and his five sisters sang about Jesus' love and salvation. Thirty people crammed into the kitchen and there they heard the message and prayed. These precious children prayed hard. Their surrounding community was devastated before Katrina ever struck their city. Their devastation was the alcohol and drug culture that imprisoned them. These children prayed for their loved ones who were lost and in prison. They prayed for America, New Orleans, and for the corrupt politicians in city government, for their schools, and for deliverance. Four years they met in the kitchen of Herbert's house.

When Katrina hit, Herbert, his mother, and his five sisters were forced from their home. Now eighteen and the man of the house, he watched as their house floated away and the seven of them were evacuated to the Superdome. It was there that they witnessed dead bodies, suicide, rape, knifings, shootings, looting, and continuous cries for rescue and help. A physical hurricane had damaged their lives, but much greater was the hurricane of despair! Herbert asked God what to do and how to help those living in despair inside that superdome. As he prayed, God filled Herbert with his holy presence and began to show him what he wanted Herbert to do. Herbert started to march around the dome singing gospel songs and choruses. Little by little, people joined him, and before long there was a second line doing the same. Then people began to pray audibly, calling out to God for help. Herbert knew then that this is what God had led him to do. He talked to people in small, impromptu Bible studies. Within one day there were fifty groups meeting informally both in the morning and in the evening before curfew.

From those meetings, people caught a spark of hope and words of encouragement. Herbert's message was simple and came right from the heart of Jeremiah who told the people, "... blessed is the man who trusts in the Lord, whose confidence is in him" (Jeremiah 17:7 NIV).

Finally, Herbert and his family were relocated to Lake Charles, Louisiana. But again tragedy struck as yet another hurricane hit — Hurricane Rita — and once again they were evacuated. But God was filling Herbert's heart with his presence. After a short time far away in Iowa, God used a congregation that was yielded to him to carry Herbert, his family, and several others from his little congregation to that state where they assisted them in housing, food, and help.[3]

God will fill us with courage and hope as we continue to trust him in our hurricanes of life!

Exist With God In Life's Hurricanes (Jeremiah 17:7-8)

Jeremiah says in verse 6 that they will be like a desert shrub that exists in the desert parched land. Their lives are like the uninhabitable salt land that not only lacks water, but is poisonous to most plants, and is lonely and sterile. However, to exist with God is to be blessed by God as verse 7 indicates. The word "blessed" is *baruch* and it means "to kneel" so as "to ask God for a blessing." What Jeremiah desires is to live a holy life dedicated to God from the inside out and not outward prosperity or living life from the outside inward. We must live in God's grace.

> *Grace is not only a gift; it is a grave responsibility. A man cannot go on living the life he lived before he met Jesus Christ. He must be clothed in a new purity and a new holiness and a new goodness. The door is open, but the door is not open for the sinner to come and remain a sinner, but for a sinner to come and become a saint.* — William Barclay[4]

To be "a saint" to live from the inside out means that we will:

• listen to God's directions,
• enjoy the fellowship of God,

102

- master the world and not allow the world to master you,
- move steadily toward God,
- conform to God's character,
- be passionate for Christ,
- receive the power of the Holy Spirit to conquer the ravages of sin, and
- radiate the love of Christ to others.

To exist in life's hurricanes is to exist in Christ!

Examine The Heart In The Hurricanes Of Life (Jeremiah 17:10)

Jeremiah confesses his own inadequacy to know himself. It is exciting to learn that what God tells Jeremiah is that he (God) knows. Andrew Blackwood Jr. states that "God knows the thoughts and feelings, and gives to a man according to his actions." Jeremiah isn't judging someone else's heart or mind but rather wants to examine his own heart!

So what should be in our hearts as we encounter God? It should be a heart that is:

- sensitive to God;
- rejoicing in the Lord;
- a living sacrifice for God, yielded on the altar of faith;
- allowing God to touch and change the heart;
- giving to offer self for others; and
- thanking God for his grace.

How is your heart?

Hurricanes do come and they hit hard and sometimes persistently. I want my life to reflect what William Henry Channing who was a clergyman and reformer (1810-1884) wrote:

To live content with small means; to seek elegance rather than luxury, and refinement rather than fashion; to be worthy, not respectable, and wealthy, not rich; to listen to stars and birds, babes and sages, with open heart; to study hard; to think quietly, act frankly, talk

gently, await occasions, hurry never; in a word, to let
the spiritual, unbidden and unconscious, grow up
through the common — this is my symphony.[5]

Let me hear God's music in my heart while the storm passes over! Amen.

---

1. Couples Devotional Bible NIV (Grand Rapids: Zondervan Publishing Company, 2000), p. 821.

2. David M. Edwards, *Encountering God* (Grand Rapids: Baker Books, 2008), p. 13.

3. Joyce Williams, compiler, *Quiet Moments for Ministry Wives* (Kansas City: Beacon Hill Press of Kansas City, 2006), pp. 161-165.

4. Albert M. Wells Jr., compiler, *Inspiriting Quotations* (Nashville: Thomas Nelson Publishers, 1988), p. 87.

5. Jan Karon, *A Continual Feast* (New York: Penguin Group, 2005), npn.

Breaking The Cycle —
God's Answer In Forgiveness

People often mistake forgiveness for a feeling, but it goes much deeper. Basically it boils down to a choice, an act of free will. A prime example of forgiveness from the scriptures is Joseph.

Joseph, the elder of the two sons of Jacob by Rachel, comes to the pages of the biblical account at age seventeen (Genesis 37). He is first seen tending his father's flocks with his brothers, the sons of Bilhah and the sons of Zilpah, Jacob's other wives. The biblical account does not go into detail about what happened while in the fields, but Joseph comes back from helping tend the sheep with "a bad report" about his brothers.

Jacob loved Joseph and favored him over the others because he was the youngest and was born to Jacob in his old age. Jacob enjoyed spoiling Joseph. After the incident with the "bad report" Jacob infuriates his other sons by giving Joseph a long tunic with sleeves that young people of the richer class wore (Genesis 37:2).

The hatred of Joseph's brothers increased when he related a dream he had that all of the family would bow down to him. The insult wedged the relationship between him and the others to a breaking point.

The Bible tells us that Joseph's brothers had gone to graze their father's flocks near Shechem, and Jacob asked Joseph to go check on them and their exact location. After arriving there, he discovered that they had moved their flocks to greener grass toward Dothan.

Catch the drama of the scene.

*So Joseph went after his brothers and found them near
Dothan. But they saw him in the distance, and before
he reached them, they plotted to kill him. "Here comes
that dreamer!" they said to each other. "Come now,
let's kill him and throw him into one of these cisterns
and say that a ferocious animal devoured him. Then
we'll see what comes of his dreams."*
— Genesis 37:17b-20 (NIV)

Reuben, the oldest of Jacob's sons, came back into the circle
and discovered what was being said and quickly stopped their murderous plot. He devised a plan to throw Joseph into an empty cistern with plans to return and rescue him. When Joseph arrived at
the site he was seized, stripped of his robe, and thrown into the
cistern. Reuben had returned to the flock. While he was gone a
caravan of Ishmaelites came from Gilead on their way to Egypt.
Brother Judah decided that instead of killing him, why not make
some money on the side by selling Joseph as a slave. His price?
Twenty shekels.

When Reuben returned to the camp, he discovered what had
been done and immediately tore his clothes (a sign of being totally
distraught). Another plan was devised to lie to Jacob by telling him
that his favorite son was dead.

One sin leads to another.

Joseph's life after these events changed forever! He was probably mistreated by the Midianite slave traders. He ended up as a
slave, was lied about, and was imprisoned for a minimum of two
years before a glimmer of hope shone through, only to be dashed
again as a longer stay ensued. After two more years, Joseph's deliverance came. Pharaoh dreamed an unusual dream and needed
an interpretation. Finally, someone remembered Joseph could interpret dreams and he was rescued! His meteoric rise came only
after years of frustration, pain, and suffering.

After several years and a complicated series of intrigue, Joseph meets his brothers again. He is no longer the same Joseph in
physical appearance. The years of hardship took the edge off his
arrogance, and God worked on his heart as well. He could have
been bitter and hated his brothers, but forgiveness ruled.

106

Forgiving involves acknowledging your hurt, releasing your thoughts about the violation and giving up the desire to pay the offender back ... forgiving has more to do with your own spiritual and mental health than it does with your spouse's. Forgiving releases your spouse from your wrath, but — more importantly — it frees you from the bondage of unforgiveness.[1]

Forgiveness releases us from the bondage of an unforgiving spirit from anyone a mother, father, sister, brother, son, daughter, colleague, pastor, church member, or anyone else. The principles of forgiveness remain steady.

Today's scripture text reveals some of those basic principles.

God Helps Us Break The Cycle Of An Unforgiving Spirit As We Acknowledge Our Attitude

Dr. Norman Wright states, "If we don't forgive, that means we are carrying resentment and bitterness." Resentment and bitterness mimic a physical cancer that eats away at the healthy body cells and can cause death. Resentment and bitterness can destroy our emotional, psychological, and spiritual life if left unchecked and unhealed.

The New Testament word for bitterness is from the root *pic* and means "to cut or prick." Literally it is pointed, sharp, or pungent in its action and feelings. Bitterness manifests itself as prejudice, an acrid tongue, exaggerated lies, and revenge.

Chuck Swindoll illustrates this in his book, *Seasons of Life.* He writes that during his time in the Marine Corps he and his wife rented a studio apartment from a man in south San Francisco named Mr. Slagle. During World War II Mr. Slagle was captured at Wake Island and for years he languished in a prison camp. It was in the prison camp that an enemy soldier struck him with a rifle butt and injured his back, which plagued him the rest of his life.

Swindoll tells that every single time he visited his landlord he would relate story after story of how barbarically he had been mistreated. Using vile language and intense emotion, he spoke of the tortures he endured at the hands of his Japanese captors and his utter hatred for them. His pain and misery were constant reminders of his hatred.

107

But there was another factor which made his existence even more lamentable. Our landlord became a bitter man. Even though (at that time) he was thirteen years removed from the war ... even though he had been safely released from the concentration camp and was now able to carry on physically ... even though he and his wife owned a lovely dwelling and had a comfortable income, the crippled man was bound by the grip of bitterness. He was still fighting a battle that should have ended years before. In a very real sense, he was still in prison.[2]

You cannot conceal bitterness because it raises its ugly head often. The root of bitterness bears the fruit of bitter actions. Bitterness imprisons us as we refuse to forgive a friend, relative, or stranger for a sinful, foolish, or sometimes ignorant act. Inner torment will ride alongside us every day of our lives until we forgive. When we decide to disclose the problem to Christ, that is the beginning of forgiveness and healing.

Paul had it right when he wrote,

Let all bitterness and wrath and anger and clamor and slander be put away from you, along with all malice. And be kind to one another, tender-hearted, forgiving each other, just as God in Christ also has forgiven you.
— Ephesians 4:31-32 (NASB)

God Helps Us Break The Cycle Of An Unforgiving Spirit As We Acknowledge Our Need Of Forgiveness

The Bible states, "Forgive as the Lord forgave you" (Colossians 3:13). As we battle forgiving others we should remember that we are forgiven individuals when we yield our lives to Christ. God sets the standard and mentors us in the process of forgiveness.

- Forgiveness is a debt of sin cancelled. Everything that we have done against him all of our lives is forgiven when we ask for his forgiveness.
- Forgiveness is a journey. The awful gulf of sin that separates us from God has been bridged by the death and resurrection

of Jesus Christ. We can continually walk across that bridge as necessary. When the mind or emotion resurfaces those feelings, we can go immediately to God and ask him to help us deal with the feelings. The fact that forgiveness has taken place does not necessarily mean that feelings don't resurface. It is a process.

- Forgiveness is also a choice. I choose to forgive as part of my willingness to give it up. Forgiveness is not done without our knowledge. It is not a surprise! It is a choice.
- Forgiveness allows God's love to flow through me to someone else. As a Christian I cannot horde Christ's love, but rather, I must give it away. Even when hurt comes I want to demonstrate God's love. I have to be practical in my response, but I must love.

God Helps Us Break The Cycle Of An Unforgiving Spirit As We Acknowledge Our Need To Move Forward

Joseph could have been harsh and taken his revenge out on his brothers in response to their actions. He chose to move forward instead. Once he reveals himself to them he tells to them to go back and bring his/their father to Egypt where all of them will live in comfort and peace. Joseph does not renege on his promise or on his forgiveness.

> *So Joseph settled his father and his brothers in Egypt and gave them property in the best part of the land, the district of Rameses, as Pharaoh directed. Joseph also provided his father and his brothers and all his father's household with food, according to the number of their children.* — Genesis 47:11-12 (NIV)

He certainly doesn't sound like a man who is holding a grudge or hatred in his heart. So how do we continue in the journey of forgiveness? Joseph gives the answer.

> *Do not be distressed and do not be angry with yourselves for selling me here, because it was to save lives that God sent me ahead of you. For two years now there*

has been famine in the land, and for the next five years there will not be plowing and reaping. But God sent me ahead of you to preserve for you a remnant on earth and to save your lives by a great deliverance. So then, it was not you who sent me here, but God.... Now hurry back to my father and say to him, "This is what your son Joseph says: God has made me lord of all Egypt. Come down to me; don't delay."

— Genesis 45:5-9 (NIV, emphasis mine)

The answer to the question, "How do we continue in the journey of forgiveness?" is God.

As Chuck Swindoll wrote in his final paragraph about Mr. Slagle.

For your sake, let me urge you to "put away all bitterness" now. There's no reason to stay in POW camp a minute longer. The escape route is clearly marked. It leads to the cross ... where the only one who had a right to be bitter wasn't.[3]

Amen.

---

1. Couples' Devotional Bible (Grand Rapids: Zondervan Publishing House, 2000), p. 782.

2. Charles Swindoll, *Season of Life* (Portland: Multnomah, 1983), p. 166.

3. *Ibid*, p. 167.

Restarting Joy — Rejoice

Joy does not depend on the external events of life. Adversity may hit us with gale-like force, but the joy in our hearts will be determined by the will of our souls. Joy is a choice!

In his book, *Laugh Again*, written in 1991, author Charles Swindoll relates that he was on the Dallas Theological Seminary's Board of Regents as they interviewed the first woman faculty member. Her name was Lucy Mabery.

Swindoll chronicles the incredible journey of Professor Mabery on her ride to being a faculty member at Dallas Seminary. He writes that Lucy was rearing a family, teaching Bible classes, and was engaged in a dozen other activities while married to Dr. Trevor Mabery. Dr. Mabery was a successful physician in the Dallas area. At the zenith of his career he was also working with Focus on the Family ministry as a volunteer. He attended a retreat in Montana where he and three other men from the Dallas area had met with Focus on the Family Director, Dr. James Dobson. They discussed plans for the future of the organization and prayed for God's leadership and the direction Focus on the Family should take over the next year. As they were flying back from their retreat meeting, something went terribly wrong with the airplane. The plane lost altitude and power then crashed, killing all four men on board.

Their deaths sent shock waves throughout the Dallas community as all four men were highly respected public figures. Their widows and families were left to pick up the pieces and restart their own lives.

Dr. Swindoll writes that Lucy Mabery chose to do it with joy. Without a moment's hesitation or warning, grief tore into the Mabery family like a tornado.

> But, determined not to be bound by the cords of perpetual grief, Lucy remained positive, keen thinking, and joyful. How can a person in Lucy's situation recover, pick up the pieces, and go on? How does anyone press on beyond grief? How do you still laugh at life? How do you put your arms around your children as a new single parent and help them laugh (see joy) in the future? It comes from deep within — because people like Lucy Mabery set their sails for joy regardless of how the wind blows.[1]

This is how Isaiah must have felt. His beloved Israel had to fight the foes of hatred, prejudice, and misery from external circumstances, but Isaiah says to hang on. He writes, "You will go out in joy and be led forth in peace; the mountains and hills will burst into song before you, and the trees of the field will clap their hands" (Isaiah 55:12 NIV).

How can we set sail for a life full of joy?

We Set Sail For Joy By Rejoicing In The Redemptive Goodness Of God (Isaiah 55:10)

God's goodness comes through his creative powers. Isaiah reminds us that we receive the rain and the snow because it is from God. He has absolute control over the weather as well as all the earth produces. It is from his hands and heart that we live. Our confidence is not in the external experiences of life, but in the God who is at work in us and who is in control of everything in our lives. Does that mean temptation or evil or harm will not come our way? Absolutely not! But I can rejoice because I know that God's goodness will override the negative. He will help us discover how to work through the tragedies of our lives and give us direction to make an impact on others. This is not a giddy happiness, but a deep-rooted joy in the midst of trouble kind of experience because we have the goodness of God at the center.

On June 2, 2007, Kelsey Smith ran an errand at a department store in a Kansas City suburb. Kelsey graduated ten days earlier from her high school and was well loved by her family and friends. While at that parking lot she was kidnapped and murdered with her body thrown out near a lake several miles away.

In a *Kansas City Star* newspaper article on the one-year anniversary of her abduction, the reporter wrote that for more than three days, her family and friends had no clue what had transpired. In the hot sun, they walked the neighborhoods within a five-mile radius of the Target store's parking lot where she was abducted, determined to find Kelsey.

They were too late. Her kidnapper had already carried out his evil deed. So how did they deal with this tragedy? They created the Kelsey Smith Foundation as a way to carry on her name. Their goal is to educate people on how to avoid becoming victims by teaching them safety tips and defensive tactics.

What the Smith family is doing provides an example that can help others when the rain comes. They are just one story. Multiply their story thousands of times with cancer survivor walks, golf outings, friends or relatives of victims starting grief programs or raising money, and it demonstrates that in the midst of tragedy God's goodness and God's love can be demonstrated.

We Set Sail For Joy By Rejoicing In The Word Of God (Isaiah 55:11)

The Holy Bible is the sacred book of Christians, and its first major division is also the sacred book for the Jews. Christians of all denominational stripes refer to it as the word of God.

The English word "bible" is derived from the Greek word *biblion*, which means "a written volume, roll, or little book" (cf. Luke 4:17, 20; Revelation 10:9). The word came to be applied to the entire collection of Christian sacred writings.[2]

Evangelicals believe it to be the final and sufficient authority in all matters pertaining to salvation and Christian living. The Bible is filled with exhortation, inspiration, promises, both personal and community, relates salvation history, discloses God throughout its pages, and shares how to receive salvation and sanctification for anyone asking and receiving.

Many years ago lecturer and authoress, Ann Keimel, summed up the joy of receiving God's word.

> *I think the thing that altered my life was when some-body said to me, "Ann, the Bible absolutely is truth, and it is the power of God speaking to us. You can talk, others can talk, but unless you know his word and read it, it doesn't become a real deep part of you." All I know is that God put it within my heart to read his word, and if I were going to try and encourage somebody to read the Bible, I would ask them to pray for the desire to read the word. I think only God can put that desire in the heart of a human being, and put the desire in that heart so deeply, that he or she will truly be hungry and thirsty for it. Only then does it take on meaning. You have to seek that. You have to want it. And I guess be-yond that, I want to love it so much, and I want to say "change me," that without holding it up and admon-ishing people to read it, they will watch my life; they will see the sparkle in my eyes; they will feel the sun-rise in my life; they will hear me laugh; they will see me cry, pick myself up, and go on. They will see all of those things in my life that exude love and power and hope, and that will draw them to God's word, and they will know that's how I got to where I am.*[3]

Do you know the joy of God's word? Have you made it a light on your Christian journey?

We Set Sail For Joy By Rejoicing In Growing In God (Isaiah 55:13)

Gardening becomes a hobby with a passion for many people. It could be said that for some it is an obsession, not just a passion. The work can be intense and time consuming, commencing with soil preparation right on through the planting of the seed or plant. The ultimate goal is harvesting the fruit of the labor, but it is so much fun (and frustrating) with the middle part of watching it grow!

Excitement over someone making a commitment to Christ and becoming a follower should cause every Christian to rejoice. But the excitement should also cause Christians to surround the newborn convert with encouragement, love, and support. Our support of him/her should help in their growth.

Celebrating the Lord's Supper or Eucharist together is a celebration of the growth and the joy of that growth for each of us. Christ came to earth with one specific goal: to die for a lost world. The end was nearing, and the stress, strain, and suffering as the human/divine sacrifice on the cross lay ahead of him. At the Passover table, Jesus reviewed the reason for his coming. He bared his concern with his followers in those closing hours. Two emotions can be detected in that event ... joy and celebration.

Interwoven in the conversation between Jesus and his disciples is the assurance and confidence of the new kingdom of promise, hope, and life. Thanksgiving was offered through blessing and prayer. Throughout the bleakness of the night, the light of spiritual victory pulsates in the words of Jesus. Communion celebrates the victory that Jesus would win for everyone who participates in his sacrifice. Every time the Eucharist is celebrated it is a reminder that we can grow closer to God. It is a confirmation of our acceptance by God through Christ, of our acceptance of Jesus into our lives, and our acceptance of one another. It is the celebration of a spiritual seedling growing into a strong fruitful plant.

Celebration of growth in communion bears the fruit of dignity, purpose, and hope. Come, accept God's invitation to partake in the elements of growth. Bear fruit with a joyous heart! Grow in grace. Rejoice in life!

---

1. Charles Swindoll, *Laugh Again* (Dallas: Word Publishing, 1991), p. 35.

2. Richard Taylor, editor, *Beacon Dictionary of Theology* (Kansas City: Beacon Hill Press of Kansas City, 1983), p. 70.

3. King Duncan, *Lively Illustrations for Effective Preaching* (Knoxville: Seven Worlds Publishing, 1987), p. 68. Used by permission.

Strengthening Your Grip On Prayer

In 1982, Chuck Swindoll wrote a book titled *Strengthening Your Grip*. The introduction chronicles his maturing years from his birth in 1934 through his ministry of the early 1980s.

> *Face it, ours is simply not the same world as it was a few short decades ago. The full picture hidden in the puzzle is still unclear, but the border is in place. The scene has changed drastically ... I found myself having to face the frightening facts of reality. We cannot drift on the ship of aimless indifference very long without encountering disaster.*[1]

One of the frightening facts is that we have drifted away from a biblical understanding of prayer. Swindoll continues, "... for too long, too many of them have been buried under the debris of tired clichés and predictable talk of yesteryear."

He then tells his readers that they need biblical fixed points to hang onto that are firm with solid handles to guide our lives into a life of purpose. "What we really want is something to grab — believable, reliable truth that makes sense for today's generation, essential principles for our aimless world."[2]

The puzzle was in God's hands during the 1980s and the puzzle is still in God's hands today, nearly thirty years later!

One area that needs strengthening the grip is prayer ... communicating with God. Solomon had a good grip on this important aspect of spiritual life. Today's text will help strengthen our grip on prayer!

Strengthening Our Grip On Prayer As A Lifestyle

David Polish wrote, "Prayer is not an investigation, it is experience. Prayer is not a shopping list in the supermarket of the universe. We should not pray, 'Help me win,' but rather 'Help me live.' "[3]

Solomon had a continual experience with prayer as a lifestyle. It came from his heart. In their book, *Fully Alive*, Jerry and Larry Hull remind us that people are to live a life of "wholeness."

This wholeness includes "integration," meaning that life is built around a single purpose or unified focus. At an early age, Solomon's life was influenced by a variety of circumstances and people. The future king was put under the care of Nathan, the prophet of God. It was Nathan who had rebuked David for his adulterous affair with Bathsheba. Influencing and molding Solomon's life would be his mother, Bathsheba, and his father, David. Solomon's brother, Absalom, revolted against their father, David, and the royal family and entourage of priests, Levites, and prophets were driven from Jerusalem. After the revolt was quelled and they returned home, the influence of the priests, Levites, and prophets continued to mold young Solomon. They pointed him to God. It was these influencers who helped him understand that prayer to the master of the universe should be a lifestyle. As you read Solomon's story in the scriptures, the observation of that lifestyle of prayer is quickly observed. Solomon's life was integrated with God.

This wholeness includes the wholeness of "harmony," living with inner tranquility and peace in a proper relationship to the creator and the creation. This produces a balance in life. The Hulls define it as steadiness and stability in all areas of life.

This lifestyle should not be arduous or stagnant. In Jesus' day prayer had become liturgical, standardized, and routine. It was always formal. Swindoll in his book, *Strengthening Your Grip*, states that prayer had become ritualistic, long verbiage, repetitious words and phrases that caused a sense of pride. We can ask, "Is it any wonder that prayer had lost its value?"

Bottom-line prayer is the type of prayer that Jesus modeled for us. The ingredients include honesty, spontaneity, heartfelt, down-to-earth communication with the Lord of life! The results are that we have full confidence and a calm assurance that our God is in complete control of our life. That's the kind of prayer Solomon offered on that day of dedicating the temple. The kind of daily dedication we must have is inside our living temple — our hearts!

Strengthening Our Grip On Prayer With A Persistent Lifestyle

Paul Cedar quotes Wesley Duewel's hard-hitting words.

> *The great need of our world, our nation, and our churches is people who know how to prevail in prayer. Moments of pious wishes blandly expressed to God once or twice a day will bring little change on earth or among the people. Kind thoughts expressed to him in five or six sentences, after reading a paragraph or mildly religious sentiments once a day from some devotional writing, will not bring the kingdom of God to earth or shake the gates of hell and repel the attacks of evil on our culture and our civilization. Results, not beautiful words, are the test of prevailing prayer.*[4]

Our task in a lifestyle of prayer is not to twist God's arm into doing what we want but to singly let God know of our needs. In his great prayer of dedication in verse 28, Solomon uses three words for prayer that should fit into our lifestyle of persistency.

The first word is *tepilla* meaning "intercession or supplication." When a need is perceived spiritually, physically, economically, or in the family, we go to God through Christ and help take on their burden.

The second word is *tehinna* meaning "an earnest plea for mercy." At its deepest level, mercy is a combination of righteousness and love.

> *Many Bible scholars are inclined to translate the word as "steadfast love," implying that God has entered into a covenant with his people. The results of this relationship are a readiness on God's part to relieve the oppressed and pardon the guilty ... Mercy is compassion in action.*[5]

Solomon pleads for mercy for his people. We have the opportunity to plea for mercy on our behalf, and God pardons us from our sinful behavior and lifestyle. He cleanses our hearts by faith as we plea for his sanctifying grace. Though hell was our destination, because of God's merciful listening to our plea he not only pardons us, but gives us a new destination ... heaven!

The third word is *rinna* and indicates "a wailing cry or petition." It is a list of requests that I cannot do by myself and I humbly need your help, God! Theologian Henri J. M. Nouwen wrote, "Only by deep, strong, and persistent prayer can we escape the illusion of self-importance."[6]

Solomon demonstrates that persistent lifestyle ... do you possess it?

Strengthening Our Grip On Prayer With A Listening Lifestyle

Several years ago, a close friend of mine was having difficulty hearing. Even after people repeated themselves he still had a hard time hearing them. He noticed that it was especially difficult hearing his wife. She suggested that he make an appointment with a hearing aid company that rented office space where she worked. The equipment was attached and the monitoring process began. After the appropriate tests were given, the man administering the tests gathered the results. My friend was nervous because he was afraid that he would have to have to purchase at least one hearing aid and as bad as his hearing was maybe two would be needed.

The man entered the room and informed my friend that he had "perfect" hearing. There was nothing wrong with his physical hearing. He said that my friend's problem was not uncommon especially among men. He said that my friend's wife's voice was being tuned out! He had what the expert called, "selective hearing!" The expert said that my friend needed to do the following things when it came to hearing people speak ... and especially his wife.

- Focus on the speaker.
- Tune into the voice of the speaker.

- As much as possible avoid "other voices" ... television, radio, outside distractions.
- Ask for the question or statement to be repeated if necessary.

What a difference his suggestions made to my friend.

Unfortunately many of us do the same with God — we tune out his voice. We allow "other voices" to distract us from what God is saying to us. My challenge is for you to listen and focus intently to God! It is amazing what he has to say if we just listen.

Strengthening Our Grip On Petitioning Prayer As A Lifestyle

In 1 Kings 8:22-53, Solomon gives a series of short petitions to God. Petitions are requests that one makes to a caring, listening God. Solomon asks:

- God to keep his promises (vv. 23-26).
- God to accept the prayers of his people as they worship (vv. 27-30).
- God to send showers of blessings upon the land and the people (vv. 35-36).
- God to help in times of disaster and calamities (vv. 37-40).
- God to listen to the prayers of all people (vv. 41-43).
- God to give victory in battles against pagan forces (vv. 44-45).
- God for mercy and forgiveness during difficult surroundings (vv. 46-51).
- God to answer those who respond to him (vv. 52-53).

What requests would you ask of God if you had the opportunity? Oh, yes, you DO have the opportunity daily! Please do not forget!

In the name of Jesus Christ, who was never in a hurry, we pray, O God, that you will slow us down, for we know that we live too fast. With all of eternity before us, make us take time to live ... time to get acquainted

with you, time to enjoy your blessings, and time to know
each other.   — Peter Marshall[7]

Amen.

---

1. Charles Swindoll, *Strengthening Your Grip* (Waco: Word Publishing, 1982), p. 14.

2. *Ibid.*

3. C. Neil Strait, *The Speaker's Book of Inspiration* (Atlanta: Drake House, 1972), p. 135.

4. Paul Cedar, *A Life of Prayer* (Dallas: Word Book, 1998), pp. 151-152.

5. Richard S. Taylor, editor, *Beacon Dictionary of Theology* (Kansas City: Beacon Hill Press of Kansas City, 1983), p. 334.

6. Albert M. Wells Jr., compiler, *Inspiring Quotations* (Nashville: Thomas Nelson Publishers, 1988), p. 160.

7. Jan Karon, *Patches of Godlight* (New York: Penguin Books, 2001), npn.

The Transfiguration Of Our Lord
(Last Sunday After Epiphany)
Exodus 34:29-35

The Radiant Life

---

*We are not citizens of this world trying to make our
way to heaven; we are citizens of heaven trying to make
our way through this world ... We are not to live so as
to earn God's love, inherit heaven, and purchase our
salvation ... [these] are gifts bought by Jesus on the
cross ... We are to live as God's redeemed, as heirs of
heaven, and citizens of another land: the kingdom of
God. Because of God's redemption we are now on a
journey home! "... a home we know will have the lights
on and the door open and our Father waiting for us
when we arrive." The writer comments that all of this,
"... means in all adversity our worship of God is joyful,
our life is hopeful, our future is secure. There is nothing we can lose on earth that can rob us of the treasures God has given us and will give us."*
                                    — The Anglican Digest[1]

We who have a relationship with God — a covenant with him
— understand that God will dwell with us! What an exciting discovery we make when we grasp that truth. When Moses comes
from the mountain where he and God had been in communion,
Moses reflected the very presence and glory of God. He even had
to put on a veil so that his face would not blind people as he spoke
to them. Wouldn't it be exciting if we had such a brilliance and
radiance about us after our time of prayer and communion with
God?

Today is Transfiguration Sunday and is the time when the church universal celebrates the Messiah as the glorified Son of the Father (Matthew 17:1-5). Moses is seen as the reflection of God's glory, but Jesus, the Messiah, is authentically the glory of God.

Both the Exodus passage and the transfiguration passage from Matthew remind us of the radiance that is in God and shows through the lives of those who follow him.

The Glory Of God Is Revealed In Change

Myron Augsburger tells us that the word "transfigured" stems from the word "metamorphosis." This metamorphosis occurs in the core of a person's spirit.

It affects the internal change when an individual's life has been transfigured and transformed by a relationship with God.

The internal and external changes occur when Christ comes to dwell in the heart by faith bringing salvation to us. We become a new creature ... a newborn in Christ (2 Corinthians 5:17). There are some "new" things that occur.

- New hope — with Christ there is a confident expectation of things seen and unforeseen!
- New home — with Christ there is now a place to go for safety, love, and care.
- New attitude — with Christ there is a new inclination to live right.
- New heart — the sinful heart has been replaced by a clean heart!

> The newborn shakes his head, blinks, looks around at his first glimpse of new life, and he can hardly believe it. And the world? Why, of course, it rushes on. Unconcerned, busy, preoccupied; it has to "stay on schedule." Someone's eternal new birth has occurred. Although it doesn't attract a second glance from those standing around. God's kingdom is being silently enlarged. It happens every day in our vast world. It even happened today. For all you know, maybe two minutes from your own front door.[2]

We need a change of heart in the core of our existence. When we experience the authentic power of God, our lives take on a new glow. Our faces shine with the presence of God as our hearts become white when the light of God enters.

The Glory Of God Is Revealed In The Fulfillment

There is no recorded conversation between Moses, Elijah, and Jesus on the mountain that day. The best speculation is that their conversation was a confirmation of Jesus' authority and fulfillment of the Old Testament law and prophets.

Moses represents the law of God and with him is the revelation of understanding right from wrong. Elijah represents the prophets and brings us to an understanding of the spirit of ethics and morals. Jesus synthesized the two and fulfilled them as the pinnacle of truth.

At that time Jesus heard the familiar voice of his Father. It was the moment when the Father confirmed verbally his satisfaction with his Son. When the Father said, "Listen to him," it was not only for those three disciples on the mountain that day but for all people for all time!

The Glory Of God Is Revealed In Worship

The disciples impulsively fell on their faces in awe of Jesus. The "awe" of God was on Moses' face. When we are in the presence of God the most natural response for us is to fall on our faces in worship.

Patrick Morely wrote that his family once attended a tawdry, gimmicky, religious meeting. He says that the minutes painfully ticked by ever so slowly. He said that he even fell asleep in his chair as the speaker drawled on for what seemed forever. According to him the organizers created a freakish, carnival-like atmosphere similar to a midway sideshow with a "barker-like" man hawking religious souvenirs with Brother Love's zeal.

I couldn't help but wonder, Would they be a bit embarrassed if they learned Jesus had sat on the front row? *He then says that when we know God is on the front*

row, *"our first reaction is to hide from the awfulness of his presence. We want to see the face of God, until the presence of his glory draws near. Then, we want him to hide us in the cleft of a rock. His presence is like peals of thunder and the fierce winds of a violent storm, and we reconsider the foolishness of our whim to see him. He is a holy God. Not only holy, but holy, holy holy...."*
— Revelation 4:8[3]

When we come to worship our God, we come to consider who he is through his ...

- holy power — Edmund Steimle said, "Do you really want to see divine power at work? Then discard your human notions of power and look at the way Christ lived and died."[4]
- holy wealth — he owns everything!
- holy wisdom — nothing is hidden from God. He is the all-wise, all-knowing God.
- holy love — who else would send their one and only son to take on the sin of all humanity?

Let us approach him with praise and thanksgiving in holy recognition that we are in the presence of the holy. As we approach the throne of grace we do so with confidence, respect, and admiration! We need to pause and mediate as we enter his presence with praise and honor!

The Glory Of God Is Revealed In The Personal Touch
The people of Israel were in awe of Moses. The disciples on the day of Jesus' transfiguration were also awed and fearful. Christ and Moses both used the personal touch to dispel their fears.

In the case of Jesus he would die for the whole world, but the whole world is composed of individuals like you and me.

In 1880, Fanny Crosby wrote the words to the song, "Tell Me The Story Of Jesus." The third verse says:

Tell of the cross where they nailed him writhing in anguish and pain.

126

*Tell of the grave where they laid him; tell how he liveth
again.
Love in that story so tender clearer than ever I see.
Stay, let me weep while you whisper; love paid the ransom for me.*[5]

On our journey of faith each of us must come to a personal
relationship with Christ. Love ... Christ ... paid the ransom for our
lives. We do not come to Christ by osmosis, wishful thinking, or
parental inheritance. It is a willful decision to accept the terms of
Jesus and to surrender to him. As we give up our plans, our desires,
our wills, and our sins our goal is to become his followers. He will
replace them with a much better plan for our lives because he will
be at the control center directing, guiding, and challenging us to
live life to the fullest.

Today Jesus can transform our lives if we allow him to do so.
He will not force, coerce, or destroy our will, but will gently ask us
to come to him. Jesus said, "Here I am! I stand at the door and
knock ..." (Revelation 3:20a NIV).

*For God so loved the world that he gave his one and
only Son, that whoever believes in him shall not perish
but have eternal life. For God did not send his Son into
the world to condemn the world, but to save the world
through him. Whoever believes in him is not condemned,
but whoever does not believe stands condemned already
because he has not believed in the name of God's one
and only Son.* — John 3:16-18 (NIV)

God personally wants to touch your life. Will you let him?
Amen.

---

1. Jan Karon, *Patches of Godlight* (New York: Penguin Books, 2001), npn.

2. Charles Swindoll, *Growing Strong in the Seasons of Life* (Portland: Multnomah
Press, 1983), p. 118.

3. Patrick Morely, *Walking with Christ in the Details of Life* (Nashville: Thomas Nelson Publishers, 1992), p. 18.

4. Albert M. Wells Jr., compiler, *Inspiring Quotations* (Nashville: Thomas Nelson Publishers, 1988), p. 157.

5. "Tell Me The Story Of Jesus" words by Fanny J. Crosby, 1880. In the public domain.

Sermons On The First Readings

For Sundays In
Lent And Easter

God All Along

David J. Kalas

Trumpet Medley

Listen to the sound of the trumpet. What do you hear?

Sounds evoke feelings, of course. And so what you and I hear takes place as much in our hearts as in our eardrums. What a sound elicits in our hearts depends upon our experience and association with that sound.

Some sounds, you know, are so inherently appealing that their effect is almost universally positive: a baby's giggle, for example, or the sounds of nature on a quiet summer evening come to mind. By contrast, certain other sounds have a predictably negative effect: the proverbial fingernails on a chalkboard or the deliberately unsettling sound of a smoke alarm.

Of course, you and I live in a time when we can be rather selective about the sounds that we hear. Much more so than previous generations.

It used to be that every telephone sounded essentially the same. Today, however, we can program our phones to play all sorts of pleasing or amusing personalized ringtones. Even the term is becoming a misnomer, for the younger generations may not associate phones with "ringing" at all.

My wife's cell phone, for instance, used to be set to meow like a cat when someone called it, which generated some memorable reactions in certain group settings when the phone rang. I have friends whose phones offer a brief excerpt of classical music. I've heard teenager's phones that are programmed to say something when someone's calling, like "Pick up the phone" or "It's for you." And we can even program specific ringtones for specific callers.

Likewise, the alarms we set to awaken us in the morning is another area of tremendous variety now. Once upon a time, alarm clocks simply rang. Then some electronic versions offered an alternative: the buzz. Now, however, we can awaken to all sorts of sound effects, voices, messages, programming, and music.

Beyond all of that, with small digital devices, we can now have our chosen music with us almost anywhere we go. Our automobiles, computers, radios, televisions, and phones enable us to listen — on demand — to a smorgasbord of information and entertainment that was unthinkable a generation ago.

Still, all of the freedom and selection we presently enjoy when it comes to the sounds we hear only serves to reinforce the same basic truth: namely, that sounds evoke feelings. Strong feelings. That's why we find it so desirable to be able to choose our sounds.

Some sounds, of course, are neutral. Or at least situational. My spirit may always be cheered by the sound of a baby's innocent giggle, and I may always be annoyed by the shrill and strident smoke alarm; but some other sounds are more variable. They evoke different feelings on different days.

Let us imagine, for example, a teenage girl, who is awaiting a phone call from the boy she likes at school. Rumor has it that he may like her, too, and is thinking of calling her to ask her out on a date. Meanwhile, let us also imagine that, living in that same house with the girl is her middle-aged father, whose doctor recently ordered a certain battery of medical tests. Those test results will serve to confirm or refute the doctor's grim suspicions and the father's worst fears. The doctor has promised to call with the results sometime this afternoon.

When the telephone rings in that house, what happens?

The teenage girl and her father hear the same sound. It is the same pitch and decibel level for both. The sound waves that reach each one's ears are identical. However, the internal reaction of the two people is vastly different. The sound of the phone instantly fills the teenage girl with excitement. The same sound grips her father with apprehension and anxiety.

Well, the prophet Joel called for the sound of a trumpet. What feelings would that evoke? How did the trumpet sound?

The prophet Joel speaks from the vantage point of late Old Testament history. We consider some earlier Old Testament texts and settings to see how trumpets had been used in ancient Israel. We find there a wide range of uses for trumpets. The instrument and pitch could have been the same in every instance, but precisely how it sounded to the people who heard the trumpet depended upon the setting and the circumstance.

The first mention of a trumpet in scripture is found in Exodus 19. The setting is Sinai, the daunting mountain of God. To the children of Israel gathered there, we observe that the sound of the trumpet meant the appearance of the Lord. The trumpet is mentioned several times in the account (see Exodus 19:13, 16, 19; 20:18), although interestingly there is no reference to a human trumpeter. This is, apparently, a supernatural trumpet, perhaps corresponding to the trumpet that will accompany Christ's return and the great resurrection of the dead (1 Corinthians 15:52; 1 Thessalonians 4:16). For the people in Sinai's shadow, the trumpet signaled the awesome presence of God.

To the later generations of Israelites, who lived in observance of the Mosaic Law, the sound of the trumpet meant the beginning of some festival, some holy day, or a meaningful religious observance. Most notably, the trumpet marked the beginning of the year of jubilee, which came around once every fifty years. It was an occasion of liberation for Israel, as debts were cancelled, slaves were released, and family land was returned. Charles Wesley famously captured the feel of the moment in a hymn, saying, "Blow ye the trumpet, blow, the gladly solemn sound. Let all creation know to earth's remotest bound: The year of jubilee is come, the year of Jubilee is come. Return, ye ransomed sinner, home."[1]

Generations later, the psalmist declared, "Blow the trumpet at the new moon, at the full moon, on our festal day" (Psalm 81:3). That suggests to us that the trumpet was used routinely to signal the beginning of special times and sacred observances. What the ringing of the church bell has meant to so many souls in more recent generations would have held the same meaning in the trumpet sound for the ancient Israelites on so many holy days.

To the people who served in the armies of Joshua or Gideon, meanwhile, the sound of the trumpet had a very different association. Trumpets, you recall, were literally the instruments of victory in the famed conquest of Jericho, as well as in Gideon's later defeat of the enemy Midianites. The trumpets did not merely signal the attack: The trumpets achieved the victory.

To the associates of Nehemiah, on the other hand, the sound of the trumpet signaled a warning (Nehemiah 4:1-20). Those who endeavored to rebuild Jerusalem's walls lived under a constant threat. The coworkers were stretched out over a considerable distance around the perimeters of the vast building project, and so the trumpet became the means of communicating an urgent message quickly to all involved. The trumpet blast indicated an attack, and it called the people together to mobilize against the common foe. The sound of that trumpet would have had the alarming quality of a civil defense siren in our day — a piercing warning of trouble and danger.

What we hear goes beyond merely the vibrations of the sound waves against our ear drums. What we hear penetrates our hearts.

Dr. Ivan Pavlov, for all of his assets and accomplishments, is most famous for his dog. "Pavlov's dog," you recall, was trained to associate the sound of a bell with feeding time. Consequently, Dr. Pavlov discovered that the sound of the bell eventually prompted his dog to salivate.

I suppose that if Dr. Pavlov had habitually beaten his dog after ringing the bell, the sound of the bell would have come to mean something quite different for the poor animal. His reaction to the bell would likely have been to recoil rather than to salivate.

On this Ash Wednesday — this first day of the season of Lent — we are invited to hear the sound of the trumpet. God spoke through the Old Testament prophet Joel, calling out, "Blow the trumpet in Zion." Indeed, he says it twice.

And when the people heard the sound of the trumpet, what did they hear?

"Let all the inhabitants of the land tremble," Joel said, "for the day of the Lord is coming, it is near" (v. 1). So the trumpet in that day must have sounded like the trumpet at Sinai: The signal of the breathtaking prospect of the coming and the presence of the Lord. The sound of the trumpet triggered reverence and awe.

"Blow the trumpet in Zion," Joel said, "sound the alarm on my holy mountain! ... Like blackness spread upon the mountains a great and powerful army comes; their like has never been from of old, nor will be again after them in ages to come" (vv. 1-2). So Joel's trumpet announces not just the coming of the Lord, but also the coming of an army — a frightening and devastating army. The trumpet was a warning, as it was in the hearts of Nehemiah's companions. The sound of the trumpet evoked alarm and fear.

"Yet even now," the Lord said through Joel, "return to me with all your heart, with fasting, with weeping, and with mourning; rend your hearts and not your clothing. Return to the Lord your God, for he is gracious and merciful, slow to anger, and abounding in steadfast love, and relents from punishing" (vv. 12-13). Fear and alarm are not the goal in themselves, you see; they are a means to an end. By awakening the hearts of the people to impending danger, they will be prompted to call upon the Lord. Since they have distanced themselves from him by their sin, that means repenting and returning to him. The sound of Joel's trumpet, therefore, carries a tune of liberty and relief — the sound of freedom and forgiveness for the people, as with the jubilee trumpet.

"Blow the trumpet in Zion," Joel says again. "Sanctify a fast; call a solemn assembly; gather the people. Sanctify the congregation; assemble the aged; gather the children, even infants at the breast. Let the bridegroom leave his room, and the bride her canopy" (vv. 15-16). Joel's trumpet signaled a great convocation. Like the ancient trumpets that inaugurated holy days and festivals, this trumpet told the people that it was time to come together to worship. The trumpet was an invitation.

On this first day of the season of Lent, God's word to us comes through Joel, and Joel calls for the blowing of the trumpet. Listen to the sound of it. What do you hear? We hear a whole medley of instructions and emotions: as we are duly awed by the presence of the Lord, as we are rightly alarmed by our sinfulness, as we rejoice in the freedom and forgiveness God offers us, and as we set aside all else in order to come together in sacred assembly to worship him. Amen.

---

1. "Blow Ye The Trumpet, Blow" words by Charles Wesley, 1750. In the public domain.

Anatomy Of A Testimony

You see a man busily writing. His face reveals the intensity of his focus. He sometimes smiles as he writes, then stops to think again. At times he shows some dissatisfaction, and he goes back to rewrite some sentence or phrase. Clearly, he wants to get this just right.

We hesitate to interrupt his concentration, but we can't restrain our curiosity. "Excuse us," we say. "What is that you're working on so diligently?"

He looks up from his work and smiles. "I'm writing a toast. It's a toast that I'm going to give at a party."

"Ah, I see. It must be for someone very important."

"Oh yes," he says. "It's for my wife!"

"That's very sweet. What's the occasion? An anniversary?"

"Yes, that's right," the man replies. "Our silver anniversary!"

Our smile slowly gives way to a more quizzical look. "Silver anniversary," we ask. "Doesn't that mean 25 years of marriage?" We are understandably confused, for the young man doesn't even appear to be 25 years old himself. How could he possibly be celebrating his twenty-fifth anniversary?

"Yes," he says blissfully, "25 wonderful years of marriage."

"But ... but," we stammer. "I'm sorry, but how can you have been married for 25 years? You can't possibly be old enough."

"Oh, no, I haven't been married for 25 years yet," he concedes. "In fact, we haven't been married at all yet. Our wedding is next month. But I want to be sure to get this right: All that I want to say to her and about her on the occasion of our silver anniversary!"

Does such a scene sound sweet? Perhaps a little foolish? Well, that is essentially the scene portrayed in the passage we shared earlier from the Old Testament book of Deuteronomy.

Deuteronomy is a long good-bye. Moses has led the children of Israel from their bondage in Egypt, through the series of plagues, and the Passover. He has led them across the Red Sea, to Mount Sinai, and received on their behalf the law and covenant of God. He has led them through the wilderness and to the border of the promised land, where they balked in their faith. He continued to walk with them and lead them through their forty-year sentence of wilderness wandering. He led them through hunger and thirst, through worship and battles, through births and deaths. And now, some forty years after the original generation left Egypt under Moses, their adult children stand poised to enter the promised land across the Jordan River. Finally, old Moses will pass the baton of leadership, having completed his very long leg of the journey. Before Joshua succeeds him and the Israelites march across the Jordan, Moses says his farewell.

Deuteronomy is that farewell.

For what amounts to more than thirty chapters, Moses reminds the people about all that God has said to them and done for them along the way. He reminds them of the consequences of their disobedience, as well as the benefits of their righteousness. He reminds them of God's rules and regulations for holy living. And, in the passage we share together today, Moses writes for the people the script of their testimony.

"When you have come into the land that the Lord your God is giving you," Moses instructs the people, "and you possess it, and settle in it ..." (v. 1). Then he proceeds to prescribe for them what they are to do and to say.

I wonder if these instructions didn't seem a bit premature to the Israelites. After all, Moses was taking so many things for granted. At this point in time, the people were still camped on the far side of the Jordan River, gazing across at the seemingly impregnable great walled city of Jericho. That battle by itself must have seemed so improbable to the people, and it was only the first of many. There were so many other towns, cities, fortresses, and armies to be encountered, unseen beyond the horizon. Yet Moses was fast-forwarding past all of those battles, as well as past the whole process of settling the land.

"When you have come into the land ... and you possess it, and settle in it," Moses says. Talk about something easier said than done! It seems almost impertinent for Moses to refer so casually to the long ordeal that lies ahead, to reduce all of the challenges ahead of them to a mere dependent clause in a sentence.

Casually say to the graduate student, "When you have completed all of your course work, finished your research, written your dissertation, and successfully defended it, then here is what you should say on the occasion of your graduation." Blithely say to the pregnant young woman, "When you have given birth to your baby, weaned him, and raised him through all the years of childhood and adolescence, then here is what you should write on his birthday card when he turns 21."

For the unmarried young man to begin to compose the toast for the celebration of his silver anniversary may seem sweet, but it also seems terribly naive and premature. There are so many years and experiences, so many challenges, so many struggles, and so much growth between now and then.

Still, there in the trans-Jordan region, Moses passes quickly by all of the challenges and obstacles that lie ahead for Israel, and he cuts right to the toast. "When all of that other stuff is done," he says, "then here is what you need to say and do on that occasion." It may seem premature — even impertinent or naive — but I suspect that Moses learned it from God. Way back when Moses first encountered God, at the burning bush more than forty years earlier, the Lord told him, "I will be with you; and this shall be the sign for you that it is I who sent you: when you have brought the people out of Egypt, you shall worship God on this mountain" (Exodus 3:12).

At that point in the story, Moses had not even agreed to take the job God was offering — to go to Egypt as God's agent of deliverance for the Hebrew slaves — and already God was talking to Moses about what would happen when the mission was accomplished. "Whoa, there! Let's not get ahead of ourselves, Lord!"

Still, all of this premature talk has its own sort of beauty. It is the beauty of certainty — Babe Ruth calling his shot or Joe Namath guaranteeing victory in Super Bowl III. It is President Kennedy pledging a man on the moon. It is the beauty of certainty, and it is most splendid when the promise comes from God, for his guarantees are absolute.

Moses confidently fast-forwards past the challenges, the struggles, and the battles, and he says to the people, "When you have come into the land that the Lord your God is giving you as an inheritance to possess, and you possess it, and settle in it...."

Yes, then what?

Then comes the toast! Only in this case, the toast is a testimony.

Moses tells the people to take an offering to the place of worship: first fruits from the harvest of the land. The offering represents the people's gratitude to God, for the harvest reminds them of God's provident care. The same God who had fed them with manna from dew and water from rocks throughout their wilderness sojourn would also be responsible for the bounty enjoyed through the cycles of planting and harvest.

Giving to God a portion of the first fruits is a lovely way of honoring and thanking him. Imagine the five-year-old daughter who, upon receiving from her parents a gift of new crayons or markers for coloring, makes her first project an "I love you" note and picture for her mommy and daddy. This is the quality of the first fruits offering: let the first thing I do with God's gift to me be a way of saying "thank you" and "I love you" to him.

Then, upon presenting the token produce at the place of worship, the Israelites were to recite a certain script: "Today I declare to the Lord your God that I have come into the land that the Lord swore to our ancestors to give us" (v. 3). It was a confessional statement — an expressed recognition that God had, indeed, kept his promise, and that the worshiper himself was a beneficiary of that promise.

And then, in the next moment, the person with the offering was to make this longer statement: "A wandering Aramean was my ancestor; he went down into Egypt and lived there as an alien, few in number, and there he became a great nation, mighty and populous. When the Egyptians treated us harshly and afflicted us, by imposing hard labor on us, we cried to the Lord, the God of our ancestors; the Lord heard our voice and saw our affliction, our toil, and our oppression. The Lord brought us out of Egypt with a mighty hand and an outstretched arm, with a terrifying display of power, and with signs and wonders; and he brought us into this place and gave us this land, a land flowing with milk and honey. So now I bring the first of the fruit of the ground that you, O Lord, have given me" (vv. 5-10).

This is the toast, you see, written long before the anniversary. This is Israel's testimony: how God had found them, saved them, led them, and prospered them. The testimony tells the marvelous story of what God had accomplished. For what began as "a wandering Aramean" has become an entire nation, settled and established. What had been a helpless group was miraculously helped. What was once a bunch of slaves in a foreign land is now a free people in their own land. And here is some of the produce of the land to prove it!

This is always the quality of a testimony, of course. Just like those early worshipers in ancient Israel, our testimonies are stories. They are stories of where we were when God found us and the place to which he has brought us. Stories of how he has led us and what he has led through. Expressions of our gratitude to God for his faithfulness and provident care.

All of us who have traveled some miles with God have those stories. They are meant to be declared in the place of worship. And even for those of us who have not yet reached the place we believe God has in store for us, it's not too early to start writing our toast.

A Resume Of Righteousness

Statues don't perspire. The characters portrayed in stained-glass windows don't blink. And so we are tempted to forget that the people they so nobly represent were human beings, just like us. In the statue's solidness and in the window's beauty, they cannot do justice to the blemishes and the frailties of the men and women they depict.

We have seen so many of our biblical heroes portrayed in art: in glorious stained glass, in noble statues, and in sweet portraits on Sunday school room walls. Those depictions have so often been glorified and idealized. Long before contemporary magazine covers were offering us airbrushed images of celebrities, Michelangelo carved for us a perfect David and a magnificent Moses.

The portraits painted by scripture, however, are not so touched-up. While men like Moses and David are celebrated, they are not romanticized. We see the men and women of scripture through a very candid lens. Moses is remembered as peerless (Deuteronomy 34:10-12), yet his epitaph comes to us from outside the borders of the promised land because of his own sin and failure. David symbolizes both a golden age past and a messianic age to come, yet the biblical author does not protect his reputation from the lust, the deviousness, the foolishness, or the pettiness he exhibited along the way. While Solomon is remembered for his splendor, his fingerprints are left forever on the tragic division of the kingdom after his death.

Likewise in the stories of Jacob or Elijah, of Joseph or Mary, of Peter or Paul. They rank among the great heroes of faith, but the

Bible does not pretend that they were perfect. On the contrary, it is generous with the evidence of their humanness and imperfections. And so it is, too, with the character at the center of our Old Testament reading today. Four thousand years after he lived and died, Abraham is remembered and honored by untold millions around the globe. So many of the pivotal promises of God trace back to him. And from him come nations and faiths that remain at the center of current events so many centuries after his sojourn in the holy land.

Abraham is a towering figure on the world's stage. The particular episode that we read from the book of Genesis this morning is one of the watershed events in Abraham's life and experience. But not only for Abraham, it is a watershed for us, as well. Four thousand years later, that event in Abraham's life proves to be a landmark in our experience, too. For the apostle Paul points back to this episode as a crucial turning point in understanding the salvation that you and I have in Jesus Christ.

The issue at hand is no less a question than how it is that we are saved. How is it that a sinful human being can be put right with a holy God? The standard assumption within the contemporary Judaism of Paul's time was that the key to righteousness was compliance with God's law. Perhaps it was just a formal ancestor of the "just try to be a good person" emphasis that prevails in so many of our churches today. The Jews recognized that God's law articulated God's will and his covenant with his people, and so they understood that thorough conformity to that law was the definition of righteousness.

However, Paul, who was himself a Pharisee — zealous in his adherence to the law — had discovered that the law was unable to make him truly righteous. The law could only serve to diagnose our sin; it couldn't cure our sin. Consequently, the law could not make us right with God; it only proves our unrighteousness before him.

Paul looks back to this moment in Abraham's life, and he sees there the real key to real righteousness. The writer of Genesis reports that Abraham "believed the Lord; and the Lord reckoned it to him as righteousness" (v. 6).

"The Lord reckoned it to him as righteousness." So it was that Abraham, hundreds of years before the Mosaic law was even given, was somehow made righteous before God. How? He believed God. And that, Paul realized, was the answer to our relationship with God and to our righteousness: believing God. In a word, faith.

In his letters to the Christians in Rome and to the Christians in Galatia, Paul makes repeated reference to this moment in Abraham's life. He sees in it profound proof that our salvation is by faith. We are not made right with God by our works, by our circumcision, or by the law. Rather "we know," Paul wrote, "that a person is justified not by the works of the law but through faith in Jesus Christ. And we have come to believe in Christ Jesus, so that we might be justified by faith in Christ, and not by doing the works of the law, because no one will be justified by the works of the law" (Galatians 2:16).

So here is Abraham: this immensely important figure, whom Paul identifies as "the ancestor of all who believe" (Romans 4:11). The Lord comes to him one night in a vision, and that night continues to endure for four millennium as a defining moment in salvation history. Given that it is such a vitally important event — and that Abraham himself is such a considerable figure — let's zoom in and take a closer look.

We observe that just three sentences are attributed to Abraham in this momentous scene. Two of them are questions. The other might best be described as a complaint — or at least a statement indicating concern and dissatisfaction.

The scene begins with God's initiative. That is almost always the case in our relationship with God. In this particular instance, we read that the word of the Lord came to Abraham in a vision and told him, "Do not be afraid, Abram, I am your shield; your reward shall be very great" (v. 1).

What a marvelous word to hear from God! It is encouraging, it is reassuring, and it is generous. We might reasonably expect Abraham to respond with some psalm of thanksgiving or hymn of praise.

But not so. Instead, Abraham responds with a question. In fact, combined with his subsequent statement, it amounts to a rather pointed question. "O Lord God," Abraham replied, "what will you give me, for I continue childless, and the heir of my house is Eliezer of Damascus? You have given me no offspring, and so a slave born in my house is to be my heir" (vv. 2-3).

Is this the quote we have from the hero of faith? Is this the response from our paragon of righteousness? In candor that seems to border on irreverence, Abraham presumes to question God's future plans by questioning God's past performance. The Lord has made a grand and generous promise to Abraham, yet the pragmatic old man responds with a rather negative calculation. "What good will any gift from you do me," Abraham asks in effect, "since you haven't given me an heir to whom I can leave it?"

Long before, the Lord had uprooted Abraham from what had been his homeland and the land of his ancestors. He moved Abraham to a foreign land and promised that he would give him much land and many descendants. To date, however, he owned no land, and he had no descendants.

I don't necessarily hear bitterness in Abraham's voice. But he does have a concern, and he is not reluctant to voice it to God.

Meanwhile, the only other words ascribed to Abraham in this scene form another question. The Lord says to him, "I am the Lord who brought you from Ur of the Chaldeans, to give you this land to possess" (v. 7). And in response, Abraham asks, "O Lord God, how am I to know that I shall possess it?" (v. 8).

It's an interesting response on Abraham's part, because he seems to be missing the point. The Lord is simply identifying himself. We recognize the format, for it is essentially the same as the Lord's opening words in the Ten Commandments. Just before listing his commandments, he says, "I am the Lord your God, who brought you out of the land of Egypt, out of the house of slavery" (Exodus 20:2). He is identifying himself to the people. He is saying who he is in light of what he has done for them, and that forms the context for the commandments that he gives to them.

Likewise here in this episode. God is identifying himself to Abraham in terms of what he has already done for Abraham: "I am the Lord who brought you from Ur of the Chaldeans, to give you this land to possess." But Abraham humanly fixates on one part of that statement of what God had done for him: namely, the part that wasn't done yet. He had not yet possessed the land. Not even an acre of it, really. And so he wants to know: "How am I to know that I shall possess it?" He's looking for a little proof, a guarantee, a sign.

That concludes the words of Abraham in this watershed moment. Two questions and a complaint. That's it.

We think of far more heroic and exemplary words by other characters at other times. We think of Joseph's integrity when he was seduced by Potiphar's wife. We think of Joshua and Caleb among the whining spies. We think of David before Goliath or Shadrach and company before the fiery furnace. We think of Stephen being stoned or Paul on trial. There are so many marvelous statements of faith and faithfulness in the face of trouble. Yet here, presented with the generous promises of God, all Abraham can muster is two questions and a complaint.

We are inclined to ask, "What's so great about Abraham? How is it that he ranks so high?"

Simply this: Abraham believed God in spite of past disappointments and future uncertainties. In spite of all the questions and laments he may have felt in his own soul, Abraham believed. In spite of his own human inability to connect the dots from his present circumstance to God's promises, still he believed God. And the Lord reckoned it to him as righteousness.

Statues don't perspire, and stained-glass characters don't blink. But heroes of faith do have doubts. True believers have their questions. Paragons of righteousness have some concerns. We discover from Abraham — as well as from Jeremiah, Habakkuk, the psalmist, the importunate widow, and others — that the candid expression of those doubts, questions, and concerns to God is itself an act of faith. We have faith that he cares and faith that he can and will do something about it. For in the end, though perspiring and blinking, Abraham believed God. Amen.

RSVP

When you and I send out invitations to events we are hosting, we typically include at the bottom of the invitation certain initials. "RSVP" is what we customarily print at the bottom of our invitations. It's an abbreviation for a French phrase, which means, "Please respond."

It's always disappointing, of course, when someone we had wanted to include in an event is unable to attend. But at least we want to know. We need to know who is coming and who is not. It is common practice to ask people to respond to invitations. "RSVP" — please respond.

Some of the things that we get in the mail or that we pick up to read do not require a response. A lot of what we read is purely informational. Some is just for our interest or amusement. Some pieces of mail get almost no attention from us at all before we toss them into the wastebasket.

However, a personal invitation is different. It is not meant to be tossed away casually. It is not merely for our information or amusement. It requires some response on our part. Someone is waiting to hear from us. They need to know: Are you coming or not?

As a gentle reminder, we put the initials at the bottom. "RSVP" — please respond.

Perhaps we should print those initials in our churches, as well.

We sometimes do include other initials in our churches, you know. Perhaps you've seen a stained-glass window, an altar, or a cross in your church that has "INRI" or "IHS" on it. Like our RSVP, those church initials originated in other languages. The "INRI" is borrowed from the Latin initials for the phrase that was posted on Jesus' cross: Jesus of Nazareth, King of the Jews. The "IHS," meanwhile, is an adaptation of the first three letters of the name of Jesus as it appears in Greek.

Likewise, we would do well to add these initials to our churches. It would be entirely appropriate to carve "RSVP" into our altars and our crosses, for we ought to be reminded continuously that God has extended an invitation to us and that he is waiting for our response.

The passage that we read together this morning from the Old Testament prophet Isaiah is an invitation from God.

We should be astonished that God extends invitations at all. After all, does a sovereign need to invite? Isn't it his prerogative simply to command, to summon, to give orders? The mere fact that God extends invitations to us at all bears witness to the kind of relationship he endeavors to have with us. It would be overstating the case, to be sure, to suggest that it is a relationship between equals. It is, however, a relationship in which we are elevated beyond our merit; and one in which he voluntarily condescends.

The Bible offers us a variety of images to describe our relationship with God. He is shepherd, and we are his sheep. He is a master, and we are his servants. He is the king, and we are subjects in his kingdom. Yet none of those authoritarian images for God quite captures the whole truth. For his communication with us is not solely orders and instructions: He also invites!

This is a testimony to how he created us. Namely, he made us free. If you and I were not free, he would not need to extend invitations to us. We would simply be programmed to come and go according to his will. But, in his sovereignty, he made the choice to create us as free and independent creatures, and in the process he limited his own sovereignty! He chose to make us in such a way that we are out of his complete control. We have the capacity to cooperate with his will or not.

So it is, then, that we are eligible to have a meaningful, love relationship with him and he assumes the posture of one who extends invitations to us. So it is that we may respond to those invitations, or not.

We ought, therefore, to carve the initials into our altars and crosses: RSVP — please respond!

Here is our situation. God loves us so much that he wants us to love him back. To that end, he made us free. To that end, he condescends to enter into a relationship in which we might spurn his love. And, to that end, he extends invitations to us and waits for us to respond.

The image of God waiting for us to respond is portrayed poignantly in two New Testament passages. First, there is the marvelous picture of Christ standing at the door and knocking, waiting for us to open up and welcome him in (Revelation 3:20). Second, there is the heartache of Jesus weeping over Jerusalem: "Jerusalem, Jerusalem, the city that kills the prophets and stones those who are sent to it! How often have I desired to gather your children together as a hen gathers her brood under her wings, and you were not willing!" (Matthew 23:37).

The first picture embodies the opportunity. The second picture raises the specter of missed opportunity.

For our purposes, that opportunity is expressed by the Old Testament prophet Isaiah. Now the Old Testament sometimes gets a bad rap in the church. We tend to be more fond of our impression of God in the New Testament, while we caricature him in the Old Testament as a kind of supernatural grouch: angry, judgmental, and destructive. We do well, therefore, to correct that misapprehension by seeing the kindness and generosity of his heart as articulated by this Old Testament prophet.

The invitation begins in the original Hebrew with a strange little word: a sad interjection that we variously translate alas, woe, ah, and ho. It is a word that appears about four dozen times in the Old Testament; all but one of which come from the prophets. The word amounts to little more than a sound: a grunt, a sigh. But that little sound conveys grief, lament, exhortation, and warning.

Thus begins the invitation from God through Isaiah. It is an invitation as broad and generous as Jesus standing at the door and knocking, yet as potentially sad as Jesus weeping over Jerusalem if we do not respond to that invitation.

The invitation is very specifically addressed: "Everyone who thirsts ... and you that have no money" (v. 1).

That sounds familiar, doesn't it? That is always the nature of the Lord's target audience, isn't it? He is, after all, the one who comes to seek and to save the lost. The physician who comes, not for those who were well, but for those who are sick. The shepherd who leaves the 99 in order to search for the one lost lamb. And the one who throws open his arms to those who are weary and heavy-laden.

It is here that God extends an invitation to those who are in need: the thirsty and the poor. We are reminded by his words to that people at whose door he knocked in Revelation that many folks may be in need — spiritually poor and thirsty — without fully realizing it (3:17-18). His invitation, therefore, is extended to a broader audience than we might have first suspected.

What precisely does he offer to those who are poor, hungry, and thirsty? He extends an invitation to receive freely the very refreshment and satisfaction that they so deeply need and desire.

Next, he broadens his invitation to an audience that may be close to home. "Why do you spend your money for that which is not bread," he asks, "and your labor for that which does not satisfy?" (v. 2).

He's talking to a lot of people, isn't he? A whole lot of folks who do not regard themselves as needy in the sense of being hungry, thirsty, or poor would admit, in a moment of vulnerable candor, that they have often spent their labor on things that don't satisfy.

Let us go out into the world — into our neighborhoods, our workplaces, our schools, and our stores — and let us ask for a show of hands: How many here are poor? How many are hungry and thirsty? We won't see many hands, but let us ask how many are unsatisfied, and then I suspect we would see a terrible, sad show of hands.

Indeed, we don't have to ask for a show of hands: We can already see how unsatisfied so many folks are. We see it in their restlessness and their discontentment. We see it in both the harmless and the harmful ways that they try to fill their emptiness. We see it in their manifold means of distracting and numbing themselves. Day after day, year after year, they've labored away, yet for that which has not really satisfied.

God has good news for them. He has good news for us! An invitation to come to the waters, to eat what is good, and to delight ourselves in something that really fills and satisfies. And, of course, it is all for free, for that is always the offer of grace!

The invitation continues. "Let the wicked forsake their way, and the unrighteous their thoughts" (v. 2). Ah, another familiar target audience for the urgent exhortation and gracious invitation of our God. And what does the Lord offer to them? "Let them return to the LORD, that he may have mercy on them, and to our God, for he will abundantly pardon" (v. 76).

We are accustomed to the gospel according to Matthew, Mark, Luke, and John. Here we hear the gospel according to Isaiah. Eight centuries before the birth, death, and resurrection of Jesus, we already see the gracious heart, the kind will, and the generous invitation of God. It is an invitation to those who are thirsty, needy, sinful, and unsatisfied. It is an invitation to turn around and come to him — an invitation to be welcomed pardoned, filled, and refreshed.

And all of it is his treat; all of it is at his expense.

So the only question is: Are you coming or not? Please respond! Amen.

Joshua's New Diet

What do you or your family pray at mealtime? When I was growing up, our family typically recited the "God is good, God is great" prayer that so many folks use as a table grace. At Christian camp settings as a teenager, I grew accustomed to singing the Johnny Appleseed song before we ate. My children are fond of singing the doxology at the dinner table. And over the years I have heard a great many people offer mealtime prayers, thanking God for his bounty, for fellowship, for the hands that prepared and the homes that hosted, and praying that God would bless the food to our bodies and us to his service.

Perhaps you have seen the famous 1918 photograph taken by Eric Enstrom. Simply titled, "Grace," the photo shows an old man, Charles Wilden, sitting at a small table, with a simple meal before him, with folded hands and bowed head, saying his thanks to God before eating.

Painted versions of the original photograph hang in countless homes and churches. For generations, it has been a cherished image of the table grace, and more recently it has been designated as the official state photograph of Minnesota (where it was taken).

This morning I'm picturing another man bowing his head to pray before he eats. He, too, is an old man, with perhaps the same sort of white beard and weathered face as the subject of the famous Enstrom portrait.

This man's prayer is not original with him; rather, it is a customary prayer of his people. "Blessed art thou, O Lord our God," he begins, but then he pauses. He says nothing. Nothing.

Has he forgotten the next line? We open an eye from our seat across the table to see what is wrong. And through our squint, we discover that the old man has stopped as he is trying to regain his composure.

After a deep breath, he resumes, deliberately and meaningfully pronouncing each word: "Blessed art thou, king of the universe, who bringeth forth bread from the earth." His voice cracks as he prays, and when he has finished, he reaches up to wipe away the tears from his eyes and cheeks.

Perhaps we have heard people break down and cry when they're sharing their testimony. Perhaps we have seen people tear up when singing a cherished hymn. But saying grace? Repeating a simple table prayer? Ah, but this prayer is a testimony! For the old man is Joshua, and when he thanks God for bringing forth bread from the earth, it is a testimony, indeed.

You and I know what it is to experience a new diet.

At the very least, we all made the transition some years ago from mother's milk or formula to the solid and varied food of children and adults.

Meanwhile, those of us who have traveled to other countries or cultures — perhaps even lived for a time in a foreign setting — have encountered new diets, sometimes bold and sometimes bland. For that matter, even spending time in another region within our own United States can introduce us to a different sort of menu — the seafood of the east coast, the Cajun food along the Gulf, the meat-and-potatoes of the Midwest, the Tex-Mex of the Southwest, the brats of Wisconsin, and the ludefisk of Minnesota, and on and on.

As we've aged, we may have entered another new diet or two. By doctor's order, perhaps, we have had to grow accustomed to a diet with less salt, or less fat, fewer carbohydrates, or fewer calories.

Old Joshua has just begun a new diet — a wonderful new diet! In order for us to appreciate the menu, however, we have to turn back the clock a bit to see his earlier fare.

Joshua was born in Egypt. He was not Egyptian, mind you, but he and the rest of his Hebrew people were captive slaves there in the land of Egypt. Their ancestors had come during the halcyon days of Joseph, and they were treated originally as VIP guests in the land. Now, however, they had suffered under centuries of cruel bondage. Labor under the lash: that is the life into which Joshua had been born. His life and body existed purely for the benefit of his taskmasters, and his toil did not accrue to his own benefit but to Pharaoh's.

We do not know what the ancient menu was for those Hebrew slaves. The biblical account, significantly, devotes more attention to the details of their deliverance than the details of their misery. We may reasonably assume, however, that the best that the land had to offer was set aside for others — for Pharaoh, for his court, and for his countrymen — but not for the slaves.

There is, meanwhile, one meal Joshua ate in Egypt that we do know about. After the arrival of Moses, the confrontations with the Pharaoh, and the gradual battering of Egypt through the plagues, the time had come for Joshua and the Hebrews finally to be set free. On the eve of their deliverance, they sat down to eat a meal prescribed by God. We know it today as the Passover meal: a menu filled with symbols of the people's bondage and God's deliverance.

Centuries before Americans invented "fast food," God had instructed the children of Israel to eat their own sort of fast food that night. They were to eat with their coats on and their walking sticks in hand. They were to eat unleavened bread — the bread of haste — because their departure would be so sudden and hurried that it wouldn't have time to rise.

Then, after that fateful night, Joshua embarked on a new diet. Call it "the wilderness diet," for it was the providential but rather limited menu that sustained the Israelites in the wilderness. The staple of that diet was manna. It was the miraculous "bread from heaven" that the Israelites could go out and gather in abundance each morning. And while the trip to the promised land — and, therefore, the supply of manna — was only meant to last a matter of weeks, it turned into a forty-year misadventure because of the faithlessness of the people. And so the people saw and ate a lot of manna.

In 1980, Keith Green famously made fun of the Israelites' discontentment with their all-manna-all-the-time diet. In his song, "So

You Wanna Go Back To Egypt," Green took on the persona of the wilderness wanderers and sang about all of the manna foods they were served. Look online for the hilarious lyrics to this song.

All joking aside, however, the situation of Joshua is a truly poignant one. As a younger man, we see him as the constant companion of Moses, and a man of intense devotion to God. Furthermore, when the Israelites first reached the border of the promised land, Joshua was one of the twelve men chosen to go in and spy out the land. When that reconnaissance mission was complete, all twelve spies reported on the beauty and desirability of the land. But ten of the twelve — everyone except for Joshua and a man named Caleb — lamented about the impossibility of conquering the land and defeating its inhabitants.

The congregation of Israel, predictably, sided with the peddlers of despair, and the Lord was displeased. Even after much exhortation from Joshua and Moses, the people persisted in their faithlessness and with terrible consequences.

When it was all said and done, the entire nation of Israel was sentenced to a generation of wandering in the wilderness: ample time for the faithless generation to die off and their children to grow up. Then, God guaranteed, he would bring that next generation into the land of his promise.

Though he himself was innocent and exemplary, Joshua spent most of the rest of his life in the wilderness. Joshua spent most of the rest of his life gathering manna every morning and eating manna every evening. His hair turned gray in the desert. His face wrinkled and his children grew up in the desert. He watched every one of his peers (except Caleb) die in the desert.

Finally, after forty long years, we come to the scene portrayed in our Old Testament reading today. The people have crossed the Jordan River, and they have paused on the other side to worship and rededicate themselves to God. As Joshua looks over the crowd, which he now leads, he sees only one man his own age: Caleb. No one else has been all of the places they have been, or seen all the things they have seen. No one else there knew Egypt and left Egypt as an adult.

The man born in Egypt now leads the conquest of Canaan. The

one raised in slavery stands now on the property of God's promise. And the one who has spent a lifetime eating manna from the desert floor now gazes over the land flowing with milk and honey.

There, at that sacred moment on the other side of the Jordan, the Bible reports, "On that very day, they ate the produce of the land, unleavened cakes and parched grain. The manna ceased on the day they ate the produce of the land, and the Israelites no longer had manna; they ate the crops of the land of Canaan that year" (vv. 11-12).

See the old man as he bows his head to pray. His face and hands are weathered by time and the wilderness. His voice cracks, tears fill his eyes, and he recites the simple table prayer, which is his testimony: "Blessed art thou, O Lord our God, king of the universe, who bringeth forth bread from the earth." Amen.

Heisman In The Hudson

In December of every year, the Downtown Athletic Club in New York City awards the coveted Heisman Trophy. Voted on by over 800 media members, the Heisman is awarded to the most outstanding college football player during that season. Past recipients have included such notables as Roger Staubach, Marcus Allen, and Barry Sanders. It is a great honor, and it represents the broad and non-partisan recognition of a player's outstanding season.

In the case of this particular young man, let us say that he has just completed a record-breaking campaign. He is a quarterback, and he has led his team to an undefeated record. They are the odds-on favorites to win the national championship. He has passed for more yards, more completions, and more touchdowns than any other college quarterback. Indeed, many observers have credited him with the greatest single-season performance by any player in college football history.

Typically, several different eligible candidates are invited to New York City for the award ceremony, and there is more or less suspense about which one of them will be awarded the Heisman. This year, however, there is no suspense, at all. Even the other three players who have made the trip to New York for the occasion are under no delusions: It will be his trophy and probably by unanimous vote.

Given all of that, now let us imagine this scene following the Heisman ceremony.

The honored young man is chauffeured in a limousine from the site of the ceremony to a television studio for the first of many interviews. On the way, he looks out the window of the limousine and notices that they are traveling alongside the Hudson River. "Stop the car," he calls out to the driver. When the car is stopped, the football player emerges from the backseat, Heisman in hand, and proceeds to walk over to the bank of the river. Then, with his famed throwing arm, he tosses the Heisman well into the river, where it promptly sinks out of sight.

"What in the world did you do that for?" asks the bewildered driver as the football player gets back into the car.

"Because I want everyone to forget what I've done," he says, with surprising serenity. "I don't want anyone to think about or talk about this past football season."

"Why?" exclaims the driver. "It was one of the most amazing individual performances by any football player ever!"

"Yes," concedes the young man, "but I'm going to do even more and even better next year."

It is an unimaginable scene. It is the job applicant, who tears up the resume that everyone fawns over, saying, "You ain't seen nothing yet." It is the much-recruited high school senior, who wants to disown his sterling GPA and board scores, confident that his achievements in college will eclipse them. And it is the God of Israel, who says, "Do not remember the former things, or consider the things of old. I am about to do a new thing" (vv. 18-19).

The setting for this unimaginable word from the Lord is the era of one of the great empires of the late Old Testament period. Perhaps the generation of the Assyrian threat or of the Babylonian exile.

The Jews of that day were a victimized lot. Too weak to fend for themselves, they needed constantly to cast their lots with neighboring nations, hoping to stay afloat by holding onto someone else's driftwood. Perhaps the Arameans could stave off the Assyrian onslaught. Perhaps the Egyptians could intercept the Babylonians. If only the Edomites had not been so duplicitous.

Long gone were the conquering days of Joshua, the heroism of Samson, the strong reign of David, and the golden age of Solomon. Now their kings were not collecting tribute from others put paying ransom to keep their thrones. Little by little the palace and the

162

temple were stripped of their treasures, and little by little the people were stripped of their dignity. Finally, during the Babylonian period, the people saw their king blinded and hauled off in chains; they saw many of their fellow citizens and family members taken captive; and ultimately they saw their capital city and the house of their God destroyed by invading pagans.

What are people to do in the midst of such misery? Where do they turn in such a crisis?

Well, when the present is painful, we human beings typically look in two directions. We look to the past, when it's fond. And we look to the future, when it's hopeful.

For the tormented people of Judah, it was hard to imagine a very hopeful future. All the trend lines worked against them. But they did have a fond past. A wonderful past! The people of God enjoyed a celebrated history of the Lord's heroism in their deliverance from Egypt, for example. At that earlier time, when they were weak and oppressed, the Lord bared his holy arm, defeated their enemies, and established his people in freedom and peace. Much of their law, their ritual, their hymnody, and their national testimony dated back to that exodus.

Now, as the Lord speaks to this later generation of Jews, he recalls those former days — those miracles and that deliverance. He identifies himself with those events: The Lord "who makes a way in the sea, a path in the mighty waters, who brings out chariot and horse, army and warrior; they lie down, they cannot rise, they are extinguished, quenched like a wick" (vv. 16-17). These are all clearly references to the exodus experience in the generation of Moses, some 500 or 600 years earlier. Specifically, they recall the final nail in Egypt's coffin when the Lord parted the Red Sea for his people to cross over, only to close the waters in on the chasing chariots of Pharaoh.

God reminds them of what he has done in the past, and that seems to be a useful and encouraging thing. After all, might not the miracles of the past engender faith in the present and hope for the future? Surely one of the recurring themes of Moses and the law, of the worship liturgy found in psalms, and of the prescribed holy day celebrations was to encourage the people to remember the past.

If they would just recall what God had said and done in the past, that would inform their faith and guide their future. The great risk to be guarded against was that future generations would forget what God had done in the past. Then they would become easy prey for every sort of sin and temptation, pride and ingratitude, idolatry and doubt.

Then comes the surprising moment when the quarterback throws the trophy into the river. God, who had commanded his people to remember and who had built reminders into their daily lives and annual rituals, now tells them to forget. "Do not remember the former things," he says, "or consider the things of old." Just as the congregation rises to sing, "O God, Our Help In Ages Past," the Lord interrupts. "Stop the music!" he insists. "I want you to forget about the past, and I want you to stop thinking about what I've done for you in the past."

It's unthinkable advice. The past is precious to us. Recalling the past — and, specifically, recalling what God has done for us in the past — brings tears to our eyes. It's our history, and it's our testimony.

Ask an adolescent what his favorite song is, and it will likely be a current hit, a relatively new song. But ask anyone over the age of forty what his favorite song is, and he will likely choose some song from years and years before — a song that represents another time and place. He'll likely choose a blast from the past that evokes sweet memories, nostalgia, and gratitude.

For men and women of faith, that natural human nostalgia has an additional layer: the sweetness of miles traveled and years lived with God. My favorite songs are songs about him and songs that remind me of times and experiences with him. Could it possibly be that he is telling me to forget them? To stop singing them?

"Do not remember the former things, or consider the things of old," he says, for "I am about to do a new thing." That's good news. For as unsettling as the instruction to forget may be, the promise of something new is certainly welcome. Then comes the critical question: "Now it springs forth, do you not perceive it?" (v. 19).

Ah, there's the rub. There is nothing wrong with the past, unless it becomes an impediment to the future. There's nothing bad about the old until it blinds us to the new.

I have attended a lot of musical concerts through the years, including a few by singer/songwriters who have been around for a while. In those instances, I have noticed an interesting phenomenon within the audience. They cheer loudest and longest for the old songs, while they are comparatively impatient with the artist's newer stuff.

Is it that the new songs are inferior? Not necessarily. It's just that we are so sentimentally attached to what is already familiar and loved that we are not interested in hearing anything new.

How frustrating that must be for a musician, and how frustrating that must be for God.

We see the phenomenon manifested in the ministry of Jesus. The people around him were so tied to what they had seen and known in the past that they were unwilling or unable to recognize fully who and what Jesus was.

The people of Nazareth were so locked into Jesus' family of origin that they couldn't receive him as anything more than the ordinary son of Mary and Joseph. Herod was so burdened by the guilty memory of John the Baptist that he could only imagine that Jesus was John come back to haunt him. The speculating crowds could only guess that Jesus was Elijah, Jeremiah, or one of the prophets.

And the artist wanted to call out from on stage, "No, forget about the greatest hits from twenty years ago. Listen to this new song!"

I am very fond of the past. More than that, I am very grateful for the past, and for what God has done in the past. However, you and I serve a God who does not rest on his resume. You and I belong to a God who keeps writing new songs. And you and I follow a Lord who tosses the old trophies away, assuring us, "You ain't seen nothing yet!" Amen.

Profile Of A Savior

In the century and a half that cameras have been around, photographers have done us the great favor of capturing moments. Previously, artists could endeavor to recreate great moments on canvas, in wood, or in stone. Photography, however, enables us to capture the actual instant, and to show us certain individuals at significant and telling moments.

In 1945, Alfred Eisenstaedt photographed the celebration of VJ Day in Times Square in New York City. With his camera, he captured the sight of a sailor embracing and kissing a nurse there. The faces are not recognizable, but the passion and the exuberance are. That picture has ever since symbolized the moment and the occasion.

A few months earlier, Joe Rosenthal photographed perhaps the only picture from 1945 that is more famous than Eisenstaedt's "The Kiss." On February 23 of that year, he captured the moment when five Marines were raising the flag of the United States on Iwo Jima. The portrait of that instant was so compelling that it became both the inspiration and the model for the United States Marine Corps War Memorial near Arlington Cemetery.

Nearly two decades later, photographer George Tames arrived at the White House to take an official photograph of President John F. Kennedy. When he entered the Oval Office, he found President Kennedy standing, facing away from him, stooped over his desk. The from-behind, black-and-white silhouette of a contemplative Kennedy against the Oval Office window makes a poignant memento of the man.

167

We are indebted to the photographers through the years whose eye and whose timing have caught and preserved for us significant moments in history. And, at a somewhat different level, we are similarly indebted to the Old Testament prophet Isaiah.

Isaiah did not have a camera. Still, he gives us a dramatic and personal portrait of an individual and a moment.

The irony is that Isaiah was at such a distance from his subject — over 700 years away, in fact — and that he may not have recognized fully just what was he was portraying. That is often the case with inspired prophecy, of course. We sense it in Psalm 22, in Isaiah 53, and in Zechariah 9.

Likewise, we wonder if the ancient biblical authors could have possibly recognized the picture that their dots — spotless lambs and scapegoats, high priests and blood sacrifices, a serpent on a pole and a son carrying up a hill the wood on which he would be sacrificed — would one day connect to make.

We find this particular portrait in chapter 50 of the Old Testament prophet Isaiah. Far ahead of its time, we discover that this portrait is actually more like a film clip — a moving and talking picture. And in it, we hear the subject talk about himself and his situation.

The first thing we discover is that the subject of the portrait is a teacher. "The Lord God has given me the tongue of a teacher," he reports. He is a teacher with a strong sense of divine giftedness.

That detail makes all the difference, of course. For as soon as we recognize that what we are and what we have comes from God, then the orientation of our lives changes. Career becomes vocation, and activity becomes stewardship. If what I have is wholly mine, then I suppose I may do with it as I choose. But if what I have has been given to me by someone else — specifically, by God — then there may be a purpose beyond my own personal agenda. I presume that he gave me what he did for a reason, and I must use what he gave me to fulfill that divine will.

The divinely gifted teacher in our portrait has a sense of that purpose: "that I may know how to sustain the weary with a word." What an unexpected and lovely mission statement. We surely know from personal experience the dramatic difference that a word can make. There is the word that deflates and discourages, the word that belittles or condemns. On the other hand, we have known the word that blesses and encourages, the word that refreshes and revives. For all of our culture's devaluation of words, they remain a surprisingly potent force. And the subject of this portrait understands that he has been gifted with a certain kind of a tongue, and that that tongue was meant to bless and edify, not to curse and destroy.

"Morning by morning," he continues, "he wakens — wakens my ear to listen as those who are taught" (v. 9). We begin to sense the intimacy between this man and his God. It's a close and daily relationship. We sense, too, the sweetness of his spirit. For not only does he see that the Lord has given him a teacher's tongue, but he has also given him a student's ear. His tongue has a sweet and gentle purpose, and he maintains the humility to listen and to learn.

Then, quite suddenly, the lovely tone of the portrait is interrupted by a discordant note. "The Lord God has opened my ear, and I was not rebellious," he continues. "I did not turn backward. I gave my back to those who struck me, and my cheeks to those who pulled out the beard; I did not hide my face from insult and spitting" (vv. 5-6).

What a strange disconnect. For all of the sweetness and humility of this man, we discover that he is the object of great opposition. No, more than mere opposition: violence and cruelty. It is a grim scene, indeed, that seems to include being whipped on the back and struck on the face. His antagonists mock him and spit at him. He appears to be alone against a crowd — ganged up on by a mob that is out to get him.

Yet he does not seem to be a victim, does he? There is a kind of serenity in his report, as though the turn of events, which surprises us in our reading, does not come as a surprise to him. It's as though he saw them coming down the road, yet he "did not turn backward." He did not endeavor to escape either, but rather surrendered himself willingly to the beating and abuse. And all of this reads like a function of his obedience to God, for he says that he "was not rebellious (and) did not turn backward."

The source of his serenity comes next. "The Lord God helps me," he says. "Therefore I have not been disgraced; therefore I have set my face like flint, and I know that I shall not be put to shame; he who vindicates me is near" (vv. 7-8a). In keeping with the subject's dependence upon God, we see that he is at peace in the face of trouble and suffering because of his confidence in God. Interestingly, though, his expectation is not so much that God will protect him as that God will vindicate him.

Those are quite different things, of course. To be protected is to be kept safe from trouble. To be vindicated, on the other hand, suggests some justice and recompense after the trouble. The subject does not expect to be spared so much as delivered.

Consequently, his attitude seems to be, "Bring it on." "Who will contend with me?" he asks fearlessly. "Let us stand up together. Who are my adversaries? Let them confront me. It is the Lord God who helps me; who will declare me guilty?" (vv. 8b-9a).

That's how Isaiah's portrait concludes. It is a powerful picture of a godly man: a man whose own spirit and purpose are entirely admirable, and who faces undeserved opposition and suffering with faith and confidence in his God.

One detail in the portrait helps us identify the backdrop of the picture: the context of the man and the moment. "I have set my face like flint," he says along the way. We recognize that feature, for eight centuries later the gospel writer uses almost precisely the same language to describe Jesus.

The watershed moment in the gospel comes near the middle of Luke 9. Jesus was alone with his disciples in the northern country when he asked them two questions. First, he asked who the crowds said that he was. Then, as a personal follow-up, Jesus asked who they — his followers themselves — said that he was. It was at that crucial moment that Simon Peter stepped forward to offer his great answer: the Messiah of God (Luke 9:20).

Jesus affirms Peter's answer and confirms his identity. Then, in the next breath, he goes on to explain just what that messiahship will mean, and its startling news. Specifically, Jesus explains to his disciples that he would suffer greatly, be rejected by the leaders of the people, and be put to death (9:21-22).

170

That occasion marked the first time that Jesus predicted the suffering and death that awaited him in Jerusalem. From that moment on, all of the words and actions begin to move and point toward Jerusalem.

In the very next scene, we witness Jesus' transfiguration. Moses and Elijah appear with him on the mountain. More than that, they talk with Jesus there. Luke does us the great favor of reporting the subject of their conversation. They "were speaking of his departure, which he was about to accomplish at Jerusalem."

Finally, just a few verses later in the same chapter, Luke reports this detail: "When the days drew near for him to be taken up, he set his face to go to Jerusalem" (9:51).

Jesus on his way to Jerusalem — which is to say, Jesus on his way to his passion and death — that is the moment that Isaiah captured in his portrait. He knows what is ahead, and yet he sets his face with determination to encounter, to endure, and to overcome all that awaits him.

Congregational minister and scholar, Samuel Ralph Harlow, put the portrait in poetry: "We marvel at the purpose that held thee to thy course while ever on the hilltop before thee loomed the cross; thy steadfast face set forward where love and duty shown, while we betray so quickly and leave thee there alone."[1]

We owe a great debt to those photographers who have captured significant moments for us. And here we have before us one of the most significant moments of all: the look of Jesus on the way to the cross. In this instance, Isaiah has the kind of high-powered lens available only through the Holy Spirit. Isaiah is at a distance, but he allows us to see Jesus up close. In that picture of that man in that moment, we see the profile of a Savior. Amen.

---

1. "O Young And Fearless Prophet," words by S. Ralph Harlow, 1931. In the public domain.

Maundy Thursday
Exodus 12:1-4 (5-10) 11-14

Prelude To A Sacrament

We have a table before us. It is a familiar table; we have gathered around it together countless times before. It features the cherished elements of bread and wine; and taken together, those elements on this table form a sacrament.

Across the many traditions within the Christian church, we call this sacrament by different names. The Roman Catholics refer to the Mass, while the Eastern Orthodox church uses the Divine Liturgy. A number of Protestant denominations call it the Eucharist, others holy communion, and still others the Lord's Supper.

Whatever the terminology in the twenty-first century, however, we all trace the sacrament back to the same event in the first century. The table that is before us tonight recalls a different table from 2,000 years ago. Each time we partake of this sacrament, we recite, recall, and reenact that particular meal shared by Jesus and his disciples.

It was Thursday night — the eve of Christ's atoning death. He clearly knew what was ahead, though the disciples seem to have been largely unaware. On three different occasions prior to this night, Jesus had plainly told them what would happen to him in Jerusalem. Again, on this occasion that we call his Last Supper, he was very straightforward about what was going to happen.

Interestingly, Jesus saw a connection between what was going to happen and the meal that they were sharing. The story is so familiar to us that we may miss the element of surprise. After all, what correlation can there possibly be between an evening meal, on the one hand, and an execution, on the other? Yet Jesus made a connection.

As they ate together, Jesus took two of the elements of their meal and associated them with what was to come. He took bread, broke it, and identified it with his body — specifically, with his body being broken. Similarly, he took a cup of wine, shared it, and identified it with his blood — specifically with his blood being poured out.

You and I come to this table from this side of the cross and the empty tomb, and so we have some understanding of Jesus' words. But those first disciples must have been entirely bewildered by what he said.

Furthermore, Jesus expressed an assumption on that occasion that his followers would continue to eat that bread and drink from that cup indefinitely into the future. He instructed them always to do that eating and drinking in remembrance of him. Again, a mystifying thing to say at that moment.

Ever since that Thursday night, however, Jesus' followers have done just what he said. We have shared the bread and cup of communion in remembrance of him. We have remembered his broken body and his shed blood. We have understood and received the connection between the meal on Thursday night and the atoning death on Friday afternoon.

The table that is before us this evening has an antecedent. Our table here is an extension of that table in Jerusalem, where Jesus and his first followers shared the bread and cup, 2,000 years ago.

Even that table was not the original. That famed table where the disciples gathered for Jesus' Last Supper had its own predecessor. When they sat down to eat, they had an eye on a still different table from long before. That Thursday night was no ordinary evening meal. It was the Passover meal.

Most holidays, you know, are celebrations of some past event. At a personal level, we celebrate the day when some family member was born or the day a couple was married. As a nation, we celebrate the day when certain battles were won, when significant historical figures were born, or when our founders declared their independence. In the church, we celebrate the day when Jesus was born and the day he rose, among others.

Passover, likewise, was a holy day set aside each year to celebrate a past event. Specifically, Passover was Israel's festive remembrance of the night that God had delivered them from their bondage in Egypt. That night is the setting for the Old Testament scripture reading that we shared this evening.

The children of Israel had been slaves in Egypt for 400 years. That is an almost unimaginably long time for us. After all, we have only been a nation for 230 plus years. Rewind our history 400 years, and we find ourselves back in days of the Jamestown settlement. William Shakespeare was still finishing up his career 400 years ago. Can we fathom, therefore, what it would be like for a people to go into slavery during the age of Shakespeare and finally meet their release today?

The family of Jacob — who was renamed Israel — had moved to Egypt during the ascendancy of Jacob's son, Joseph. They lived there for a generation as honored guests in the land. After that generation had died, the new Egyptian regime did not look so kindly upon the very large family of foreigners occupying some of their best land. The Pharaoh turned their status upside down, making them into Egypt's slaves.

For four centuries, the children of Israel labored in cruel bondage. For four centuries their children were born in chains and their old men and women died under the whip. For four centuries they cried out to their God for help, but no help seemed to come.

Then one day, quite out-of-range from the Israelites' view or earshot, God encountered a man at a burning bush. And though that man was the patron saint of reluctance, God urged and encouraged him to be God's agent of deliverance for the Israelite slaves. He was to return to Egypt — from which he himself had fled some years before — and appear before the Pharaoh as God's representative. With God's instruction and assistance, he was to navigate Israel from bondage to freedom.

The process did not begin well. In fact, almost as soon as Moses took his first obedient steps, things got worse for the Israelites he sought to deliver. It was a most discouraging beginning to what

175

seemed already to be a hopeless endeavor. God needed to reassure Moses and the people of his ultimate victory.

That, incidentally, remains very much a part of the dynamic between God and his people in every generation. We are so inclined to assess the probability of success based upon circumstances. We instinctively extrapolate from how things are going so far, and we think that actually predicts the results. It does not, however, for victory is not an extrapolation of circumstances but an extension of God's promises.

So the process continued. The Nile turned to blood. Frogs and pests plagued the land, followed by diseases in both humans and animals. There was hail and darkness. Crops were destroyed and animals died. Yet, for all the devastation, Pharaoh's default setting was stubbornness and pride, and he continually refused the demands of Israel's God.

And then, finally, came that night: the night when God would deal the severest blow to Egypt, and the slaves would be set free. No, more than just set free — they would be hurried out of the land, laden with gifts and treasures. And that pivotal night — the pivotal event — was the Passover.

The saving event was God's to do. Israel did not need to strategize or fight to win their freedom. They needed only to cooperate with what God was doing, and that cooperation took two forms. First, they had to prepare the outside of their homes. Second, they had to prepare and eat their evening meal.

Significantly, the central issue for the preparation of their homes was blood. Specifically, the blood of a lamb. That blood, brushed along the sides and tops of the doors of their homes, would signal the angel of death to pass over those homes. Of course, we do not presume that the angel could not have been otherwise invested with the knowledge of which homes were to be spared, but God has always invited his people to distinguish themselves by some act of faithful obedience: circumcision, looking up at the serpent on the pole, baptism, and such. This particular act was meant to be instructive to them — and to us — as their salvation was achieved by the blood of the lamb.

Then there was the meal. The passage we read earlier provided some of the instructions about the meal, and those instructions from God were remarkably detailed. After all, is there anything more routine, more ordinary, more daily than eating? Yet, on this most extraordinary of nights, God was concerned with their menu.

Through Moses, God gave Israel a very specific recipe for that night. The elements of the meal were symbolic — calling to mind a memory of their bondage and a reminder of God's deliverance. Plus, God's recipe featured more than just the particulars of what they should eat; he also gave instructions about what they should wear and how they should eat. For everything about the meal — from the unleavened bread to the walking sticks to the hasty consumption — all spoke of hurrying. After 400 years of waiting for deliverance, now they were suddenly in a hurry, for now their deliverance was going to come quickly. Like firefighters who sleep dressed-to-go, the children of Israel were told to wolf down their food and be ready to leave, for that was going to be the night.

Finally, there was one more component to God's directions. In addition to the menu, the attire, and the speed of the meal, God also gave them instructions for the future; namely, that they were to eat that meal on that same night every year for the rest of their lives. And, beyond that, their children and their grandchildren were to eat that meal every year on that night. It was designed to be "a day of remembrance for you," God told them. "You shall celebrate it as a festival to the Lord; throughout your generations you shall observe it as a perpetual ordinance."

So it was that over 1,000 years later, Jesus and his disciples sat down at the table together to celebrate the Passover meal: A remembrance of how God had saved his people from their slavery in Egypt. On that night, Jesus reinterpreted two of the elements of the meal. They now symbolized his body and his blood, and they spoke of how God would deliver all humankind from its bondage to sin. God's people were to continue eating that bread and drinking that cup for all generations "in remembrance."

So it is that we have a table before us — indeed, it is a table from more than 3,000 years before us! Moses and the soon-to-be-free children of Israel are gathered around it. They have on their

177

coats and shoes, and they are eating in a hurry. Their meal both coincides with God saving them and represents God saving them. As such, we discover, their meal is a prelude to this sacrament. Amen.

That's Why We Call It Good

At the end of the day, God saw that it was good. Indeed, that is the recurring refrain in the story of creation. For at the end of each day, God saw that it was good.

Modern minds may like to quibble about the science of the creation account in scripture, but no one can dispute the beauty of it. Phase by phase, the beauty unfolds.

When the curtain opens on the mysterious pre-creation scene, it is a frightening blackness. We read of both chaos and emptiness, and all of it in the midst of an enveloping, impenetrable darkness. But then God begins to speak. Light pierces and dispels the darkness. There is order in place of chaos, and the former void is filled with purpose. What had been uninterrupted blackness now brims with color, splendor, and life.

Oh, the life! All shapes and sizes: an almost incomprehensible array and variety. Plants and animals, fish and birds — all of them endowed with their own peculiar beauty and wisdom of design, as well as a magnificent capacity for fruitfulness. That fruitfulness, then, makes this beauty more than a mere still-life portrait. For this life is not static: it is cascading, abounding, and reproducing.

Then, as a crowning element, finally there is one more component in the creative act: a finishing touch on the masterpiece. Humankind — the artist's personal signature. Or, perhaps even more than that.

Jan Van Eyck was a noted fifteenth-century painter from northern Europe. In 1434, he painted a portrait of the Arnolfini wedding. Visible on the back wall, between the groom and the bride, is a round mirror. A closer inspection of the mirror reveals this charming detail: a small self-portrait of the artist at work, painting the portrait.

Perhaps that is how God completed his creation: not so much with a signature as with a self-portrait. For on the final day of creating, he made man and woman in his own image.

At the end of each day, God saw that it was good. That was the recurring divine verdict on each day. Surely it was good, for, after all, each day God had been at work. His will had been done. He had brought light and life where there had been darkness and chaos, and he called the day good.

The only exception to the pattern comes on the last day of creation — the sixth day — Friday. On that day, when God had finished his work, scripture reports that "it was very good" (Genesis 1:31).

The biblical author tends to be understated. He is not given to purple prose or exclamation points. Yet, on the Friday of creation, he breaks from his characteristic economy of language to include this adverb. Now the word "good" was not good enough. God saw that it was very good. Exceedingly good. His work had been accomplished and completed, and so with the end of that day it was very good.

Some centuries later, however, we discover that God's creation is not so very good anymore. Quite the contrary: It had turned very bad. We read the details in Genesis 6 as we are introduced to Noah. The problem is not that the cosmos had lost its majesty, of course, or that the plants and animals had lost their beauty. The problem was humankind. That climactic and cherished component in God's creation had become very bad, indeed.

In stark contrast to what God saw at the end of each day of creation, the writer of Genesis reports that "the Lord saw that the wickedness of humankind was great in the earth, and that every inclination of the thoughts of their hearts was only evil continually" (Genesis 6:5). It is an emphatic statement of the human condition: a grim diagnosis, for which the only immediate prescription would be the flood.

Then, some centuries later, in the passage we read from the Old Testament prophet Isaiah, we encounter a quite different prescription. The human dilemma remains fundamentally the same as in the days of Noah. Writing on behalf of humanity, Isaiah speaks of "our infirmities," "our diseases," "our transgressions," and "our iniquities." Furthermore, he confesses, "All we like sheep have gone astray; we have all turned to our own way" (v. 6). It is a statement that could just as well have been made by some poor soul outside the ark when the first drops began to fall. For that matter, it is a statement that could have been made by Adam and Eve, as they clutched their shame-covering-leaves on their way out of the Garden.

The grand confession comes within a larger context of remedy. Those infirmities and iniquities, it seems, are not irresolvable, and those wayward sheep are not irretrievable. For "the Lord has laid on him the iniquity of us all" (v. 6b).

"Him"? Whom?

We don't know him by name in this passage. He is introduced only as "my servant," and we read at first that he "shall prosper" (52:13). But most of what follows does not sound to us like prospering. For the prophet goes on to describe a scenario of rejection and taunting, of unjust suffering, seemingly misplaced punishment, and ultimately death.

But this suffering and death are different somehow.

In this fallen world, you and I do not have to look far for examples of injustice or murdered innocents. We can read such stories in newspapers and history books. We think of the students senselessly gunned down on their school campuses, the family devastated by a drunk driver, or the old woman who is killed by a stray bullet in a drive-by gang shooting. So many heartbreaking stories of people who did not deserve to die.

Yet this suffering servant from Isaiah 52 and 53 does not seem to belong in the same category with the rest. His death is unjust, but not senseless. He is innocent, yet not victimized. He dies a cruel and undeserved death, and yet he does not emerge as a tragic figure.

181

This death is different, for behind all of the apathetic or malevolent human perpetrators involved, we see the hand of God. "Struck down by God," Isaiah reports of this man's death (v. 4). We recall further that it was the Lord who laid on him the iniquity of us all, and "it was the will of the Lord to crush him with pain" (v. 10). So this death was not senseless. No, on the contrary, this death was quite purposeful.

Isaiah is clear about the purpose. "Upon him was the punishment that made us whole," the prophet proclaims, "and by his bruises we are healed" (v. 5). Furthermore, his life is identified as "an offering for sin" (v. 10), and, in the process of his undeserved ordeal, "he shall make many righteous" (v. 11).

Quite apart from the senseless and tragic deaths of other innocent men and women in history or in the news, therefore, the death of this unidentified servant is curative. For the people who are hopelessly burdened by infirmities and iniquities find their healing, their redemption, and their salvation in him — specifically, in his suffering and death.

In the beginning, it was good. And with the creation of humankind in particular, it was very good. Then humanity turned very bad and required some remedy. Isaiah presents this servant as the great remedy for the human condition.

Finally, some centuries after the time of Isaiah's prophecy, we come to the event that the prophet foresaw. The setting is a skulllike hill outside of Jerusalem. The occasion is the crucifixion of Jesus. It is a grim scene: dark and turbulent. The atmosphere is vile, as crowds gawk and conspirators mock. There is bleeding, suffering, and suffocating: all of it unjust and undeserved. The one hanging on the center cross was, indeed, "despised and rejected" and "held of no account" (v. 3).

It is the death of an innocent man, to be sure, but it is not the stuff of tragedy. Above and beyond all the petty antagonists who arranged for his arrest, his scourging, and his sentencing, we see the hand of God. "God proves his love for us," Paul later wrote, "in that while we still were sinners Christ died for us" (Romans 5:8). And, like the death anticipated by Isaiah, this particular death is curative: "He himself bore our sins in his body on the cross," declared Peter, "so that, free from sins, we might live for righteousness; by his wounds you have been healed" (1 Peter 2:24).

Last year on Good Friday, our young daughter asked me, "If this is the day Jesus died, why do we call it 'good'?"

Why? Because it was the day when God breathed his light and life into the darkness and chaos of sin. Because on that day the most cherished but most broken element of his creation was redeemed. And because that Friday was the day when God's work was fully accomplished and completed.

And so, at the end of the day, we see that it was very good. Amen.

Easter Day
Acts 10:34-43

The Gospel According To Pronouns

The gospel of Jesus Christ is personal. If you have not yet realized that fact, then I'd like you to see it this morning. If you have recognized that truth somewhere along the way, please don't ever lose sight of it. The gospel of Jesus Christ is personal.

On this occasion, Peter had been summoned into this living room for the purpose of preaching that gospel. The audience was a God-fearing Gentile man named Cornelius, along with his family and the members of his extended household. God was eager for Cornelius and his clan to hear the good news about Jesus, and so, with the help of an angel visitation in one place and a vision in another, the Lord orchestrated this face-to-face meeting between Peter and Cornelius.

Already, before any preaching takes place, we observe this first bit of evidence that this is a personal event. For God himself, you see, had personally arranged it. He had taken care of all the necessary details in order to guarantee that Peter and Cornelius would meet so that Cornelius could hear the gospel.

You and I know that experience: that rear-view-mirror realization of God's activity in our lives. We look back on significant times and occasions, and we recognize his guiding hand, his provident care, making it all come together. We remember settings where we heard a preacher or teacher addressing a whole audience, but it was apparent that he or she was speaking directly to us. We knew that God was kindly, purposefully, and personally behind it all.

So it was for Cornelius. God personally arranged for all the pieces to be in place for this pivotal event in Cornelius' life.

185

Meanwhile, we observe another way in which the gospel is personal: God uses people to communicate it. This is particularly striking on this occasion, for we observe that God had also employed an angel and a vision. Yet those were his instruments for bringing the people together, not for proclaiming the good news. The vision prepared Peter to go to Cornelius' house, and the angel alerted Cornelius to the location of Peter. But the angel was not the one to proclaim the gospel to Cornelius. No, the angel was only sent to refer Cornelius to another person, to Peter.

We are reminded, at this juncture, of the conversion of the apostle Paul. The risen Lord himself had appeared to Saul on the road to Damascus, and yet it was still essential for Paul to be put in touch with another person — a believer named Ananias there in Damascus — in order for God's whole will to be done in Paul's life.

Here, in our story, Peter was the person selected for the assignment. He arrives at the home of Cornelius in order to share with him and his household the gospel of Jesus Christ. And we heard Peter's words in the scripture reading from the New Testament book of Acts.

As we listen to Peter's message, we are struck again by how very personal it is. That is to say, it is a message filled with people and relationships. Peter is not presenting Cornelius with a detached and theoretical philosophy. He is not speaking in vague, impersonal terms about truth, knowledge, and wisdom. Rather, Peter is telling a story — a personal story.

We get some measure of how person-filled Peter's message is by the preponderance of personal pronouns. In the nine verses of my English translation (NRSV), I count more than twenty different uses of personal pronouns. He, we, they, and you: These are the characters in the story — the gospel story — that Peter shared in Cornelius' living room.

① The first, the most frequent, and the most important of the pronouns is "him." The dozen or so references to "he," "his," and "him" in this passage are all references to the Lord. First, to God the Father, and then to Jesus, his Son. That is truly where the gospel begins: with God and with his Son.

As we hear Peter's message, we are blessed by the good news of what "he" did and does.

First, he shows no partiality. That should not surprise us, of course, since we understand and affirm that he is the creator and father of all humankind. Still, because partiality is so much a part of our experience in our human relationships, we may tend to project the same dynamics onto God's relationship with us. And, too, Peter and his first companions in the faith were coming out of a paradigm that presumed a certain favoritism on God's part. But the declaration that God shows no partiality is the first bit of very good news for Cornelius and for us.

Next we hear that God sent a message to the people of Israel and that Jesus Christ was both the subject and agent of that message. He is the one anointed and ordained by God. He is the one who went about doing good and healing all who were oppressed. He is the one who was put to death, but who rose again. He is the one proclaimed by the prophets who preceded him and by the apostles who followed him. He is the one through whom we receive forgiveness of sins. The good news, you see, is all about a person: It's all about him.

2. Meanwhile, Peter makes several references to "we" and "us." With these pronouns, of course, he is referring to himself and to the other apostles who had been eyewitnesses of Jesus' earthly work and his resurrection. "We" ate and drank with Jesus, and Jesus commanded "us" to go and proclaim the person and work of Christ.

Here, you see, is yet another personal layer of the gospel. The message does not consist merely of some rules for living handed down from on high. It is not dogmatic creedal statements to be memorized and recited. Rather, the gospel message is, first and foremost, personal testimony. It is born out of personal experience, that is, experience with a person (Jesus), told by people (his followers), to other people (Cornelius, and to the ends of the earth).

3. Then, in the midst of Peter's message, we find one reference to "they." "They put him to death," Peter reports, "by hanging him on a tree" (v. 39). The use of the third-person suggests someone who is not there. "They" is someone other than the one speaking or the ones being spoken to.

187

It is noteworthy how little attention "they" receive. Though their actions were pivotal, "they" are not central. And that in itself is a testimony to the providence and victory of God. After all, if you look at their names and titles — the chief priests and scribes, the Pharisees and Sadducees, Herod and Pilate — "they" were the people in power, "they" were the people of importance. Yet "they" are reduced to a single quick and unflattering reference in the larger story of God's saving work.

Now you and I rightly own the fact that it was "our" sin — not someone else's — for which Christ died. The hard-line reference to what "they" did, therefore, may be somewhat uncomfortable for us. But then we are further removed from the event than Peter was. For us, after all, everyone in the New Testament story is third-person. We are not immediately a part of the story, so everyone in the story is classified as "he," "she," or "they."

(4) However, Peter and the other apostles were in the midst of the story, and for Peter there was a clear distinction between "us" and "them." On this occasion among the Gentiles, we observe, Peter would shed one of his us/them paradigms. But the distinction between those who followed Jesus and those who crucified Jesus remained.

We look back on the cross, and we recognize that it was for the sake and for the sin of all humankind. Yet the event of Christ's crucifixion still reflects a difference between "they" and "we" because it represents two different responses to him. "We" heard his call and followed him. "We" believed, obeyed, and loved. "They," however, opposed and dismissed him. "They" rejected the man and his message. Ultimately, "they" conspired to have him killed.

Yes, he died for us and for them. After all, even as he died on the cross, Jesus prayed that "they" would be forgiven. Still, Peter's use of the first-person and third-person pronouns represents for us the fundamental difference between the people who did respond to Jesus as the Christ and those who did not.

(5) That distinction brings us to the final personal pronoun; the one where the gospel gets really personal: "you." For "you" has the option of aligning with "us" or "them." "You" must respond to Jesus as the Christ or not.

Peter says, "You know the message" (v. 36).

Now let us note that he didn't have to say exactly that. Peter had other equally good options for his opening phrase. He could have said, "Here is the message" or "This is the message." He could have begun with the words of the prophets and the promises of God. He could have told the story entirely from his own vantage point, "I remember the day Jesus called me as I sat with my brother in our boat on the Sea of Galilee." The possibilities are endless, really, yet Peter begins with a pointed reference to his audience: "You know the message."

Actually, it's hard for us to say just how much Cornelius and his companions knew. Perhaps Peter's statement was not meant literally, for he went on to articulate just what that message was. But the fact remains: He begins with "you."

This is the ultimately personal part of the gospel: The part that is addressed to "you." We hear it right from the beginning from the very first evangelists. On Christmas night, the angel over the fields outside of Bethlehem announced this good news: "To you is born this day in the city of David a Savior, who is the Messiah, the Lord" (Luke 2:11). Most birth announcements simply report the details of the birth — name, date, size, gender, and such. But the announcement of this birth is personalized: "to you is born."

In the case of our episode from Acts, the "you" was Cornelius and his household. We discover that, in the end, they received the Holy Spirit and were baptized by Peter. "You" responded to the gospel that day.

So it is that, from beginning to end, the gospel of Jesus Christ is personal. It begins with him. It is passed along through us. And it comes to you. What will you do? Amen.

A Tale Of Two Peters

When the curtain opens on Scene Two, we see a familiar scene. It is the austere, official chamber where the Sanhedrin hold court. The room is cold and intimidating. It feels even more so when the first characters begin to arrive on stage.

These are the members of the Sanhedrin: the leaders in the land who form the ruling council for the Jews of first-century Palestine. They are a distinguished looking group. They are well-dressed, well-manicured, and well-to-do. Their faces betray the seriousness of the purpose for which they have gathered.

After the members of the council have taken their seats along the front and sides of the chamber, two more men come in. No, actually they do not come in; they are brought in. Chained and raggedy, they are the prisoners who are being called to appear before these assembled leaders.

We in the audience do a double take when we see them. We know these men! They are Peter and John, the beloved men who were part of Jesus' inner circle during his earthly ministry. These apostles had been apprehended and kept in custody. For them, this is judgment day.

These erstwhile Galilean fishermen look so out-of-place. They find themselves in a setting they never could have imagined just a few years earlier and for a reason they never could have anticipated.

A mere five years ago, they spent their days and nights in boats on the picturesque little lake, Galilee, in the north. They lived quiet lives, far from the political intrigues or theological controversies of Jerusalem. Perhaps they made the annual pilgrimages to the temple in Jerusalem for the holy days, but that urban setting in the south was a long way from home for them.

There's no doubt that, back in their fishing days, they knew the name of the high priest and members of his household. Perhaps they knew the names and reputations of some of the other men who sat on the council, too. But there was no reciprocal familiarity. Certainly the high priest and the members of the council did not know them. Indeed, probably very few people outside of their little northern hometown of Capernaum knew them.

Now they are known. Indeed, they have become infamous within certain circles of the Jewish leaders in Jerusalem. In the wake of their recent activities — namely, healing and preaching in Jesus' name in the temple — Peter and John have been apprehended and brought on trial before the leaders of their people.

After the hubbub of whispers among the council members has subsided, the high priest rises to speak. His expression is severe, and his tone is most serious. He points at the prisoners accusingly, reminding them that they have been warned not to speak anymore in the name of Jesus or about him.

Stop to consider the dynamics of this moment.

First, there was the theological component. The point of friction between the apostles and the Sanhedrin was fundamentally a theological one. That is to say, the Jewish leaders opposed and endeavored to silence what Peter and John believed, taught, and preached. But observe that this dispute is not a cordial disagreement among equals. No, these largely unschooled laymen were appearing before the religious leaders of the land. The members of this ruling council included the professional clergy, biblical scholars, and theologians-in-residence. These were men of sophisticated training, expert in the scriptures and conversant in all matters of doctrine.

Furthermore, the culture was not the think-and-let-think atmosphere of pluralism that marks our day. No, there was an assumed standard of right and wrong, of truth and falsehood, and Peter and John stood before the men in charge of making those distinctions.

The priests and scribes, the Pharisees and Sadducees, were not always in agreement with one another. But they were the ones who drew the lines of dogma, and so when they were unanimous in calling something foul, that was the final word. They were insistent that Peter and John should cease to preach and teach in Jesus' name.

2. In addition to the theological dynamic, there was also the legal reality that these ordinary and previously unimportant men found themselves in serious trouble with the authorities. And this was no trivial matter. For they were not just appearing before the local sheriff or in the county courthouse. No, they had been hauled in before the very leaders of the land. The only situation that could have been more severe for them would have been a trial before the Roman governor of the province himself, and they had seen firsthand this same group of Jewish leaders forward Jesus' case to precisely that bar.

3. That brings us to the third and most compelling dynamic: recent history.

The episode recorded in Acts 5 does not appear to be very far removed from the Day of Pentecost. Pentecost came only a matter of weeks after Jesus' ascension. His ascension had been just a few weeks after his death and resurrection. In other words, when Peter and John stood before the members of the Sanhedrin, it may not have been very long at all — perhaps just a few months — since Jesus himself had stood on trial before the very same group.

I imagined at the outset that a curtain was opening on a scene — Peter and John on trial before the ruling council — and I called it Scene Two. Now let's rewind and take a look at Scene One. 1

The action takes place in the same chamber. The same well-dressed and serious characters are there, occupying their seats of judgment. Again, they have a prisoner dragged before them. It's Jesus.

His arrest had been a conspiracy, achieved by a covert operation at night. The charges were largely fictitious and most of the testimony a sham. But these leaders, who had been vigorously antagonistic to Jesus for some time, were determined to bring this trial to a very specific conclusion, no matter what contortions of justice would be required.

The incongruities of testimony were a nuisance, Herod's foolishness was an annoyance, and Pilate's uncharacteristic reticence to kill a man was a surprising obstacle. Ultimately, though, they got what they wanted.

Meanwhile, during the scene of Jesus' trial before the Sanhedrin in this familiar chamber, we overhear some voices from offstage. Some simultaneous dialogue is occurring nearby. We cannot make out the words, at first; only the tone. We sense accusation, and we can detect an escalating anxiety and defensiveness in one man's voice. Finally, we hear that voice loudly from offstage, and we recognize it as unmistakably Peter's. We hear him swearing and cursing as he cries out, "I don't know him!"

It had been a long and trying night, you recall.

It had begun with such festivity and good cheer. Jesus and his disciples were sitting down at table to enjoy and celebrate the Passover meal together. But the atmosphere of that supper became quite unsettling as Jesus spoke. He talked about his broken body and his shed blood. He talked about one of his close associates betraying him. He also spoke very specifically about Peter denying him.

What could it all mean?

Then they went out of the city and up into the Mount of Olives. It was late in the evening and the disciples were tired. But Jesus was eager to stay in a garden there and pray. He went off by himself, returning occasionally to awaken his drowsy followers. Then, suddenly, the quietness of the place was shattered.

It all happened so quickly: torches, spears, and clubs; menacing guards accompanied by Judas; a kiss and a confrontation; a swing of a sword and a rebuke. Then, within just a few minutes, the garden was quiet again. Jesus was gone: apprehended by the mob and the disciples were gone; they had fled into the night.

Peter had enough temerity to follow rather than flee. He followed at some safe distance, to be sure, but he wanted to see what was going to happen to his friend and Lord. And there, not far outside the chamber where Jesus was on trial before the leaders of the land, Peter warmed himself by a fire.

He was tired and cold, confused and scared. He must have felt like a spy behind enemy lines there in the courtyard, desperately hoping he would not be recognized or discovered. Then it happened; the thing he most dreaded. Someone noticed him.

He tried at first to brush aside the pointing finger as a case of mistaken identity, but he couldn't do it. There was another accusation, followed by a more insistent denial. Then, finally, a third person connected the dots between Peter and Jesus, at which point Peter swore emphatically that he did not know Jesus.

The sound of the rooster awakened Peter's conscience to what he had done, and he disappeared into the darkness, weeping bitterly.

That wasn't so long ago. There really weren't very many weeks between Scene One and Scene Two. In the first scene, Jesus was on trial in the austere chamber, and Peter waited timidly outside. He was so frightened by what was happening to Jesus that he tried to dissociate himself entirely from his Lord.

A few months later, Peter himself was in that dreaded chamber. The same men who had arranged for the arrest and execution of Jesus now point their fingers at him. And the same man, who had denied his Lord three times not long before, was commanded by the authorities to deny him once again.

That night in the courtyard, Peter was on the fringe of danger, but this time he was in the crosshairs. What would he do? How could he escape?

Peter addressed the members of the Sanhedrin: "We must obey God rather than any human authority" (v. 29). And with that bit of holy defiance, Peter went on to make his fearless proclamation about Jesus as the Christ of God: crucified, risen, and exalted.

We set the two scenes side by side, and we can hardly believe that it's the same man. How can it be that the one, who just a matter of weeks before crumbled beneath a lesser pressure, should be so courageous now in the very face of what he most feared? Is this the same Peter?

No, it's not. Not really. For two pivotal things have happened between Scene One and Scene Two. Jesus had risen, and the Spirit had come. Peter was a new man.

195

In the end, of course, all of our stories should read like Peter's. Let my story be called "A Tale of Two Davids." Let yours be a story of two Bobs or two Michelles, two Dans or two Betsys. Our before-and-after pictures, you see, are our testimonies. They are the Exhibit A in the proof of our salvation. Just as creation bears witness to the creator, so my re-creation and yours bear witness to our redeemer. The surest proof that Jesus is alive is what happens to his followers *between* Scene One and Scene Two. Amen.

God All Along

See him as he travels along the road to Damascus: the intensity in his eyes, the purposefulness of his pace. He is a man on a mission.

His name is Saul, and he is making the 135-mile trip from Jerusalem to Damascus for a deliberate and expressed purpose. He and his companions are sort of a posse, tracking down dangerous criminals in order to bring them to justice. But this is not a scene from the Wild West. No, these men from Jerusalem are a theological posse, if you will, and the criminals they seek are heretics — "any who belonged to the Way" (v. 2).

We would better recognize both those heretics and their pursuer by different names. The so-called heretics were actually the early Christians, and their chief antagonist was the man we later know better as the apostle Paul.

We so associate Paul with the spread of Christianity that it is hard for us to imagine him as one of the earliest and fiercest opponents trying to extinguish it. We read a dozen or so books in the New Testament written by Paul to encourage the believers — all from the same hand that originally endeavored to arrest them. And the one, whom we eventually see traveling great distances in order to win people to Christ, we observe here hitting the road in order to persecute and prosecute those who already believe.

Those early followers of Jesus were the target of Paul's animus. The narrator of the story offers this strong characterization of his state of mind: "Saul [was] breathing threats and murder against the disciples of the Lord" (v. 1). We can almost see him stewing and frothing as he appears before the high priest. He is looking for authoritative letters that will permit him to scour the synagogues of Damascus for any of these enemies of God.

Make no mistake: that was Paul's estimate of the Christians. We mustn't misunderstand Paul as a wicked and violent man, bent on opposing the things of God. Quite the contrary: Saul of Tarsus is an earnest and godly man. He is sincere in his devotion to God and zealous in his service. His opposition to the Christian movement, therefore, is born entirely out of the seriousness of his piety.

Let the half-baked, half-hearted man of God shrug his shoulders and do nothing about this growing perversion. Let the fool wink and smile at heresy. Not Saul. No, he recognized the Christian claims as dangerous and misleading, and so he set out to silence them.

What he did not recognize, however, was that God was behind it all.

So, see him traveling along on the road to Damascus. He is a man on a mission, albeit not the sort of mission we commonly associate with him. But the look is familiar, nonetheless. He is purposeful and devout. He is on the road for the Lord.

Then, mercifully, the Lord meets him along that road.

Paul's experience on the road to Damascus is distinctive, to be sure, but it is not unique. Rather, we may recognize it as part of a larger pattern. Specifically, it is a pattern of God's behavior, for he characteristically meets us along the way.

We see it early with Jacob. On two different and significant occasions, Jacob is simply going along his way when God graciously intrudes on his journey. As a young man, he is asleep on the ground near Luz: just an overnight stop along the way between the home he has to flee and the relatives' home that will be his refuge. But that non-descript spot becomes for Jacob "Bethel" — the house of God — as the Lord appears to him there in a dream. Many years later, on the return trip between those same two homes, Jacob is met again by God along the way. That previously unheralded spot becomes "Peniel" for Jacob — the place where he saw God face-to-face.

We see the same phenomenon later with Moses, who is simply watching the family flocks one day, when suddenly he observes a strangely burning bush. He goes closer to see, and there God changes his life. Every tomorrow from that point on was different from what Moses would have thought or planned as God interrupted Moses' daily routine to call him to God's work.

The fishing brothers — Peter and Andrew, James and John — were literally minding their own business by the shores of Galilee that day when Jesus appeared and called them. Likewise with Matthew at his tax table. Add to the list Gideon, who was just doing his chores when the call of God came. Add the shepherds, who were famously watching their flocks by night in the fields near Bethlehem when they became the first audience for the gospel and the first eyewitnesses of the Savior.

All of these, and so many more, had life-changing encounters with God, but all of them came just along the way. These were not epiphanies in the temple or theophanies in worship. These men and women were not in the midst of previously designated sacred places, and they were not engaged in some sacred business. They were in very ordinary places doing very ordinary things, and God met them all along the way.

You and I recognize that pattern, for that would likely be a part of the testimony for so many of us, too. We would bear witness to a God who does not reserve his activity to certain specified places or designated times. Rather, we have encountered him in the midst of our routines. For some of us, he has been a gracious interruption, calling to us while we were just minding our own business. He meets us, deals with us, and speaks to us all along the way.

So it was for Saul. He was traveling along the way from Jerusalem to Damascus when, suddenly, he was surrounded by a blindingly brilliant flash of light. He fell to the ground, and he heard a voice speak to him.

As the story unfolds, we discover that Paul had companions with him on this journey, but they were not blinded by the light, and they did not hear the voice. Even in the midst of a group, this was a singularly personal experience.

It was a pointedly personal experience, for the voice called him by name. This was not a public address: this was a one-on-one encounter with bystanders. "Saul, Saul," the voice called (v. 4).

Grammatically speaking, this is a double vocative, and we have seen it elsewhere in scripture. In the Old Testament, we remember God trying to speak to a young boy at night, calling, "Samuel! Samuel!" (1 Samuel 3:4). Meanwhile, in the New Testament, we think of Jesus' gentle word of correction that begins "Martha, Martha" (Luke 10:41). Somewhat later we hear him lamenting, "Jerusalem, Jerusalem" (Matthew 23:37). And at the Last Supper, he speaks a sober caution to Peter, saying, "Simon, Simon" (Luke 22:31).

At a minimum, the double vocative suggests a certain urgency. That is certainly the tone of the episode in Samuel. It reflects one person trying hard to get through to another person. And, beyond just the urgency, there seems to be a quality of sadness in each of the New Testament usages cited above. Jesus is sad about Martha's well-meaning error. He is heartbroken over Jerusalem's obstinacy. He conveys a troubling message to Peter in the midst of a troubling moment.

So, too, with Paul on the road to Damascus. The Lord calls him by name twice: "Saul, Saul." He urgently endeavors to get through to Paul. Certainly there must be a sadness in the voice: sadness over Paul's own error, as well as sadness about his misguided mission and its damage to Christ's church.

"Saul, Saul," the voice calls out from the light into Paul's darkness. "Why do you persecute me?"

What an astonishingly personal question. It is personal, as we have already observed, because it addresses Paul by name. But even beyond that, it is personal because it personalizes Paul's work.

After all, Paul's endeavor had been to rid the synagogues of heresy — to put away those Jews who were accepting and teaching what Paul understood to be a dangerous doctrine. He was not opposing an individual; he was opposing a movement, a group. If Paul was persecuting anyone, the object of his persecution was plural, not singular. If someone were to ask him why he was persecuting, the question would have to be, "Why do you persecute us?"

But that's not the question Paul heard. Not "us" but "me." "Why do you persecute me?"

From our vantage point, we can see the truth of it. We think of Jesus' familiar teaching about the sheep and the goats (Matthew 25:31-46), and we recognize the vicarious nature of our actions. What we do for the least of his brethren we do for him. And what we fail to do for them, we fail to do for him. Small wonder, then, that Paul's harassment of the church should be portrayed by Jesus as a persecution of him.

Evidently, Paul has no idea who is calling to him — or, for that matter, whom he is persecuting. So he cries out, "Who are you, Lord?" (v. 5a).

The term "Lord" is an imprecise one for our purposes. The underlying Greek word, *kurios*, was not only a theological term used to refer to God and, later, to Jesus. It was also a secular term used in day-to-day life. An individual might address as "lord" almost any authority figure. A king, a governor, a landowner, a master, and even a husband might be addressed as "lord."

Accordingly, when Paul cries out, "Who are you, Lord?" he might be addressing God, or he might be simply saying "Sir." Whatever the case, the answer he received was staggering. If Paul was not already on the ground, he would have fallen to the ground when he heard this.

"I am Jesus," the voice replied, "whom you are persecuting" (v. 5b).

But Jesus was dead.

It was Jesus' troublesome followers with whom Paul took issue, not Jesus. The Jesus problem had already been dealt with some time before by the Sanhedrin and by Pilate.

We don't know precisely what Paul thought of Jesus prior to this moment on the way to Damascus. Perhaps Paul regarded him as a failed political figure, as a heretic rabbi, as a false prophet, or as a fanatical cult leader. We don't know. But on this occasion, Paul discovered that Jesus was none of those — he was God all along.

See him as he travels along the road: the intensity in his eyes, the purposefulness of his pace. He is a man on a mission. He is making several thousand miles worth of trips — through Israel, Phoenicia, Asia Minor, Macedonia, and Greece — as he endeavors to bring everyone he can to know "the way." Amen.

The Good Works We Leave Behind

It's a poignant scene: the gathering place of mourners.

In our culture, that scene is usually played out in a funeral home, a chapel, a sanctuary, or at the graveside. In that day, however, it most often took place in the home of the deceased. And the body was there, too, similar to our visitations with open caskets; though without some of the cosmetic advantages.

So it is that the grieving friends of Tabitha are gathered together in her home. She must have died rather recently, for she hasn't been buried yet. Instead, she is upstairs; her corpse laid out on her bed.

As the sad and surprising word spreads through town, more of her many admirers arrive at the house. The initial conversations at the door are all essentially the same. "I just heard the news." "I can't believe it!" "How did it happen?" "Was anyone with her?" "She was such a wonderful person!"

The growing crowd of grieving friends and neighbors reminisce together, sharing their favorite stories about Tabitha. Without the benefit of the kind of photographs and videos that we have today, their recollections had to be entirely verbal. And so they talk on for hours, saturating themselves in the happy memories.

On the other hand, while they do not have scrapbooks to hold in their hands and picture albums to show one another, they do have something else that's physical. Something perhaps even more personal than photographs. They have the things that Tabitha herself had made.

Evidently this saintly woman was skillful at making clothes. Not just skillful, but generous, as well. Was there a friend or a neighbor who hadn't received something from her hand? The reminiscing turns into a lovely sort of show-and-tell as the townspeople bring out the tokens of Tabitha's kindness.

"She gave this to me for my last birthday," one woman tearfully reports, as she holds up a lovely shawl. "She was so thoughtful! She never forgot a birthday, you know."

"She was always thinking of other people," another chimes in.

"This robe," says another woman, drawing attention to the one she's wearing, "I'm sure she was making this robe for herself. But when I visited one day and commented about how pretty it was, she held it up against me and said, 'A perfect fit! It's yours!' "

On and on the stories went.

You and I don't get to hear those stories. And the fact is that we don't really know Tabitha. Scripture does not follow the story of her life or even any portion of her life. Indeed, the only part of her biography that is preserved for us at all is the story of this one particular day; and she was dead for most of it. We have no record of any words that she ever spoke.

And yet, for all of that, we feel like we know her, don't we?

We feel like we know Tabitha because we all have been blessed to know someone like her somewhere along the way. Perhaps it was our grandmother, an aunt, or a neighbor lady. Perhaps it was an older gentleman from church, a customer on the paper route we carried as a youngster, or a former teacher. Some saintly soul whose skillful hands and generous spirit combined to leave behind a lovely legacy of good works.

Personally, I know that all of Gladys' adult grandchildren still have Christmas stockings that she sewed for each of them when she was alive. Elizabeth's crocheted afghans are still gracing countless homes so many years after her death. Jack's carefully crafted stained-glass art hangs now in the windows of the homes of family and friends all over the country. And William built more bookcases, picture frames, cabinets, and shelves than he could remember before he died, but those of us who have pieces of his craftsmanship all remember him.

So it was with Tabitha. The family members, friends, and neighbors gathered together in her home, clothed and armed with the good works that she had left behind. Together they admired her loving handiwork. Together they fondly remembered her. Together they showed the symbols of her goodness to the apostle.

Peter, the well-known disciple of Jesus and pillar of the early church, had been staying in the nearby town of Lydda. He was just a few miles from Joppa where Tabitha had lived. And so the Christians there sent word to Peter, urging him to come to Joppa right away.

Peter did. When he arrived, he was taken immediately up to the room where the body of Tabitha lay. There he was surrounded by the grieving friends, each one with an article of clothing to show him, each one with a story to tell him. Surely the apostle's heart was blessed by the stories of this saint who had died and by the good works she had left behind.

Then he did something unusual. Peter sent them all out of the room.

I wonder if that seemed abrupt to the people gathered there. I wonder what they whispered to one another as they walked down the stairs, leaving the apostle alone in the viewing room.

As a pastor, I have seen a number of occasions when a loved one has wanted to be alone with the body of the deceased. They wanted an opportunity to say a personal and a private good-bye. They wanted an opportunity to say some things that ought not have an audience.

But this was not Peter's circumstance. He was not among the bereft that he should want to be alone with the corpse. He didn't know Tabitha; and he had not known anything about her until the past fifteen minutes. Why, then, would he send everyone away? Why would he seek to clear the room and be alone with the body?

Why? Because that's what he had seen Jesus do.

Years before, when Peter and the rest of the twelve had accompanied Jesus all along the dusty roads of Galilee, Peter had been in a similar bedroom. The twelve-year-old daughter of Jairus had died, and the house was full of mourners. But Jesus sent them away. Or at least out of the room. And then, accompanied only by a select few disciples and the grieving parents themselves, Jesus spoke to the little girl. And in speaking to her, he raised her to life.

So, now, the disciple followed the example that he had seen set by the Master. He sent the mourners out of the room, and then he spoke to the corpse. "Tabitha, get up," Peter said, and the dead woman opened her eyes. Then she sat up. And then, next thing you know, Peter is leading her out to present her to her astonished friends and loved ones.

Can we even fathom the scene that ensued? All of the warmth of the people's grief now combined with their joy and surprise at the sight of Tabitha alive to form an uncommon sort of welcome and embrace. Have tears of sadness ever turned more quickly and completely into tears of joy? The gathered mourners, who not so long before had cried over her corpse, could now hug her person. The friends who had whispered their affection and appreciation in her ear where she had layed could now say it to her face.

And then, in the midst of it all, watch the apostle leave the scene.

The grateful people are loathe to let him go. They hug and thank him repeatedly. They cling to him in their appreciation.

We human beings are accustomed to saying thank you for routine things: a door held open, a compliment, a gift. But how do we adequately thank a person who has brought a loved one back from the dead?

Peter goes on his way, on to the next place where he will stay, where he will preach, where he will heal. He leaves Tabitha, alive and well, behind in Joppa. She is among the good works that Peter leaves behind.

Earlier, we caught a glimpse of the good works that Tabitha had left behind. Tunics, cloaks, robes, shawls, and such. But Peter has his own profound collection. Healed bodies, saved souls, and a living Tabitha — these are among the good works that the apostle leaves behind.

Peter's example and Tabitha's example challenge us. We see what each left behind, and we ask, "What is it that I leave in my wake? What is the impact and effect of you or I having been in a community, a church, a school, a workplace, a family?"

Where Tabitha had been, she left behind symbols of love and generosity, tokens of thoughtfulness and sweetness. Where Peter had been, he left behind life and health, gladness and rejoicing.

We consider the example of Tabitha, and we observe that the good works she left behind remind us of her Lord. For he is the original artisan, after all, and he has generously shared his handiwork with us. We see both his skill and his sweetness in what he has made. The works of his hands inspire our praise and adoration.

Likewise, we consider the example of Peter, and we see that the works he left behind also remind us of his Lord. We follow Peter, and we remember the one who sent his followers out "to proclaim the good news ... Cure the sick, raise the dead, cleanse the lepers, cast out demons. You received without payment; give without payment" (Matthew 10:7-8). We remember the one who went about doing good (Acts 10:38) and then told Peter and the rest that they would do the works he had done and even greater works (John 14:12).

The deeds and lives of his people, you see, remind us of him. For in the end, they are — we are — the good works that he leaves behind. Amen.

Look Who's Talking

Professional sports has no statistic for measuring talking. Yet talking can be an important part of the game.

We can measure how fast a player pitches or serves. We keep statistics on batting averages, shooting percentages, and quarterback ratings. We track yards-after-catch, on-base percentages, and shots on goal. We record height and weight, wins-and-losses, and times in the 40-yard dash. But we have no way of measuring a player's talking.

Nevertheless, even though it doesn't show up on the scoreboard or in the record books, and even though the Elias Sports Bureau doesn't track it, every sports fan knows what an important part of the game talking can be. The famous face-to-face yelling matches between managers and umpires. The trash-talking on the field or on the court between players. The ill-advised comments in an interview that become bulletin board material for the other team. The over-the-line remark that earns a technical foul. Talking is a major part of most athletic competitions.

John McEnroe was notorious for his talking to the judges during matches. Michael Jordan was well known for trying to get into his opponent's head with his talking. Brett Favre is still famous for his playful conversations with members of both his own team and the opposing team. And Mohammed Ali turned pre- and post-bout talking into an art form.

Of course, who does the talking and what they have to say can change dramatically during the course of a game, much less a season. Players typically do more talking when they're winning than when they're losing. The player or coach who finally wins "the big one" is often said to have silenced his critics.

Talking is a major part of our story from the New Testament book of Acts. Over the course of that story, we see a dramatic and marvelous change in who does the talking and what they have to say.

(1) The first people we hear talking in this episode are these critics.

We know how that sounds, don't we? Every one of us here recognizes that familiar and unpleasant sound: the talk of the critics.

For people whose lives and careers are played out in the public eye — entertainers, professional athletes, politicians, and so forth — the critics are plentiful and loud. They have newspapers and magazines. That have television and radio shows. If a public person cared to listen, he could hear himself being criticized virtually every day of his life.

Most of us get to live our lives more privately, so we are not subject to such broad and constant critique. Still, we know the sound. We hear it from the customer or the supervisor who is displeased with our work. We hear it from the neighbor who takes issue with something we've done on our property. We hear it at times from a friend or family member: the criticism that is most personal, and therefore the most painful.

Indeed, for some poor souls, the sound of the critics talking has become so hurtful that they live their lives in almost constant response to it. Not that they are so constantly criticized; but rather, they have been so hurt by criticism that they are constantly afraid of it. So many of the day-to-day choices they make reflect their developed instinct to do whatever it takes to navigate around or away from possible criticism.

The first people we hear talking in this episode are these critics. Specifically, they are the Jewish Christians from the headquarters church in Jerusalem. They are critical of Peter because he has recently fellowshiped with Gentiles.

This was, you see, some of the most unpleasant brand of criticism, for this came from the people who were close. Perhaps the public figure can write off the impersonal criticism of the pundit, the commentator, the blogger. But this criticism of Peter was more personal. It came from his own brothers and sisters in Christ at his home church. These are the folks who were supposed to be on his side. These are the close associates whose instinct and reflex toward him should have been support and encouragement. Peter could well have expected criticism and opposition from the Sanhedrin, from the Gentiles, and eventually from Rome. But not here; not within this tight-knit fellowship of believers. Criticism there had to hurt.

Furthermore, this was some of the most unpalatable kind of criticism because it was so off-the-mark. We may be irked by the critic who has put his finger on our fault, but there is a limit to the hurt and indignation we may feel when the criticism is correct. When, however, the complaint is dead wrong, that's hard to live with.

This complaint was dead wrong. It was wrong because Peter had only been serving and obeying God. It was wrong because it reflected a deep-seated problem in the hearts of the critics themselves.

Notice in the text what it was the believers back in Jerusalem had heard: the impetus for their criticism of Peter. "Now the apostles and the believers who were in Judea heard that the Gentiles had also accepted the word of God" (v. 1).

If the news that had reached their ears was simply that Peter had been in the wrong kind of place with the wrong kind of people, then we might fault their standards, but we would at least concede that they were being true to their standards. In this case, however, they simply reveal that they had entirely wrong standards; that they had missed the priorities of God.

These people were supposed to be the at-all-costs followers of the one who had commanded them to love their enemies and who had instructed them to be his witnesses to the very end of the earth. For them to respond to the news of someone's conversion, therefore, with such parochial exclusiveness — to be so blinded by prejudice that you cannot see the work of God — is a frightening error.

We must be cautious in our critique of the critics. Such evaluation of others should always come with a mirror close at hand.

Let us not be too eager to point out their specks until we have considered our own logs.

Is there some group of people for whom we feel such distaste or disdain that we do not care for their souls? Is there a kind of person whose conversion *we* would not welcome because, frankly, it is a kind of person we do not welcome? Is there a group whose exclusion is more acceptable to us than their inclusion?

The apostles and believers in Jerusalem had heard the news that the Gentiles had accepted the word of God. They did not rejoice at that news. Instead, they criticized Peter for having anything to do with that out-of-bounds group.

The first people we hear talking in this episode are the critics. Then comes Peter's chance to talk.

What follows is commendably charitable. Peter's tone is not defensive, and his purpose is not self-justification. It seems to be our natural human instinct, when we are attacked, to defend ourselves and even attack back. While natural, though, it is not consistent with either the teachings of Jesus or the example of Jesus. We sense here that this close follower of Jesus had learned well from his master. Peter does not seek to prove himself right or to prove his critics wrong. He simply bears witness to what God had done, which makes Peter an example to us all.

Peter recounts how God had privately prepared him to think about and respond to Gentiles differently. This is the episode, then, in which God is the one who does the talking. "What God has made clean," he says to Peter, "you must not call profane" (v. 9). This is God's word on the subject of the Gentiles, and it laid groundwork in Peter for what lay ahead.

It was wise for Peter to share with his critics his own experience. After all, he had no doubt shared their initial reflex in response to Gentiles. We discover that remembering how we ourselves used to be is an essential ingredient in patience and compassion with other people.

Then, having been prepared by God, Peter set off for the home of Cornelius. Again, it was Peter who did the talking, and the talking he did was the simple sharing of the gospel message. That, in turn, gave rise to yet another kind of talking. Peter's Gentile audience began to speak — in tongues!

This clearly came as a surprise to Peter and the believers who were with him. Beyond just surprising, though, the event was confirming. Now Peter recognized how certainly God was including the Gentiles in his plan and in his work. It was precisely that new certainty that Peter shared with his critics.

(3) Then, finally, see who is not talking. The Bible reports that when the critics "heard this, they were silenced" (v. 18a). That's a certain symbol of victory, of course, when your opposition is silenced. Whether in sports, in politics, or just in an ordinary argument, when you can silence your opponent, you know that you've won.

Except that's not how God wins in the end. The entire episode ends on a happier, superior note. It does not end with critics who are silenced, embarrassed, or put to shame, which would be characteristic of a human victory. No, but rather, we read that "they praised God, saying, 'Then God has given even to the Gentiles the repentance that leads to life' " (v. 18b).

This is the sign and a symbol of God's victory: not silence, but praise. For his end-game with human beings, always and always, is not defeat but conversion. And by the end of this entire episode, we have seen three beautiful conversions: Peter's, the Gentiles', and the critics'.

We don't have statistics to measure a player's talking, but every sports fan knows what an important part of the game talking can be. Even more than the sports fan, however, you and I as Christians know how important talking can be. From creation to Pentecost, from the Ten Commandments to the Great Commission, from the dry bones that surrounded Ezekiel to the Gentiles that surrounded Peter, we know how important — how eternally important — talking can be. Amen.

The Man Who Wasn't There

I've never had a vision — at least not of the sort that Paul had. I don't know personally, therefore, what you feel the next morning. But it's clear from the story that whatever Paul felt, he felt it so strongly that he and his companions changed their itinerary immediately in response to that vision.

Perhaps this sort of turn-on-a-dime operation is acceptable for a missionary. It's a little hard to imagine in other lines of work, however. Does the salesman staying in Phoenix tell his boss that he decided to change plans and hop on a plane to San Diego instead because he had a vision of a San Diegan in the middle of the night? Of course not. Yet Paul and company instantly pulled up their stakes in Asia Minor, hopped on a boat, and sailed across the Aegean to Macedonia.

It was a major move. Asia Minor was Paul's home turf. He was originally from Tarsus, and virtually all of his missionary work to-date had been in that larger region, which we know today as Turkey. To make the move to Macedonia, therefore, was to travel into a more foreign territory.

Furthermore, it was a major move culturally and historically. Now Paul — and with him the gospel — would enter Europe. In the process, they would both move a step closer to Rome.

The voyage across the Aegean takes only a moment to read in the text, but it required at least two days to make. Imagine the excitement and anticipation of the missionaries during those days and nights on board ship. And imagine, too, the apprehension and uncertainty as they approached unfamiliar territory and unknown challenges.

With each hour of their voyage, the coastline of Asia Minor grew smaller and smaller behind them, until it was no longer visible on the horizon. With each hour of their voyage, they were further and further away from what was familiar, and they moved nearer and nearer to the unknown. Indeed, all that they knew for certain going into Macedonia was the man Paul had seen in his vision.

Just how clear was Paul's vision? How vividly had he seen that Macedonian man? Had Paul seen his face? Did he remember his look, his features, and perhaps even the sound of his voice?

I wonder, as Paul disembarked the boat there in Neapolis, if he found himself looking for that face and listening for that voice. It would have been a natural thing to do. Even if Paul was under no delusion whatsoever about his vision being of an actual person, how could one help but look for that one familiar face in the sea of unfamiliar faces? We couldn't blame Paul for craning his neck and scanning the crowd to find that one particular man: the Macedonian he had seen a few nights before.

Paul and his companions traveled inland from that port city of Neapolis, and they arrived shortly at the important city of Philippi. Upon arrival there, they sought out the local synagogue.

While Paul clearly had come to understand his mission as being especially to the Gentiles, as a matter of policy and procedure he always began with the Jews. He was one of them. He shared with them a common heritage, faith in the same God, and confidence in the same scriptures. When he would arrive in a new town, he would find the local synagogue, and begin by sharing the gospel with the folks gathered there.

When they got to Philippi, however, Paul and his companions discovered that there was no synagogue in that town.

In the tradition of a quorum, a minimal number of Jewish men was required in a place in order to form a synagogue. Evidently, however, the city of Philippi did not feature even that negligible Jewish population.

That must have been a discouraging discovery for Paul. If Macedonia already seemed foreign, now it seemed more so. The natural point of contact — the customary starting place — wasn't available. If Paul was looking for the familiar face from his vision, it surely seemed more distant and elusive now. The apostle had been beckoned over to Macedonia to help, but where were the people who wanted his help?

In the absence of a formal synagogue, there was a Plan B. Where there was insufficient population to establish and maintain a synagogue, local Jews and God-fearers would designate a "place of prayer." It had no street address or structure. It was just the site where a handful of devout folks habitually gathered. In many instances, such a place was by the local body of water. In Philippi's case, that was the river Gangites. And that is just where Paul found a group of women gathered for worship when the sabbath day came.

A group of *women*. Not only was there an insufficient number of Jewish men in Philippi to form a synagogue, it seems there were no Jewish men there at all. If Paul's instinct was to look for the familiar face of the Macedonian man in his vision, he would not see it here in this makeshift congregation.

Perhaps you have been in gatherings where someone has asked, "Where is everybody?" In most instances, it's a poorly phrased question, for clearly not everybody is missing. Some body or two is there. Indeed, I have been in a few settings where a fairly substantial number of people have been gathered, yet still heard someone ask, "Where is everybody?" Thus the question reveals that the questioner's real concern is not with everybody but with some select bodies who happen to be missing.

I saw this most plainly in my years of working with youth groups. You could have a group of twenty teens, but if certain older teens who were popular and important leaders in the group happened to be absent, others would ask, "Where is everybody?" Conversely, if those key youth were there, the group could be smaller, yet no one would ask where "everybody" was.

I wonder if Paul and his companions looked at one another that sabbath morning and asked, "Where is everybody?" Not because no one was there at that riverside place of prayer, but because the people they naturally looked for were not there.

Still, like a good golfer, the apostle Paul always shows his willingness and ability to play it where it lies. He did not find a synagogue. He did not find the Macedonian man from his vision. Indeed, he found no men that sabbath day at all. But he found a small gathering of earnest women, and he sat down and spoke with them there.

We have all known churches and movements along the way that survived only because of the dogged determination of a few women. It must have been so there in ancient Philippi. And while biblical passages have sometimes been misused to oppress women, the fact is that the New Testament shines an admiring spotlight on the role of women in God's work. It begins most notably with Mary, the mother of Jesus, and continues with the group of women who provided for Jesus and his disciples out of their means. Women were the first witnesses to the resurrection. Women were clearly instrumental in the ministry of Paul and the early church. Women were the cornerstone of God's work in Philippi. And one particular woman has the distinction of being known as the first European convert to Christianity.

Her name was Lydia, and she was among the women that Paul found gathered down by the riverside. She responded to the message she heard from Paul and his companions that day. She and all her household were baptized. She followed through on the decision of her heart with the work of her hands, extending an insistent hospitality to the missionaries during their stay in her town.

At least one of their nights in Philippi, however, was not spent in the comfort of Lydia's home. At least one of Paul's nights in Philippi was spent in prison.

The beating and confinement were entirely undeserved. And in Paul's case, as a Roman citizen, they were also unjust. But it came to pass that Paul had attracted the attention of a poor slave girl, who was demon-possessed. She had followed and hounded Paul for several days, when finally he turned and ordered the demon out of her.

While this was liberty for her, it amounted to constraint of trade for her owner. Evidently, the poor girl's condition had been exploited and turned into a profitable venture by the man who owned her, and so her deliverance interfered with his bottom line.

Paul and Silas were publicly stripped and beaten, and then thrown in jail. As they sat there, chained and bleeding in a foreign prison, I wonder what they felt and thought. Might Paul have revisited that night in Troas when he saw the vision of the man from Macedonia? He still had not found that man. He had shared the gospel with a group of women and received considerable welcome from one. He had set another woman free from her spiritual bondage. But the Macedonian men with whom he had had contact were the slave-owner who had him and Silas arrested, the public officials who had them beaten and sentenced, and the jailer who had fastened their feet to heavy blocks of wood.

In pain and in prison, you couldn't blame Paul for wondering if he had misunderstood God's direction, if he had come to the wrong place.

We imagined earlier a salesman trying to explain that he abruptly left his work in Arizona in order to fly to California because he had had a vision of a San Diegan calling to him in the middle of the night. Of course a responsible businessman wouldn't do such a thing.

On the other hand, the salesman would have done exactly that if what he had received in the middle of the night was a message from his boss giving him new instructions.

That is what Paul did. His impetus happened to be a midnight vision, but he understood it as instructions from his boss. He went to Macedonia because he believed he was following orders. And indeed he was.

Before that night was over, a providential earthquake had broken open their chains and cells. By morning, the jailer and his entire household had been converted and baptized. And within a few years, the church in Philippi had grown into one of Paul's most cherished and happy partners in ministry and fellowship with him.

But what of the vision? Was there, in fact, some person who wanted Paul to go to Macedonia or not? Indeed, there was, but it was not a man from Macedonia. It was the God who loved Macedonia so much that he gave his only Son. Amen.

The Ascension Of Our Lord
Acts 1:1-11

A Stupid Question

Generous teachers sometimes assure their students that there is no such thing as a stupid question. Personally, I'm not so sure. It seems to me that I have heard some pretty stupid questions over the years. I'm quite sure that I have asked some very stupid questions along the way, as well.

In this episode from the first days of the early church, the disciples asked a stupid question. Or, at least, they asked the wrong question. They asked Jesus, "Lord, is this the time when you will restore the kingdom to Israel?" (v. 6).

In order to understand their question, we need to see it in context.

The first bit of context is the political reality of the day. At this time, the nation of Israel had been reduced to a part of a Roman province. Long gone was the heroic age of Joshua, the golden reign of David, and the splendor of Solomon. They were now a conquered people. They had toiled under the heavy hand of Rome for two generations.

On the other hand, just prior to the arrival of the resented Roman empire, the Jews had enjoyed a century of independence and peace. This was the happy age of heroism and liberty ushered in by the Maccabean Revolt. The gilded memories of those events and days no doubt informed the hopes and influenced dreams of the people in Jesus' day.

Consequently, when the disciples asked Jesus, "Lord, is this the time when you will restore the kingdom to Israel?" they may have had that revolution and recent era of independence in mind.

In addition to that larger political context, the disciples' question also comes out of a personal context.

These men, you see, had been following Jesus for some time, traditionally estimated at about three years. Perhaps they began with a fairly traditional understanding of Jesus as a rabbi. Rabbis in that day chose and gathered around themselves disciples: students who would commit themselves to their master's life and teaching.

It was not long, however, before speculation about Jesus exceeded the ordinary assumptions about rabbis. Not only was he an uncommon teacher; he was also a miracle-worker. Soon, his disciples observed that Jesus had the fascination of great multitudes, the respect of demons, and the scorn of the Pharisees. When the moment came, therefore, for Jesus to ask his disciples what the popular scuttlebutt was about him, it was no longer just rabbi stuff; now they were talking about prophets. Now Jesus was being mentioned alongside Elijah, Jeremiah, and John the Baptist.

This was of a higher order, you see. There were many men recognized as rabbis at any given time in ancient Israel, but very few men who were recognized as prophets. Furthermore, we should recognize that prophet was, arguably, the highest office in the land. While he was not elected by the people or part of a family line, Israel's history bears witness to the high rank of the prophet. The prophet had authority to correct, not just the people, but the priests, the king, and entire foreign cities and nations, as well. The prophet's authority came from the simple recognition that he carried God's word, and that made his words most important.

Stop the average Israelite on the street in Jesus' day and ask him to list the names of rabbis. He will forget more than he will remember, and there will be a still larger list that he had never heard of at all. But then ask him to list the prophets, and he will generate a select list of significant names.

Now Jesus is being mentioned in that company.

Jesus presses the matter further. His real purpose is not to discover the common speculation of a crowd. Rather, he wants to know what his own followers understand and believe. "What about you," he asks. "Who do you say that I am?" (Matthew 16:15).

This is the occasion when Peter steps forward to make his astonishing declaration about Jesus. "You are the Messiah," Peter proclaims, "the Son of the living God" (Matthew 16:16).

To call Jesus "rabbi" was to say that he was special, yet still one among many. To call him a prophet was to affirm that he was one of a comparative few. But to call him "Messiah" was to say that he is a one-and-only. The one who was promised and prophesied and who fulfilled those centuries of promises and prophecies. The one who would sit on David's throne and rule with peerless strength and justice. The one who would defeat God's enemies, and who would establish Zion in peace, in strength, in prosperity, and as a kind of spiritual headquarters for the entire world.

That was conventional wisdom in first-century Palestine about the promised Messiah, and it was heady stuff for Peter to identify Jesus in those terms. Yet, it seems that there was more to being "Christ/Messiah" than what the conventional wisdom had anticipated. And so Jesus began to explain to his disciples, for the first time, what would happen to him in Jerusalem. He told them that he would be arrested and handed over to the authorities, that he would be beaten and would suffer, that he would be crucified, and that he would arise again.

Now, many, many months later, all of those things had taken place. The disciples gather now around the risen Lord on a hilltop, from which he will momentarily ascend out of their sight and into heaven. With all that has happened — all that they have seen and heard — the disciples now ask the question: "Lord, is this the time when you will restore the kingdom to Israel?"

After so much time, so many experiences, and so much instruction, still they are confined, you see, to their conventional wisdom.

First, they were thinking too small.

We should observe that this seems to be something of a habit. Seldom have God's people missed the mark because they were thinking too big. We see frequently in the pages of scripture, however, the people of God thinking too small.

Time and again in the gospels, Jesus had to stretch the horizons of his followers or his audience. Their own natural assumptions were too limited, too myopic. Peter, for example, assumed that seven times was the high ceiling on forgiving some repeat offender. Not even close, according to Jesus.

Similarly, the inquirer wanted to know who his neighbor was — the one he was supposed to love as well and as much as he loved himself. Jesus' answer reached over a high and thick wall, finding the hated Samaritans to illustrate true neighborly love.

So it is here, too. The disciples' question proves that they were thinking too small. Their limited focus was merely the kingdom of Israel, but the instructions that Jesus gave them were so very much broader.

He gave them an assignment that began in Jerusalem. That was a natural enough starting place for them, but it might have been a natural ending place for them, too. Reestablishing David's throne in David's city might have been the full extent of their vision.

For Jesus, however, Jerusalem was only the starting point. The next layer mentioned was the surrounding region of Judea. That, too, was fine and familiar for the disciples. But then Jesus next mentioned Samaria. Now Samaria was not far away geographically, but it was an assignment for the Hatfields to go knocking on the McCoys' door.

But even Samaria was not the end game. Rather, Jesus sends these followers, literally, "to the ends of the earth."

Go home and take a good look at your globe. See how big the world is and how many people and places are included in this epic commission from Jesus. Then twirl the globe until you find the Mediterranean Sea. Direct your attention to the eastern edge of that body of water and squint to see the tiny sliver of land designated as Israel. Then we shall see how wrong the disciples' question was, and how way too small they were thinking.

Furthermore, the disciples were not only thinking too small, they were looking in the wrong direction. "Lord, is this the time when you will restore the kingdom to Israel?" they asked.

For several years now, they had been following Jesus and watching him do things. They watched him cleanse lepers, cast out demons, feed the multitudes, and calm storms. They had seen him die and return to life. But now it was time for them to stop just watching him do things. He was about to return to his Father; now it was time for them to start doing things.

The disciples' question was about what Jesus would do next. But that was the wrong question, for his answer was about what *they* would do next. The mantle of ministry was being placed on them, and the next phase of God's work in this world was theirs to do!

Finally, the disciples had set their sights too low, for they were focused on the kingdom of Israel rather than on the kingdom of God.

This miscalculation on their part is surprising given the preponderance of Jesus' teachings on the kingdom of God. He had portrayed it as a priceless treasure; as a thing that starts almost imperceptibly small, but then grows into a grand reality; and as an end-time harvest, judgment, and banquet. Still, for all that he had taught them about God's kingdom, they remained strangely fixated on Israel's kingdom.

It's easy to find fault with the disciples in this passage. It's easy, but it's not very useful, unless I recognize myself in them. For I am disposed to the same brand of myopia and miscalculation. Perhaps you are, too.

For myself, I know that I have often been guilty of thinking too small — underestimating either the power, or the love, or the will of God. Likewise, I have sometimes been impatient for him to act in some situation when, in fact, his will is for me to act. Routinely I am inclined to focus on my little kingdom and interests rather than on God's.

So the disciples in this passage look very familiar to me. Do they look familiar to you?

I know; that's a stupid question. Amen.

The Place Of Prayer

"Where is the place of prayer?" they asked. "We're looking for the place of prayer."

It was Paul's first visit to the city of Philippi. He, Silas, Luke, and some other companions had come there to share the good news about Jesus. They wanted to start by going to the place of prayer.

Originally, you recall, Paul and his companions had not intended to go to Philippi at all. They had been traveling and preaching exclusively in Asia Minor, when one night Paul had his vision of the man from Macedonia pleading, "Come over and help us!" Taking it as a sign from God, they adjusted their itinerary, and prepared to preach the gospel in Macedonia.

That meant crossing the Aegean Sea. More significantly, that meant crossing into Europe.

They made the trip. And their first extended stop in the region of Macedonia was the city of Philippi.

Customarily, when Paul would arrive in a new city, he would go first to the local synagogue. There he would present the news about Jesus to the Jews, for they were his people, they were God's people, and they were the natural first audience for the message about God's Messiah.

In Philippi, however, there was no synagogue. Instead, Paul sought out "the place of prayer" — that is, the site where Jews in that town would gather to pray and to read the scriptures together.

Paul and his companions went down to the riverside there in Philippi, for in so many ancient cities the place of prayer was by the water.

227

That has a great personal appeal for many of us. We, too, may have found that some lake, river, or ocean has also been for us a marvelous setting of inspiration and a lovely place of fellowship with God. It's easy for us to imagine Paul and company walking down a grassy hillside, sloping down toward the Gangitis River, and meeting there a devout group of Jews gathered together on the sabbath to pray.

The missionaries shared the gospel with that little congregation, and we know that one particular woman from the group — Lydia — responded to what she heard. She is often identified, as a result, as the first European convert to Christianity. It was she who, subsequently, insisted on housing Paul and his friends in her home for the remainder of their time in Philippi.

On another day during their Philippi stay, Paul and his friends were again going to the place of prayer, but as they walked, a young woman began to follow them, making a great commotion. Apparently she was the victim of some evil spirit, and her master capitalized on her condition by charging people to have his slave-girl tell their fortunes. She was a profitable commodity. When the apostle Paul cast out the spirit that possessed the girl, he had interfered with that Philippian's livelihood.

The girl's master complained to local authorities, who in turn had Paul and Silas arrested, publicly stripped and beaten, and then thrown into the inner cell of the local jail.

About midnight that night, the Bible reports that Paul and Silas were singing and praying, and the other prisoners were listening to them. Suddenly, there was a great earthquake, which so shook the prison that the chains and bars and walls began to break apart.

Now in those days, jailers were often held personally responsible for their prisoners. Consequently, when the Philippian jailer saw that the earthquake was crumbling his prison, he thought surely that some or all of his charges would escape. In despair, he reached for his sword, planning to kill himself.

Instantly, the apostle intervenes. Paul calls out for the jailer to halt his self-destruction, assuring him that all of the prisoners were still there and no one was escaping.

By morning — by morning! — that Philippian jailer had welcomed Paul and Silas into his home, washed and bandaged their wounds, heard the gospel, and been baptized, along with his whole family.

That is the story of Paul's visit to the Macedonian city of Philippi. Let us review quickly the progression of events on that particular day.

Paul and Silas had set out for the place of prayer, but as far as we know, they never got there that day. By that afternoon, they were in trouble with the authorities. By that night, they were in jail. By the next morning, they were free, and another family in Philippi had come to Christ.

The story is a magnificent testimony to the faithfulness of these servants of God, as well as to God's marvelous versatility, able to accomplish his work and his will at any time and in any place.

In fact, the whole story of Paul's relationship to Philippi is a beautiful one. From the vision of the Macedonian that prompted the trip to the conversion of Lydia; from the liberation of the demon-possessed girl to the baptism of the jailer and his family; and, finally, there is the bit of correspondence we have between Paul and the believers in Philippi: the so-called "joyful epistle."

This morning, I want to tell you what my favorite part of the story is. In the morning, Paul and Silas set out for the place of prayer. In the middle of the night, they were in prison, praying.

Do you see? It was not where they intended to be. It was not where they expected to be. It surely wasn't where they wanted to be. They began by looking for a place of prayer, and they ended up making a foreign dungeon into precisely that: a place of prayer.

A number of years ago, driving in Green Bay, Wisconsin, my attention (and imagination) was captured by a large billboard by the side of the road. It was an advertisement for a brand of brats. (A brat, in Wisconsin, does not refer to an obnoxious child; rather, it is a type of sandwich made of bratwurst.) The billboard's message was simple: "Another perfect day for grilling." Interestingly, however, the billboard also had built into it a device that indicated the current temperature.

As a result, when you drove by the sign, you would see the current outdoor temperature, and you would read that it is "another perfect day for grilling."

It struck me as a rather bold gesture on a billboard located in Green Bay, Wisconsin. Perhaps in Orlando or Phoenix or San Diego you could make such a static, year round claim that it's another perfect day for grilling. But to have a built-in thermometer that draws attention to just what kind of day it is — and it might be a very cold one in Green Bay — and still make the claim that it is a perfect day for grilling. Whether it's 70 degrees, 50 degrees, 30 degrees, 10 degrees, or worse, the article of faith remains the same: It's a perfect day for grilling.

Clearly they were committed to the proposition that any day is a perfect day for grilling, and I have met some folks along the way who would concur. I had a good friend in another parish who embodied that attitude. He cheerfully cooked out on his grill in every season and in any weather. He would agree with the billboard: Any day is a perfect day for grilling.

I imagine that the apostle Paul could have carried around with him a sign that he could have stuck in the ground wherever he was: a sign that read, "Another perfect place for prayer." He proved it in Philippi.

If he was in the sacred space of a synagogue; or if he was in the loveliness of the grassy slope by the river; or if he was naked and bleeding, hands in chains and feet in stocks, in a dungeon, in the middle of the night, in a foreign city — wherever — it's another perfect place for prayer.

Twenty years ago I was teaching a children's class in a vacation Bible school in Virginia. As I walked through the curriculum with the kids, I came across an exercise that I found rather disturbing. The curriculum had a prayer time built into the end of each day's class session. On this particular day, the teacher's book said something like this: Have the children sit on the floor, close their eyes, and imagine a beautiful, peaceful place. Then invite them to imagine that Jesus comes and meets them there and talks with them in that place.

It all sounded very nice, but I regarded it as a frighteningly misleading approach to prayer. The testimony of scripture is not that God meets us in imaginary, beautiful places. Rather, the profound and magnificent truth is that God meets us in very real places — some beautiful and some dreadful.

I didn't want those children growing up to think that they needed to escape to some make-believe place in order to meet with God. Rather, I wanted them to discover that they were known and loved by a God who would meet them any place and every place.

Whether it was by the riverside with Lydia or in the dungeon with Silas. Whether it was in the Judean wilderness — "a dry and thirsty land" — with David or in the middle of a storm at sea with Peter. Whether it was in the middle of nowhere, where Jacob slept outside with his head on a rock, running away from home to leave his troubles behind him; or at the River Jabbok, where Jacob wrestled all night, as his troubles were just a day ahead of him. Wherever it is, it is another perfect place of prayer. It is another perfect place to walk or talk, to cry or wrestle, with God.

I don't know where you are today. Perhaps it's exactly where you wanted and expected to be. Perhaps not.

Likewise, I don't know where you'll find yourself tomorrow. Perhaps it will be exactly where you wanted and expected to be. Perhaps not.

But wherever it is — in your marriage, in your work, in your finances, in your health — Paul and Silas would assure you that it is the perfect place of prayer. Amen.

Sermons On The First Readings

For Sundays
After Pentencost
(First Third)

God's Playful Wisdom

Stephen P. McCutchan

This work is dedicated to my wife
Sandra Jo McCutchan
who has loved me
supported me
and edited my writings
all of which has strengthened
and enhanced my ministry

The Day Of Pentecost
Acts 2:1-21

Birthdays And Marriages

It is common to speak of Pentecost as the birthday of the church. I want to add to that the image of marriage. As most of you are aware, marriages do not just happen with the signing of a contract. There is the courting period and the public declaration of engagement before the formal ceremony takes place that lifts up the importance of the couple's commitment to each other. Even the formal ceremony does not make a marriage.

A marriage without a period of courting is based on blind chance. It may work, but the percentages of its success are greatly lessened. A marriage without the public declaration and ceremony may work as well, but it tends to have an ephemeral quality about it. It is as if somehow the couple is not sure enough to publicly and pridefully declare to the world that they are committed to working out the delicate and difficult dimensions of a truly intimate relationship. The public ceremony invites a larger community to not only celebrate the couple's declaration of commitment to each other but also to support them in fulfilling that commitment.

A marriage is developed as we live out that commitment to each other, discovering our differences, our commonality, and developing that third something that did not exist until we came together. There are moments of joy, friction, boredom, and ecstasy as a couple begins to utilize every experience as an opportunity to deepen their relationship.

Those same sorts of dynamics are present in a healthy church community. Like in a marriage, members of a church discover that they carry into the community a lot of unconscious assumptions having to do with values, relationships, roles, and responsibilities. When I am counseling a young couple in preparation for marriage, I often suggest that they are entering into something like the formation of a new architectural partnership whose first contract is to design a new community. Fresh out of their respective schools of architecture, replete with all of the individual quirks of their professors who trained them, they enter into their new project with full enthusiasm.

Soon they begin to notice points of tension and disagreement over apparently trivial things. What they need to be aware of and openly discuss is that their training came from different schools of architecture. In those schools they absorbed, unconsciously, different customs, values, and manners of working that each assumes to be generally true of everyone. Since they assume what they believe is generally acceptable truth, they see as irrational behavior or resolute stubbornness the partner's insistence on doing it a different way.

Those same tensions often occur in a church among members and between members and their pastor. Each acts on assumptions and customs that they believe to be true and cannot understand any reason for changing. It is only as they learn to value the presence of diverse assumptions that they will begin to build a truly healthy church.

With that image in mind, let us turn to Pentecost. As I mentioned, Pentecost has often been referred to as the birthday of the church. The book of Acts records that the disciples and followers of Jesus were gathered together in Jerusalem following the events of the cross. Most likely they were a motley, disorganized, frightened group of people. Their hopes had been raised so high by this man Jesus, then dashed to pieces by his execution as a criminal on the cross. Then some among them spoke of having experienced Jesus alive again. But even if that were so, he was not among them now to give them direction. The world outside seemed cold, inhospitable, and unresponsive. If people would not listen to Jesus and in fact had rejected both him and his message, what hope was there for this small, frightened group of people to have any effect on the world?

236

Aware of their many weaknesses, confused as to their role in the world, and disoriented as to the direction they should move, they gathered for the feast of Pentecost. Pentecost was the Greek name for the second of the three great religious feasts of the Jewish year. It was originally an agricultural festival celebrating the completion of the harvest — something like our Thanksgiving. But as Israel became more urbanized, it became a time for celebrating the renewal of the covenant or agreement between God and God's people.

It was a time for the people of God to recognize that God's original covenant was with all of creation. That in the beginning God breathed the breath of life into Adam — the closest equivalent we have for that word in English is earthling or humanity. God formed the earthling out of earth and then breathed the breath of life into this inert body. By sharing God's breath with humanity, God formed a special relationship with them and made them partners in the fulfillment of God's purpose in creation.

In the course of time, people were continually seduced by the powers about them into distorting God's original intention of their role in creation. Therefore, in a series of calls and covenants, God formed a special people amidst all the peoples of the earth to be a sign for the rest of the world. Each year this people of God gathered at the feast of Pentecost, both to give thanks to God for God's bountiful blessings and to reflect upon and rededicate themselves to their part in this covenant between God and humanity. It became a time of renewal, of new beginnings in their attempt to be a sign to the world.

Then, after years of the Jewish people celebrating this Pentecost festival, a motley group of frightened Jews who had followed Jesus sought to rededicate themselves as part of the people of God. They wanted to make a new beginning as followers of "the way" in which Jesus had instructed them. Like their Jewish ancestors before them, they wanted to reflect upon their covenant with God and to seek new direction for their life together.

Once again, as it had happened at creation, God breathed God's breath upon this people who had the form of a community and the form took on life as a community of faith. Like any totally new experience, they could only describe it by analogy to old experiences. It was like the breath of God breathing life into Adam. It was like the violent wind and fire of the experience of Moses on Mount Sinai when God formed the people of Israel out of the escaped slaves of Egypt. It was unexplainable, and it was unearned. It was a gracious gift of God that enabled them to do far more than they believed possible. They measured themselves against the world and felt powerless. Yet they trusted in God and received the power to become part of God's people.

They became a sign of a new humanity that placed the enhancement of the lives of people above the preservation of structures. They were able to speak a new language that reached across the barriers that the world had erected of language, custom, race, class, national origin, and ideology. They were, if just for a moment, able to reverse the experience of the tower of Babel and catch a vision of the direction toward which the world must strive. Just as the first life created by the breath of God was made in the image of God, so they were also made to reflect God in creation. It was this new life, again as the result of the breath of God, which empowered them to be a new reflection of God's purpose for the world. It was the birthday of the church, as a people who, by the gift of the Spirit of God, were enabled to be a sign to the world that the barriers dividing them could be transcended.

Like those first followers of Jesus, the church today celebrates Pentecost with a mixture of hope and uncertainty. We are all aware of our weaknesses when compared to the power that many other institutions in this world can wield. We too often find ourselves subject to their power rather than transcending it. We tremble when the voice of economics cautions us against performing a ministry that it considers unfeasible. We conform all too easily when the voice of class differences suggest that certain people should go to one church while others would be more comfortable in another church.

All across this world we repeatedly witness Christians succumbing to their respective national pressures to forgo authentic communion with brothers and sisters in other lands that differ ideologically. We wait in frustration while national church structures tell us the time is not right to heal the shameful divisions of Christians in this land. Too often, instead of searching for a language that transcends such barriers, we name a language that is comfortable for us and then demand that others accept our language as the universal language.

How should Christians respond? We come to celebrate, as did those first Christians, well aware that we do not know the actual dimensions of our role and the direction that we are to go. Yet, we come in faith that God does have a role for us and a direction for us to move. We celebrate the birthday of the church as a beginning of our lives together and as a time for renewing our commitment as individuals and a community to being a part of the people of God as we are given to understand it. We rededicate ourselves to try to listen to the word of God, to try to hear how God is trying to express himself in our lives, and to try to discover whatever gift of language God seeks to give us that will enable us to speak across a barrier that divides this world.

Good marriages take lots of hard work, lots of forgiveness, and lots of thanksgiving for the gifts we have been given. It is the same with the church. Amen.

The Holy Trinity
Proverbs 8:1-4, 22-31

God's Playful Wisdom

If I mentioned Sophia to you, what memories would it evoke? Would you think of a movie called *Sophie's Choice*? Or perhaps you know of someone whose name is Sophia. Some of you might think of a controversy stirred up several years ago at a women's conference that was exploring feminine images for God. Some who objected to their ideas accused them of pagan worship when they used Sophia to refer to the feminine side of God.

If you are from the Eastern Orthodox branch of the church or even have good friends who are, you are aware of churches named Sophia. The Eastern Orthodox church has always been more familiar with the role of Sophia in the faith than the Western branch of the church.

For Christians, our understanding of the role of Sophia in the faith can be traced back to this passage from Proverbs 8. Here Sophia, the Greek word for wisdom, is personified as a woman who was with God before creation. It's sort of a pre-creation story. "The Lord created me," says Sophia, "at the beginning of his work ... before the beginning of the earth" (vv. 22-23).

This personified wisdom then goes on to describe how she was an intimate part of every aspect of the creation. Some manuscripts describe how she was "beside (God) like a little child ... daily (God's) delight, rejoicing before him always" (v. 30).

If you allow your imagination its freedom, you can almost see this little girl, Sophia, skipping around delighting God as God proceeds with creation. For those of you who have little children, you may be able to fill out that image.

241

When we get to the New Testament, the gospel of John develops this understanding of Sophia as the spirit of truth. "I still have many things to say to you, but you cannot bear them now. When the Spirit of truth comes, [she] will guide you into all the truth ..." (John 16:12-13). This spirit will reveal to us things Jesus chose not to reveal to us during his time on earth.

What we learn is that God accommodates God's message according to our level of understanding. It should not be a surprise that there are areas of truth that God knows but humanity, at any particular stage of life, could not understand. Jesus could not, for example, have explained the truth of space travel or computers to his disciples. John is not talking about scientific knowledge but a greater knowledge in the area of faith. Jesus did not speak directly to many of the issues that we face in today's church, so as the body of Christ we have to seek that truth together. Sophia nurtures us in our journey of faith as we mature and our culture advances.

The image of Sophia as a child also reminds us of the gospel admonition that unless we become like little children, we will not enter the kingdom of God. What is it about a child that is instructive to us in the faith? One of the great characteristics about children is that they know how to play.

Consider the last time you allowed yourself to play with your faith. When children play, they are not afraid to fantasize different possibilities. They can imagine radical possibilities because after all, they would explain, it is just playing. Children might be unafraid to ask: What if God doesn't exist and Jesus was just a made up story? What they are exploring is how such a truth would affect their lives. Or they might ask: What if God does exist and Jesus' commandments that you must love your enemy and forgive those who offend you are truths by which you will be judged? How would that alter life? In adult language, they are asking which truth would bring about a more radical change in their life. Sometimes play clarifies reality.

How often have churches failed in their reflection of the good news of Christ because they took themselves too seriously and forgot how to play? Imagine a church — let's call it First Community Church. First Community has been having a very serious struggle within the leadership. All factions are sincere and serious in believing that their way is the way of truth and righteousness.

Then one Sunday two of the elders from different factions find themselves assigned to watch the first-and-second-grade room. They suggest to the children that they play a game together.

One of the children says, "Let's play church."

Another child says, "I want to play the good preacher."

"That's no fair," said another, "you played the good preacher last time. Why don't you play the preacher who gets told to go away?"

"I don't want to go away," said the first child. "I'll be the preacher to one group. You can be preacher to the other group, and we will tell each other what is wrong with the other."

A third child speaks up and says, "Our group wants to have a party."

"You can't have a party in the church," says another. "Church is for God, and God doesn't like parties."

"Uh uh," says another, "I have a storybook that says Jesus liked to go to parties with tax collectors and spenders."

"But if Jesus liked parties, how come our church never has parties?" asked another.

As the two stunned elders watched, they saw mirrored before them the child's perception of what it was like to be a church. Suddenly one of them began to laugh.

Immediately one of the children turned toward him and stuck out her finger and said, "Stop that laughing, you are in church. We don't allow laughing here."

"I think," said the elder, "that our church needs to learn from you to laugh and play more so that God can delight in us."

Is the elder right? Do we need to play with our faith and our church more so that we might be a delight to God? Think of what might happen if we were more open to playfulness as we face issues in the church.

It is no accident that science advanced in those parts of the world where either Jewish or Christian thought predominated. By the nature of our faith, the physical world is not something to be worshiped. We can probe and explore it, and we believe that God wants us to grow in our understanding. That developed because we weren't afraid to play with possibilities.

My concern is that we have shown an inability to "play with" the possibilities in other areas of life. When we have faced issues like abortion, race, war and peace, homosexuality, and more, we have quickly chosen up sides and refused to play with possible solutions the same way we did with issues of science.

We refused to allow Sophia to play with possibilities and trust that God would continue to delight in us as we probed for the truth. Churches have chosen to split over many such issues. We choose to violate God's commandment that we love one another rather than risk that we might not see the truth clearly.

I understand we live in a world that is experiencing a flood of change and would like to have some solid truths to hang onto. And there are such truths.

- God is the holy, sovereign Lord of history.
- God seeks to create a world of justice, mercy, and love and bids us to seek to bring that about in our world as well.
- God does provide for us that which we truly need to both sustain and grow in our lives.
- God offers us forgiveness for our sins and bids us do the same for others.
- God understands that we face temptations and seeks to deliver us from evil.

We can put those same truths in a form that is easier to remember: Our Father who art in heaven, hallowed be thy name. Your kingdom come. Your will be done, on earth as it is in heaven. Give us this day our daily bread. And forgive us our debts as we forgive our debtors. Lead us not into temptation, but deliver us from evil. Amen.

Proper 4
Pentecost 2
Ordinary Time 9
1 Kings 18:20-21 (22-29) 30-39

Mugwumpers

In certain streams of Christianity, it is common to speak of people being "born again." The phrase comes from an exchange between Jesus and a Pharisee named Nicodemus in the third chapter of John. In that exchange, Jesus contrasts being born of the flesh with being born of the Spirit.

To be born of the flesh is to be shaped by the genes of your parents and their background. You come into this world with a heritage as a given. Because you live according to the demands of the flesh, you also possess the bodily desires and needs, emotional fears, and human vulnerabilities that all humans experience.

To be born of the Spirit is different. To be born of the Spirit is not a given but a choice. We can choose to respond to a force that is beyond the natural universe. Often this Spirit enables us to rise above some of the more base elements of the flesh and choose to not be guided by our fears or our desires. Rather, we are guided by God's purposes that often cause us to resist self-centered desires and not be driven by our fears.

The story of Elijah's contest with the prophets of Baal provides us with an outline of the choice that is before us. Elijah was a prophet. A prophet is one who speaks the word of God, a word that comes from beyond our physical universe. A prophet is able to clear away the smoke and help us see the real choices before us. Sometimes the prophetic word does not come to us in the form of a person. Rather, it comes in the form of an historical event like a recession or a personal event like a sudden illness or a troubled marriage.

245

In our story, the prophetic word came out of a dispute that Elijah had with King Ahab. Ahab, the ruler of Israel, wanted to please his wife, Jezebel, by including her gods in Israel's life. Elijah, on the other hand, declared that only Yahweh, the God of Israel, was acceptable in Israel. As a way to settle their dispute, Elijah challenged Ahab to gather all of Israel to witness a contest on Mount Carmel. Then he summoned the 450 prophets of Baal and the 400 prophets of Asherah. The fact that so many prophets existed reveals that this was a well-established religion in Israel. The idea was to demonstrate to all the people which god was real and which was merely created by humans.

Baal and Asherah became effective symbols in the Hebrew scriptures of what Jesus and Paul meant when they talked about living according to the flesh. These gods were essentially fertility gods that attempted to provide some way to understand and manage the dynamic forces of both humans and nature. We are all aware of how we can be captured by our desires and driven by our fears. We are also aware of how the sudden powers of nature can disrupt our orderly lives. What the Canaanites had done was to raise these often-disruptive forces to a godlike status and attempt to appease and manipulate them through religious rituals and sacrifices.

Many people in Israel tried to cover their bases by participating in rituals that responded to both the Canaanite gods and the God of Israel. Elijah challenged the people to choose who they truly worshiped. "How long will you go limping between two different opinions?" (v. 21) or as one translation has it, "How long will you continue to sit on the fence?" To use an 1884 political term: How long will you be *mugwumpers* — that is people who like to keep their *mug* on one side of the fence and their *wump* on the other side?

Remember that to worship something means to give high worth to it. In our society, one of the dynamic forces that requires our worship is the force of economics. Like the fertility gods in Israel, the economic realities of our society demand that we give them high priority. Like the Israelites, we try to give worth or worship to both the power of economics and to God who has blessed us with our wealth. For the most part, we try to avoid honestly facing which one has highest priority in our lives.

Each year in most churches you are offered the opportunity to take a snap quiz on which power you trust most in your life. In most churches it is called either a stewardship campaign or a pledge campaign. You are asked to decide between your *mug* and your *wump*. Beginning with Abraham, the Jewish faith instructed believers to give a tithe or 10% of their wealth back to God. The wisdom of the tithe is that it is not just loose change after all the important bills have been paid. It is a significant enough commitment that one has to decide whether you see what you have in life as a blessing from God or as a possession that you have earned. Like the choice in Elijah's contest with the fertility gods of Canaan, you have to decide whether you see life as made up of things that you must possess to assure security and pleasure or as a reflection of the blessings of God who can be trusted for the future. You are challenged to declare by your pledge whether your life is shaped by Baal or God.

Elijah set up a contest between the gods. Both groups would set up a sacrifice on an altar at the top of Mount Carmel. The real God would receive the sacrifice by fire. Fire was a common symbol of the power and presence of God in the Hebrew scriptures and the New Testament. At Pentecost it was the tongues of fire that symbolized the presence of God empowering the frightened disciples to overcome their fears and go forth boldly into the world.

The prophets of Baal set up their sacrifice and exhausted themselves with prayers and ritual dances to call upon their god to receive the sacrifice. Despite all of their efforts, they were not able to command such a god to act. When you see people who literally exhaust themselves in all sorts of work and societal rituals in order to attain security and happiness in life and yet continue to come up short, you know that the story of the Baal prophets points to a reality in our lives as well.

When it was Elijah's turn, he took twelve stones, one for each tribe of Israel. Symbolically he was gathering together the history of their life's experience. These were the stepping stones that had brought them to this decisive point in time. Like Elijah, our response to the promise of God is not something that happens out of the blue but is built on all our experiences within the church community. If you look at the major turning points or stepping stones of your life, both good and bad, God has been silently present nurturing you to respond to promise rather than despair.

It is the altar of our lives upon which the prophet lays the sacrifice bidding God to receive it. Then, we are told, Elijah poured gallons and gallons of water on the sacrifice. There was to be no human explanation if God received the sacrifice. If you think about the times when you were grasped by a power from beyond you and given a sense of calm in the face of fear or grief, you know there is no human explanation. Yet, for a moment, you were born of the Spirit. Life was sustained not by your wisdom or material resources but by something divine.

Elijah's prayer was: "Lord God of Abraham, Isaac, and Israel, answer me and let this people know that thou art God and that thou hast turned their hearts back." Abraham, Isaac, and Jacob recalled the stepping stones of the community's faith. Abraham was the one who left everything behind to respond to the promise of God in faith. Isaac means God's laughter and reminds us of the need of humor that keeps us from taking ourselves too seriously. Israel was the name given Jacob and means one who wrestles with God. It is in our response in faith to the promise of God, to the humor of life and the joy of God, and our willingness to wrestle at decisive points in our lives with the presence of God that we experience the power of God in our lives.

It was then that fire fell and consumed the sacrifice. It is then that the power of God's presence absorbs our fears, insecurities, and empowers us to face life in the power of God's Spirit. To be born again is to suddenly recognize how our mugwumping has been ineffectual in enabling us to experience the depth of life. To be born again is to realize that our attempt to secure ourselves against the insecurities of life and to satisfy our desires through indulgence is hopeless. When each of us reviews the journey of our life, the stepping stones that have brought us to this moment, it begins to dawn on us how often there has been a hint of the divine presence waiting silently for us to respond.

Then, in promise, laughter, and struggle, we slowly begin to open ourselves to be guided by a power that is beyond us. We begin to allow ourselves to be grasped by a truth that empowers us to overcome our anxieties and to trust in the faithfulness of a love that transcends even our fear of death. It is this new life that was revealed to us by Jesus who lived in response to God's Spirit even though he was tempted by the same human realities that we are.

It is a new birth, a new beginning to life. It is a life lived in response to the promise of the Spirit rather than a life lived in response to the fears of the flesh. It may happen in an explosive experience that seems to overwhelm us or, for many of us, it may slowly dawn on us through a series of experiences that confront us with what we really trust in life and nurtures us into greater and greater trust in God whose love increasingly sets us free for the promise of life lived in the Spirit. Amen.

Proper 5
Pentecost 3
Ordinary Time 10
1 Kings 17:1-24

The Sinner And The Sinned Against

Each of us experiences the world as both sinner and the sinned against. When we act in a way or even refuse to work against a condition that violates our relationship with God, other people, or the natural world, we are sinners. When we experience the painful result of a sinful world, whether it be a disease, poverty, a tragic accident, prejudice, or the violence of war or crime, we are the sinned against. Most often we are both sinners and the sinned against. At different times we are more one than the other.

When we are the sinner, the gospel is clear that we must repent or turn our lives around and stop sinning. The story of Elijah is helpful in knowing how to respond when we are the sinned against. The first thing that you note in the story is that God cares for the faithful. When Elijah told Ahab of the coming drought he, too, would be subject to those conditions. It was God who directed him to go to the Wadi Cherith, which was east of the Jordan, and hide himself. There he found water to drink and the ravens fed him. It is interesting that the term for ravens can mean Arabs. We are either experiencing God's love through a miracle of animal behavior or through the power of God's love to heal the human barriers that separate us.

The next thing we learn from the story is that God's care does not mean we are free from danger and suffering. Even though at first he was fed by the ravens or Arabs and had water to drink at the Wadi Cherith, eventually that resource also dried up and Elijah was faced with the problem of survival. Not only that, but he faced

251

the very real danger of the armies of Ahab who were searching for him.

God sent him to a foreign land. Elijah fled to Phoenician territory, outside the territory of the faithful. It raises the question for us of when God's people, Jewish or Christian, become so faithless that we must flee from them for protection.

(3) When God sent Elijah to Zarephath, foreign territory, he made clear that God was already at work preparing for his care. God's actions were not restricted to the faith community or the territory where they were active. It is also clear that God's ministry comes to us from the least expected and most unlikely sources. The person to whom Elijah was to go was a widow with a small child. Elijah was told that this foreign widow would feed him.

The conventional wisdom is that if you need help go to the strong, the resourceful, or the affluent. God did not send Elijah to an Israelite who could at least offer national and communal loyalty. God did not send him to a member of the community of faith who could offer him the resources of faith. God did not send him to a rich person who could offer material resources. God did not send him to someone who was self-sufficient and could teach him survival skills and strength. God did not even send him to one who was aware of God's calling. At least then that person could offer a witness of reassurance. God sent Elijah to a poverty-stricken widow who could not even provide for herself and her son. God sent Elijah to the weak rather than the strong.

(4) That leads to the fourth lesson that we learn from the story. God's ministry does not always come from people who are aware that they have something to offer. When Elijah asked the widow for help, her response was that she had nothing to give. "As the Lord your God lives, I have nothing baked, only a handful of meal in a jar, and a little oil in a jug; I am now gathering a couple of sticks, so that I may go home and prepare it for myself and my son, that we may eat, and die" (v. 12). The widow of Zarephath believed that her condition robbed her of having anything to offer. She was only aware that she was one of the sinned against.

Faith, in the form of Elijah, approached the widow, not as a sinner who needed to repent but as one who was sinned against.

252

She had been sinned against by the prejudice in a society that consigned women who had lost their husbands to the forgotten of the world. She had been sinned against by poverty because she had no earning power and was slowly descending to the point of starvation. She had been beaten down in the world, and she was prepared to die.

When faith approaches the sinned against in us, those times in our lives when fate has dealt us a cruel blow, we are called upon to recognize that we are of value. Faith brings us the strength and resources to resist the evil that threatens us.

Faith, in the form of Elijah, gave the widow a renewed awareness of her own value. Elijah treated her as someone who had something to offer. He encouraged her to resist the evil that threatened to consume her and her son.

> *Do not be afraid; go and do as you have said; but first make me a little cake of it and bring it to me, and afterward make something for yourself and your son; For thus says the Lord the God of Israel; "The jar of meal will not be emptied and the jug of oil will not fail until the day that the Lord sends rain on the earth."*
> — 1 Kings 17:13-14

His message was that she should not give in to the power of death. Reach out to me, he said by his request, and God will not forget you.

The columnist George Will once wrote a column called "Disposable Relationships" in which he lamented how willing we are to dispose of relationships that seem to offer the possibility of unpleasantness — whether it is a rocky marriage or a handicapped child. As counterintuitive as it is, how often have we heard parents of handicapped children, which the world often sees as weaker, report what a blessing that child has been to their family — the weaker feeding the stronger.

Does not the Bible repeat this theme time and again? If you think you are too old or too young, too weak, too sick, too weary, too inarticulate, too pressed down by the woes of the world or the burdens of your own life to experience the truth of God, go first not to the wise, the articulate, the self-sufficient, but rather make a renewed commitment to reach out to the weaker, the sicker, the more oppressed. Regardless of whether their condition is because of the structure of society or because of some tragedy or disease, they are the sinned against of the world. Reach out to the sinned against; treat them with value; encourage them to resist that which is beating them down; offer to share with them what strength you have, and you, too, will be fed. Amen.

Proper 6
Pentecost 4
Ordinary Time 11
1 Kings 21:1-10 (11-14) 15-21a

On Loan From God

Sometimes it is hard to understand what it is in human nature that allows people to become so crass in their dealings with each other. We have all had the experience of being treated like a thing — a nonperson whose only value is to be used by someone else to accomplish their goals. No one likes that. We all want to be treated with the dignity that we believe belongs to humans.

I think that some of the problem may be that we have forgotten how to treat things with proper respect. The degradation of the environment is ample testimony to our failure in that respect. When we do not know how to treat things with respect, it becomes doubly confusing when we then try to treat people with respect.

The story of the interchange between King Ahab, the anointed king of Israel, and his neighbor, Naboth the Jezreelite, can serve as an effective parable for what is happening in our society. To properly hear this story I would ask you not to identify with Naboth too quickly. Ahab is known as the anointed one of Israel. The Hebrew word for anointed is *messiah* and in Greek it is christ. As Christians we are called to be God's anointed or Christians. Therefore, the story becomes a cautionary tale about us.

One day Ahab looked out his palace window and saw a vineyard owned by Naboth the Jezreelite. As he gazed at the vineyard, it occurred to him that this small piece of land next to his palace would make an excellent garden. A curious feature of this story is that vineyards are usually planted on rocky soil and, also, they make the soil too alkaline to make a good vegetable garden. Right

255

away we know that Ahab was no farmer. It was not for love of the land but for the love of possessions that Ahab was motivated.

Ahab is not an evil man. Like many of us he simply saw what he wanted and evaluated his ability to obtain it. Being a relatively honorable king, Ahab went to visit Naboth himself. Imagine the president of the United States visiting you personally to negotiate a deal.

Ahab began his negotiation from a generous position. "I would like to have your vineyard for a vegetable garden and in return I will get you an even better piece of land. Or, if you are tired of working the land, I will give you an excellent price in money."

Being the king and accustomed to getting his way, Ahab concluded his offer and began to suck on a grape as he let it dawn on Naboth how generous and fair his beloved king really was. What would you have done if you were Naboth?

What Naboth did was explode in anger. "The Lord forbid that I should give you my ancestor's inheritance." Right away you know that there is something more going on than merely the commercial value of the land. We do not have the dialogue to explain Naboth's reaction, but because we know the Israelite faith, we can imagine it.

"I can understand how some pagan king who has no sense can make such an offer, but how can the king of Israel say such a thing? You should know that this land does not belong to me any more than the land your palace stands on belongs to you. All land belongs to God."

"But," said Ahab, "what would God care if I took your land and gave you another equally valuable piece of land in return?" For Ahab, the issue is value for value on a monetary basis.

"Land in Israel," responded Naboth, "is on loan from God for the sake not just of your present family but to sustain all the generations of your family line in the future. How we care for the land, what we do with it is a way of honoring or dishonoring God. God has provided each family line in Israel with enough land to provide for the basic necessities of food, shelter, and clothing. You know how the prophets rail against those who gather great land holdings at the expense of others who are left landless. We even have the

256

year of jubilee every fifty years to redistribute the land in order to make sure that the generous provisions of God are not distorted by the greed of humanity."

"But," sputtered Ahab, "I will give you another piece of land, even a better one. You will be better off."

"Don't you understand our own faith?" responded Naboth. "God gave this land to my ancestors in trust for me. I, in turn, must provide for the children yet to come. It is a sacred trust."

Was Naboth wrong in clinging to this ancient tradition? Are we not free to see land and other parts of nature as simply things to use to benefit us? Does our faith really obligate us to consider such transactions from God's viewpoint and from the perspective of how it will affect the generations that come after us? How different our environmental debates would be if we held that perspective.

Let me attempt to provide a contemporary parallel for us. Sally leases a home on Cape Cod for the summer. It is an absolutely gorgeous setting with surf pounding the rocks below, clear summer breezes, and a beautiful blue sky. It is a wonderful place for her two teenage sons who love to sail. In the first week, they already made friends with some boys down the beach.

The owner had made a generous lease agreement because of his friendship with her grandparents. Those same grandparents had given her a cash gift for her birthday that made the whole deal possible. It was the perfect setting for some regeneration of her spirit after the loss of her husband a little over a year ago. She felt undergirded and sustained by this beautiful setting.

A week into their summer stay, a wealthy neighbor on the cape decides that the little house in which Sally and her sons are staying would be a perfect spillover for guests that he wished to have visit him during the summer. He comes to Sally and says, "Look, in the past I have not had the best relationship with the owner of this place, but I want to make a deal with you that will benefit both of us. I will find you another place with an equally beautiful setting and even more room. I will also give you a generous cash bonus that could make your summer even more pleasurable. I promise that I will take excellent care of the place. The owner will never have to know and we will all benefit."

Should Sally accept the deal? After all, who is it going to hurt? And she and her neighbor will benefit. In Sally's situation, we begin to feel the tug at our conscience. She would be taking advantage of the original owner, who, after all, had been very generous in the lease agreement. She would also risk dishonoring the friendship of her grandparents with the owner. Even if no one ever found out, the profit that she would make on the deal would be based on deceit. And, once she had made the deal, since it was based on violating the trust of the owner, she would have little control over whether the neighbor respected the property or not.

Like Naboth, we as a nation and as individuals have to decide whether what we have is a trust or a possession. If what we have received in this life is a possession, then we have no obligation to others or any future generations. We are free to exploit it for what we can get now. But, if all that we have is on loan to us for a higher purpose intended by God for all generations, then our lives are to be lived according to that higher purpose, and we are accountable. Most of us do not scheme to take someone's land away, but most of us do get the balance between trust and possessions confused.

In our marriages and our parenting we declare that our relationships come first. Yet in order to possess more things, we often sacrifice time needed to nurture those very relationships. The reason we come to worship is because we believe that our relationship with God is important. Yet the work we do to enable us to have more things often so exhausts us that we choose to sacrifice time with God to get away and get rested so that we can get back to work.

It is not easy to keep the right perspective between relationships and possessions in a world that keeps pushing things. God cares and has provided us the resources by which we might realize the fullness of life. Realizing that fullness requires time with God and each other, we dare not lose sight of that necessary balance between things and relationships. Amen.

At Points Of Despair

It seems almost inevitable that people who experience the highs of life are also going to experience the lows in life. No one lives on a perpetual high. There are always peaks and valleys. The disciples accompanied Jesus to the mount to witness his transfiguration, but after that they descended into the valley below.

Have you ever noticed how often the low comes right after the peaks? As a Christian you aren't called upon to always be on a high. Rather, you are called on to look for the presence of God in both the highs and the lows of life. That is true for individual Christians and for Christian churches.

The story of Elijah is the faith biography for many of us. Elijah was one of the great prophets of the Bible. He lived in the time of King Ahab and Queen Jezebel.

Ahab had formed a political alliance with his marriage to Jezebel. When Jezebel moved into the palace, she wanted to bring her gods with her. You can imagine Ahab at first resisting. "That's just not the way things are done here, Jezebel."

Jezebel wasn't to be easily dissuaded, however, and she pleaded, "But Ahab, your God is so stern and demanding. My gods will add a little variety and spice to the people's lives."

Jezebel was urging Ahab and Israel to mellow out and not be so exclusive in their practice of faith. The Bible is a great book but there are lots of great books. Worship is a good thing to do on Sunday morning but there is nothing like a good game of golf on a sunny Sunday. Justice and mercy are great virtues but one must recognize the practical reality that money rules the world.

Faithfulness in marriage is important but the *Bridges of Madison County* is more entertaining.

Jezebel didn't reject Israel's God but simply wanted to balance life a little and have some fun as well. Elijah, the prophet, said, "No." "How long will you go limping with two different opinions?" (1 Kings 18:21). Choose this day who you will worship.

Then Elijah challenged the gods of Baal to a contest on Mount Carmel. And when they had all built altars to their gods — sex, wealth, power, hate, selfishness — Elijah also built an altar to his God. After the other priests had tried futilely to get their gods to show themselves, after all the other passions of life had failed to satisfy the hunger of the soul, Elijah called on God to accept his sacrifice and fire came down from heaven and consumed his sacrifice.

It was a great victory for Elijah, but then it happened. Jezebel was furious at Elijah for spoiling all the fun in life. She sent him a message and said, "You are not the only one who can play rough. I'm going to have your head."

"Don't you understand," responded Elijah, "I have demonstrated that there is only one true God."

Jezebel said, "I don't care what you have demonstrated. I'm going to have your head."

Elijah had won a great victory and yet the world was still full of the same temptations and evil. What good does it do to fight the battles if nothing ever changes? Elijah ran to the desert. Elijah fled to the desert of despair. Elijah found a solitary broom tree to provide shade, and he laid down and asked God to let him die.

We work hard for some good cause. We try to solve hunger by working for the CROP walk or serving the hungry at a soup kitchen but after all that work, people are still hungry. We gather our energies together to help build a Habitat house for a worthy person, but after they move in, there are thousands like them without a home. We become worried about the marriages that are falling apart, so we organize marriage enrichment seminars and premarital counseling. Then after all that effort, marriages still fall apart.

There comes a time when we want to run to the desert. We want to retire from doing good. We want to quit tilting against windmills. We want to say with Elijah, I have tried to be faithful but it isn't doing any good. I want to retire to Arizona and play in the sun. I want to quit working in the church and let someone else do it. I'm frustrated with church conflict, so I'm going to quit going to worship.

Then, if you are lucky, like Elijah, you feel a tap on your shoulder. You can imagine Elijah saying, "Go away, don't you see I'm trying to sleep? I don't care if I ever wake up. Stop bothering me." But the tap, tap, tap is persistent.

If you really pay attention to God at those points of despair, you realize that God is ready to provide you food for the journey. "Get up," said the angel to Elijah. "You must eat and drink or you won't have strength for the journey."

Now this is the first time Elijah knew that there was a journey ahead of him. He, you will remember, had planned to just die and everything would be over. When we are feeling sorry for ourselves, when we allow ourselves to be depressed, it is natural not to consider the future.

Like Elijah, when things don't go our way, we want to slink away and lick our wounds. Yet, for the faithful, even in our despair, there is that tap, tap, tap on our shoulder. God gently tries to awaken us from our self-absorbed slumber and open us to the greater journey ahead of us.

If we will awaken, God wants to provide us food for the journey. Elijah traveled forty days and forty nights to Mount Horeb, also known as Mount Sinai. This was where Moses was given the ten commandments that formed the community of Israel. Elijah had traveled back to the source.

When a church loses its vision, it begins to turn on itself, just like a depressed person turns anger inward, and we are robbed of the energy to go on. That is the time for a church to return to the source, to enter a time of prayer and to review the basic core of the faith.

When Elijah returned to the source, God asked that terrifying question, "What are you doing here, Elijah?" (v. 9). Why have you come back to the source if you are ready to crawl in a cave and feel sorry for yourself?

261

Elijah began to defend himself. "I have been the faithful one while everyone around me has been desecrating your commandments." I have been faithful while the church has been ignoring the clear commands of scripture. I've done my work, Lord; it's the others who have let you down.

God said to Elijah, "Go out and stand on the mountain before the Lord" (v. 11).

Elijah went out. There came a great howling, screeching, rock shattering wind, but God was not in the wind. After the wind, there came a mountain-shaking, chasm-producing, earth-shattering earthquake, but God was not in the earthquake. And after the earthquake, there was rock-melting, ore-purifying, searing fire, but God was not in the fire.

Then came a sheer, deafening, overwhelming silence, and in the silence, God gave Elijah his next assignment. God was not through with Elijah yet.

It is not in the winds of doctrine that we find our God. It is not in the earthquakes of dispute that we find our God. It is not in the hot fire of debate that we find our God. Churches and individuals, as they probe the depths of their souls, find in the silence, when all the egos are put aside and we are really listening, that God is not through with us yet.

For Elijah it was to anoint kings and ordain prophets to move the world forward according to God's agenda. We were meant for God like a deer longs for flowing streams. Our soul thirsts for God, for the living God (Psalm 42).

When we reflect back on our history, how we have continued in the procession with glad shouts and songs of thanksgiving as a multitude feasting on the goodness of God, our memory drives us on. God has been faithful to this church for 2,000 years and invites us to listen for God's purpose in our life together, and we continue to move forward.

By day the Lord commands his steadfast love, and at night God's song is with us, a prayer to the God of our life. Whether we are elated or despairing about any given moment in church life, we are called to stand before God and listen to how God wants us to respond to this moment in our life together. Amen.

Seeing A Chariot Of Fire

I think that we are in a battle for the soul of the church. I'm not just talking about my Presbyterian denomination, although it certainly has its problems. I'm suggesting that we are in a battle for the soul of the whole church in our time.

Wherever you turn, the church is changing and evolving toward something new, though it is not yet clear what that new form will look like. Our forms of worship are being challenged by repeated experiments to appeal to a new generation. Denominational loyalties are falling apart and many churches are trying to distance themselves from their own denomination. Many churches have even removed the denominational identity from their name and speak of themselves as a community church.

At the time of the Reformation, there was an attempt to define what made for a true church. Their basic definition was that a true church was where the word of God is truly preached and the sacraments are rightly administered. The battles were over a doctrinal understanding of the faith. Today the battles within churches are largely over ethics rather than doctrine. We are greatly disturbed about issues surrounding abortion, divorce, or sexual orientation but do not worry so much about predestination, atonement, the definition of filioque, or the meaning of sanctification.

Consumerism has so infected us that the first question for many church programs is what will please people rather than what will please God. We are moving through a time of change and as it says in 1 John 3:2, "Beloved, we are God's children now; what we will be has not yet been revealed." The question for Christians is how to remain faithful when it is hard to tell what it means to be faithful.

I direct your attention to our lectionary passage about that great prophet Elijah. Elijah is only one of two people in the Hebrew scriptures that we are told did not die. We don't know much about the other one, but we do know a fair amount about Elijah. Elijah didn't die but was taken up to God in a chariot of fire. We sing about him in that old spiritual, "Swing Low Sweet Chariot."

Because he did not die, the tradition developed that Elijah would return to prepare the way for the Messiah. If you are fortunate enough to be invited by Jewish friends to celebrate the Passover with them, you will note that there is a vacant chair at the table. That is the chair for Elijah. In what we call the New Testament, it is suggested that John the Baptist was Elijah returned to prepare the way for the Messiah, which in Greek is called the Christ. John even dressed in garments reflective of how Elijah was described in the Hebrew scriptures.

Elijah, as a transitional figure, shows us how we are to act in times of great change. Elijah prepares the way for us when things have grown chaotic. In our scripture lesson, Elijah and Elisha, his presumed successor, knows that things are about to change. What will happen is unclear but that something significant will happen is quite plain. In preparation for whatever is going to happen, the two prophets go on a journey.

Like the church, when we experience great changes taking place, Elijah and Elisha tried to revisit the great touchstones of their faith. They wanted to get back to fundamentals. First they went to Bethel where their ancestor, Jacob, had this strange dream of a ladder extending between heaven and earth. It had been a time of critical change in Jacob's life. He named that place Bethel, which is Hebrew for house of God. Like a church that wants to return to the way things were when all seemed right, so Elijah and Elisha wanted to return to where heaven and earth seemed well connected. Surely if Elijah was being taken up to heaven, it would happen here. But nothing happened.

Next Elijah traveled to Jericho, the place where the walls came tumbling down at the sound of the trumpet. This was the great turning point in the battle that enabled Israel to enter the promised land. Elijah and Elisha wanted to relive the moment of great victory when Israel had felt strong in the faith and God had clearly been on their side. It was like a pilgrimage to a great religious shrine. Surely this is where they could be close to God but nothing happened.

So they travel on to the Jordan River, that greatest of all rivers in Israel's existence. When they arrived, Elijah struck the water and it parted just like Moses parted the waters of the Red Sea. This recalled the great moment of liberation of the people of Israel. As a church we often seek places where we can experience clear signs of God's presence, signs of great spiritual awakening on the part of members. But even when we have traveled to the spot, like Elijah's protégé, Elisha, we still face an uncertain future.

Elijah asked Elisha, "Tell me what I may do for you before I am taken from you" (v. 9). Elisha responded, as we might respond, "Let me inherit a double measure of your spirit" (v. 9). Let me have a faith that can endure all the challenges of the future. Let me grasp the truth in a way that cannot be challenged.

Elijah responded, "If you see me as I am being taken from you, then it will be granted to you but if not, it will not" (v. 10).

Here we enter the great mystery of the church on which the soul of our faith rests. Here is where we have been journeying all along. The test of Elisha's faith is whether he can see the invisible framework behind the visible reality of life.

This is what I mean. When Elijah had walked with Elisha a little further, suddenly there was a chariot of fire that separated them and Elijah ascended into heaven in a whirlwind. If anyone else had been standing there, they might have seen a great whirlwind pick Elijah up but only Elisha saw the chariot of fire behind the whirlwind. Only Elisha could see the power of God made visible in the chariot working behind the scenes to transport Elijah to heaven.

When you look at the church, what do you see? Many see a building, people, and an organization. All these things are visible and measurable. How big is your building? How many people attend worship? How many joined last year? What type of programs do you offer? But if you look through the obvious and the visible, can you see the invisible and the incredible presence of God?

As Christians we affirm the words recorded in Ephesians 1:22-23 that God "has put all things under (Christ's) feet and has made him the head over all things for the church, which is his body, the fullness of him who fills all in all." Behind the visible signs of the church as an organization of people who join together on their journey of faith, there is an invisible force that is shaping the people of God as the church.

I recognize that there are lots of storms swirling around the church as we move forward into God's future. From the outside, it may appear that the church is caught in a whirlwind that may destroy it. When Elisha saw the real presence of God behind all that was visible, he knew that whatever the future held, God held the future. Christ is the head of the body we call the church, and Christ is not going to lose that with which he has been entrusted.

As Jesus promised Peter, Christ will build his church, and the gates of hell will not prevail against it (Matthew 16:18). Behind the visible organization that will inevitably change as it has in a variety of ways in the last 2,000 years, there is an invisible presence. For those who see it, they will not be afraid. Amen.

The Naaman Syndrome

The healing of Naaman, commander of the army of the king of Aram, seems to me to provide a metaphor for our time. We live in a world in which we pay attention to power and the powerful. We look to the powerful for the solutions to our world's problems. Naaman was one of those powerful people. He was a prominent commander of the army of Aram, a neighboring nation to Israel.

Even powerful people have problems. We are told that despite all his success and honor, Naaman had a problem that he could not solve. All that power and praise could not provide Naaman that which he most needed in life. Naaman was a leper.

His leprosy, a physical malady, is an effective metaphor for those diseases of the soul that plague so much of our society today. There is something desperately sick in our society that is ripping us apart. And all our power, success, and enormous affluence can't make it go away.

It goes by many names, but it produces the same result. Our politics are a sham. Our religious congregations squabble among themselves until people walk out in disgust. Our schools spend hours arguing over the tangential and fail at the essential. Our families are falling apart and our children are killing each other.

It is instructive to notice in the story of Naaman where the first signs of hope come from. In his society, it was from the lowest of the low — a slave girl captured in battle. It was a captured slave in a class-conscious society. It was a woman in a man's society. It was not from the powerful or famous but from the place where he would least expect it that the first glimmer of hope came to Naaman.

267

Think about that — from where would you least expect hope to come for those problems that plague our society?

Sometimes you are desperate enough to pay attention to anything. So Naaman did listen to the voice of this insignificant slave girl. But note how he acted on what he had heard. Naaman was a man of the world. He assumed that when you wanted to get something done, you went to the powers that be. So he went to his king and got a letter of introduction to Israel's king. He also understood that there was no free lunch, so he took along with him expensive gifts of gold, jewelry, and fine cloths.

He would discover that the gift of healing doesn't belong to the rich and the famous. The wise and the powerful don't always have the answers you seek. You can pay for all the expensive seminars you want and order the finest exercise equipment or join the latest spiritualist fad, but the healing you seek is not there.

When the King of Israel heard Naaman's request, he rent his clothes and said, "Am I God, to give death or life, that this man sends word to me to cure a man of his leprosy?" (v. 7). It was a common saying in Israel that only God could raise the dead or cure someone of leprosy. "This man is trying to pick a quarrel with me," said the king.

Fortunately God's grace does not lack a witness even when we are looking in the wrong places. The prophet Elisha heard what the king had said, so he sent word to his king saying: "Stop acting like an idiot and send Naaman to me so that he might realize where the real power of the universe is."

So Naaman, thinking he now had the correct information, went riding up to Elisha's house with his full entourage. You can picture this great cloud of dust, the noise of numerous chariots, perhaps the clanking of armor, maybe even a trumpet or two — certainly not a subtle approach.

Naaman seemed to be saying, "I have come for a healing and I want you to know what an important person it is that is asking you for your help."

In case we missed the fact that God doesn't work according to the world's criteria and expectations, Elisha didn't even bother to go out to greet his important guest. He sent a messenger out on his behalf. This great warrior who had come with his abundant gifts didn't even merit a personal greeting.

Not only did the prophet not recognize Naaman's importance, but the message itself seemed a slap at his ego as well. "Go and wash in the Jordan seven times." An insignificant messenger told him to wash in a two-bit muddy stream in a third-rate country. Naaman was furious. "I thought for *me* he would surely come out, and stand and call on the name of the Lord his God and would wave his hand over the spot and cure the leprosy!"

Such an important person with such a serious, incurable disease, deserved a dramatic healing complete with the role of stirring drums, clashing cymbals, perhaps a few bolts of lightning, and some smoke and mirrors.

Naaman almost missed the grace of God again. This time it was one of his servants who had to set him straight. Have you ever noticed how we can let our ego get in the way of the cure we seek? We look in the wrong places for the signs of God's grace in our lives. We would far rather pay a few thousand dollars for an expensive consultant to cure our problems than to overhear the truth of faith available to us every week. And, we expect our problems to be so significant that the cure must be dramatic if it is to be worthwhile.

How many millions of dollars have companies paid to reduce stress in the lives of their executives? I'll tell you how to reduce stress for free. Set up about four or five sessions with your priest, rabbi, or pastor and seriously learn the discipline of prayer. Spend twenty minutes twice a day totally focused on God in prayer. Remember the sabbath day and keep it holy.

Do you want to cure your marital problems? Ninety percent of them don't require expensive therapy. I can give you a simple formula for free. Each day from this day forward, without fanfare, choose to do something nice for your spouse. Each day without fail, find twenty minutes to seriously listen to your spouse. And twice a day, consciously give thanks to God for this human partner who has had the grace to put up with someone like you.

The problem, of course, is that both of those formulas sound a lot like washing in the muddy Jordan seven times. Surely it requires something more dramatic than that.

I'll give you a more dramatic suggestion. Go home today and double your pledge to whatever church you belong. If it's truly God's house, that is a worthy investment. Follow the advice I have given you on stress and marriage for six months. If these suggestions are not true, ask for your money back.

God has been gracious enough to knock on your door this year. It is up to you whether you will open the door and accept what God offers you. Amen.

Proper 10
Pentecost 8
Ordinary Time 15
Amos 7:7-17

When God Measures The Church

We begin to hear about prophets in the Bible after Israel convinced God to let them have a king. It was almost as if God set up his own checks and balances system. Once the people looked to a king and the government to guide them, God also called prophets to remind the government that it, too, was subject to God.

There were apparently professional prophets in Israel who served as ethical advisors to the king, but occasionally a voice arose that challenged the very nature of the society. Amos was one of those unique voices.

By his own admission, he was not a professional prophet or one of the king's ethical advisors. He was better described as a migrant worker who trimmed fig trees in season and hired out as a shepherd at other times. He lived in Judah, the southern nation after the split that formed two nations — Judah in the south and Israel in the north.

Though he lived in the south, he had a series of visions in which God spoke to him through images and commanded him to go and prophesy at the sanctuaries of Israel in the north. He was an outsider both by geography and profession. Who would listen to such a person?

He also came with his disturbing message at a time when things looked very comfortable for Israel. There was no imminent war with any neighbor, the political situation was stable, the economy was very strong, and people were flocking to places of worship. What more could you ask for?

271

But Amos saw the shadow side of what was taking place in Israel. While there were many who prospered in Israel, there was also a widening gap between the rich and the poor. Decisions were made on the basis of economics rather than compassion for the needy in society. They bought "the poor for silver and the needy for a pair of sandals," declared Amos (Amos 8:6a).

People would use their prosperity to build both summer and winter homes and then, having spent all their wealth on themselves, were reluctant givers to acts of charity. He denounced wealthy women as "cows of Bashan ... who oppress the poor, who crush the needy, who say to their husbands, 'Bring something to drink!' " (Amos 4:1).

He denounced the courts that seemed more responsive to the needs of those with money than they were to the poor. He was a fierce critic of people who would flock to the places of worship on the sabbath but did not see any connection between their worship of God and the suffering of the poor, the helpless, and the needy.

Picture Amos coming into a full sanctuary of worshipers and declaring in the name of God these words:

> *I hate, I despise your festivals, and I take no delight in your solemn assemblies ... Take away from me the noise of your songs; I will not listen to the melody of your harps. But let justice roll down like waters and righteousness like an ever flowing stream.*
> — Amos 5:21-24

You probably have not heard a lot of sermons based on Amos. What is a preacher to do with the message of Amos? How do you think you personally would respond if a preacher tried to apply the message of Amos to our life and our culture?

You have heard repeatedly that the United States is a very religious country. Huge megachurches are filled each week with thousands of worshipers. Millions are raised for charity, and the works of compassion that are performed by church members are too numerous to count.

At the same time there is a shadow side to our lives. While we would not directly approve of selling out the poor for a pair of shoes, some of us have investments that probably make a profit from underpaid labor. Certainly we benefit from corporations that will lay off workers to make the stockholders a better profit or move a factory out of a local town in order to find cheaper labor.

I repeat that I am as uncomfortable with Amos' words as many of you are. I had a pastor friend of mine from Detroit who used to berate me for living off money connected with tobacco. I would remind him of how many people were killed in automobiles made in Detroit that could have been made much safer if they weren't so interested in making a maximum profit. The truth of the matter is that we are all living in an ambiguous world. Few of us have the ability to cast the first stone.

So what is a preacher to do with the words of the prophet? For that matter, what is a congregation who wants to be faithful to do with such uncomfortable words in our Bible?

Prior to this passage, Amos had two other visions in which God declared a judgment against Israel — one by locust and another by fire. Each time Amos begged God to forgive rather than punish the people for their sins. I do find that an appropriate task for a pastor. I do beg God to forgive us as a congregation and as a nation and not to punish us for our sins.

Then came this third vision. Amos saw God holding a plumb line against a wall. God announced that he was setting a plumb line in the midst of his people, Israel. God was going to measure Israel against his standards of justice and compassion. Amos was called to enter the largest sanctuary in Israel and proclaim his vision.

He proclaimed that the great sanctuaries would become desolate, and the king of Israel would be killed and the people would be led off into exile. While eventually this all happened, at the time it sounded harsh and unrealistic.

As you might imagine, neither the people nor the high priest, Amaziah, were pleased with Amos' message. Amaziah attacked Amos for being an outsider, suggested that he was a paid troublemaker, and questioned whether or not he was a traitor to the society. We aren't told whether they arrested or even killed Amos when he refused to shut up, but we can certainly understand that, at best, he might be dismissed as a crackpot and, at worst, a threat to the well-being of a prosperous society.

So I return to the question, "What are we to do if God is measuring us as a church against God's standards of faithfulness?" Even before we get to God's demand that we "let justice roll down like waters and righteousness like an ever flowing stream," we find ourselves frequently falling short on God's demand for keeping the sabbath and returning a minimum of 10% of what God has given us.

In Luke 10:23-37, we have the parable of the good Samaritan. You know the basics of the story. A man fell among robbers and was left by the side of the road. Along came a priest and a Levite who both passed him by on the other side. Then came a Samaritan, who didn't belong to the faith. This Samaritan outsider had compassion and went out of his way and at great expense to care for the wounded man.

This story, on a personal level, was similar to Amos' declaration on a national level. The message was essentially the same. Our fate depends upon our understanding that God does have a standard of justice and mercy and expects us to be responsive to it. We live in a world and society that desperately needs to hear the words of the prophets. We need to hear these words, not because they are comforting but because they shake us out of any temptation to complacency so that God might get a word in edgewise.

However hard we try, none of us are a righteous people. Life is too ambiguous for such purity. But it is only as we are honest with our sinfulness that we can appreciate the enormity of God's grace that continues to love us.

In the words of 1 John 1:8-9, "If we say that we have no sin, we deceive ourselves, and the truth is not in us. If we confess our sins, he who is just will ... cleanse us from all unrighteousness." Amen.

274

Proper 11
Pentecost 9
Ordinary Time 16
Amos 8:1-12

When The Fruit Is Spoiled

When we speak of Amos today, we know that he was one of Israel's great prophets. Yet at the time when Amos spoke, he took pains to remind us that he was just an ordinary migrant worker. What he spoke were the words God had shown him.

God spoke to him through a series of visions that came to Amos when he was in worship. As he participated in these common rituals of worship, which he and others had seen hundreds of times, this time the ritual had a clarity that it had never had before. It is the fourth vision that I want to focus on.

The fourth vision given to Amos was a basket of summer fruit. It was the annual offering of the firstfruits of the harvest. The offering was at the conclusion of the harvest and in anticipation of winter rains that prepared for fresh plantings. People would bring a fresh basket of the finest of their harvest and place it on the altar as a gift of thanksgiving to God.

The offering took place as it did each year, but suddenly something stirred within this particular migrant worker. It was as if God was saying to Amos, "What do you see?"

Amos responded with the obvious, "A basket of summer fruit" (v. 2). And there was silence as the words played over in Amos' mind.

To understand what happened next, you must understand that Hebrews loved to play with words. Punning, rhyming, and word associations were normal for them. The Hebrew word for summer fruit was *quayits*, and it had a rhyming quality with *qets*, the word for end.

275

It would be similar to Amos seeing a party with a band and dancing and God saying, "What do you see?" and Amos responding, "I see revelry" and God would respond, "Perhaps you should see reveille — the trumpet awakening the people."

For Amos, God was saying the ripe fruit suggested not thanksgiving for harvest and trust for winter rains but an "end" to the relationship with God. What looked so ripe and beautiful was on the verge of being spoiled and rotten. This last basket of summer fruit spoke of the end time. God confirmed this by saying, "The end has come upon my people Israel, I will never again pass them by" (v. 2b).

Amos' message was an angry message and hard to hear. Yet he was angry because he feared for the soul of Israel. He was fearful that God was going to reach the limits of divine patience and give up on the people. Despite the fact that people were actively participating in acts of worship, Amos believed that they were turning their backs on God.

If Amos was to parallel his message to us today, he would be focusing on how our materialistic culture is driving us away from God. Using Amos' images let me take you down that path and see what you conclude.

First Amos sees people becoming over-identified with their work and losing any vital sense that they are reflectors of God in their lives.

> *Hear this, you that trample on the needy, and bring to ruin the poor of the land, saying, "When will the new moon be over so that we may sell grain; and the sabbath, so that we may offer wheat for sale?"*
> — Amos 8:4-5

You know that the sabbath and the service of the new moon were religious festivals. Both were times when people were to cease work and refocus on their connection with God in whose image they derived the meaning of their lives. They were doing that, but Amos detected a restlessness as if their bodies were in worship but their minds were already making business plans for when the sabbath was over.

Setting aside for a moment the connection between that attitude and its impact on the poor and the needy, are there signs in our society that commercialism is more important than worship? We can easily make generalizations, but let me provide you with a simple test for yourself.

Let us say that you received two letters in the mail. Letter one said that the company was downsizing and your employment would no longer be necessary. Letter two said that the church had decided that you were not living up to what God asks of you, and therefore you would be barred from worshiping God in the future. Which letter would make you feel the most helpless?

Which would most threaten your sense of identity? Which would make you merely storm off in a rage proclaiming that no one can stop you from doing what you want to? My guess is that we are not nearly as frightened of church decisions about us as we are about secular decisions that affect our future.

We might even think that it is a silly question because we have a responsibility to feed our family and that is more directly affected by our work than our worship. We easily pray, "Give us this day our daily bread," and yet we assume it is our decisions, not God's, that will provide us with the bread we eat.

Now take the next step with Amos. He believed that when we make this disconnect between worship and work, we lose the core of our identity that can easily result in ethical lapses. When our identity is so tied up with our work, the pressure to succeed is so enormous that we push the envelope of what is acceptable. He accused the people of making "the ephah small and the shekel great, and practicing deceit with false balances, buying the poor for silver and the needy for a pair of sandals, and selling the sweepings of the wheat" (vv. 5b-6).

The *ephah* was the basket in which the wheat was measured and the suggestion was that the merchant had a deceptively small basket. The silver was weighed out with a scale with so much weight making a shekel, only here the weight was made to be extra heavy.

The result was more wheat was paid for with less money, thus shaving the profit in favor of the merchant. The sweepings of the wheat were the leftover wheat on the market floor that was to be

277

left for the poor to gather. To sweep them up for sale was to rob the poor of their food.

When your identity is tied up with your profession or work and success is measured by the margin of profit, the pressure is on to push the ethical boundaries in order to secure more profit. Most communities benefit from the charitable gifts of our local businesses. Yet as the market tightens and mergers occur, the lingering question is whether such community support will continue.

Again a personal test: You are asked to make a recommendation as to an action of your business or company. One way may be ethically fuzzy but the lawyers assure you they can win any legal case brought against the company, and it will in a manner enhance the profits of the company. The other way benefits employees but may cut into quarterly profits, which will cause stock prices to fall and therefore limit cash available to operate. On what basis do you make such decisions?

Is it even fair for Amos, or your pastor, to suggest that such decisions are connected with your worship of God? In fact, if you heard such words enough, might you decide that you wanted to find a church that would proclaim a more pleasant message?

Now comes the real difficulty with Amos' message. "The time is surely coming, says the Lord, when I will send a famine on the land; not a famine of bread, or thirst for water, but of hearing the words of the Lord" (v. 11). When we become so focused on our work that we grow restless when we are away from work, worship becomes a burden rather than a joy. Sabbath time becomes an interruption of what is important rather than a taste of heaven.

Another personal test: Which happens more often in your life?

1. You are working on a task at home or at work and suddenly your mind wanders to a moment in worship in which you experienced a sweet moment with God.
2. You are in worship and your mind suddenly wanders to a task at work or at home.

Amos confronts us head on with the question: "Who are you?" Has your life so drifted from the God who gave you birth and fills your life with meaning that your identity depends upon accomplishing tasks that can be taken from you in an instant of corporate decision making or a bad run of health?

I think Amos is right that our souls are in danger. That is not because we are evil people. We are not. It's not even because we don't wish to please God, we do. Rather, it may be because we have been so trapped in this crazy system that we don't know how to get out of it.

In the gospel lesson there is the familiar story of Jesus being in the home of Mary and Martha (Luke 10:38-42). Martha is feeling the burden of responsibilities of being host and complains about Mary who is simply sitting at Jesus' feet and listening. Jesus responds to Martha's complaint by saying, "Martha, Martha, you are worried and distracted by many things. There is need of only one thing. Mary has chosen the better part ..." (Luke 10:41-42).

My prayer for us is that we will recognize before it is too late to choose the better part. Amen.

Sermons On The First Readings

For Sundays
After Pentecost
(Middle Third)

When God Calls

Chrysanne Timm

A Marriage Made In Heaven

This is wedding season, and with the privilege of presiding at the weddings of many couples over the years, I have had the opportunity to hear how these people came to meet one another. Lately, internet dating networks have yielded more and more lasting relationships, but the majority of couples have met through the intervention of friends or family.

Once in a while a couple will meet in church, and once in a great while one or the other of them will say something like, "The Lord led me to _____." I always find those stories especially interesting because my husband and I fully believe that God was preparing us for one another and the adventure of married life and parenting that we would share.

As a pastor, I can't imagine hearing the kind of story the prophet Hosea might tell, were he and his fiancée, Gomer, doing premarital counseling with me ... can you?

> *When the Lord began to speak through Hosea, the Lord said to him, "Go, marry a promiscuous woman and have children with her...."*   — Hosea 1:2a (TNIV)

Central and core to the success of Christian marriage is the promise of lifelong faithfulness that each spouse makes to the other. But as Hosea takes Gomer to be his wife, he knows that she is promiscuous. He already knows that faithfulness will not be part of the fabric of their marriage. It seems that God is asking the impossible of Hosea in directing him to marry this woman.

283

But God has a reason for making this seemingly doomed match.

> *Go, marry a promiscuous woman and have children*
> *with her, for like an adulterous wife this land is guilty*
> *of unfaithfulness to the Lord.*   — Hosea 1:2 (TNIV)

Haven't we always been taught to trust that the Lord will do what is best for us? Haven't we been told that God will never give us more than we can handle? It would seem that when we are talking about challenging marriages, God has a very high opinion of Hosea, son of Beeri.

This isn't the first time that God has commanded a person who is faithful to God to do a very difficult thing.

In Genesis 6:14, the Lord commands Noah,

> *Make yourself an ark of cypress wood; make rooms in*
> *the ark, and cover it inside and out with pitch.*
> — Genesis 6:14

At first glance, this doesn't seem like such a difficult task, but we can only imagine how the rest of Noah's family reacted to his mission. And trying to gather two of every species of animal and loading them onto this ark? No doubt, Noah was the laughing stock of his neighbors as they watched his efforts.

In Genesis 12:1 we read about the first of God's commands to Abraham (then Abram).

> *Now the Lord said to Abram, "Go from your country*
> *and your kindred and your father's house to the land*
> *that I will show you."*   — Genesis 12:1

The land of Canaan that God would show Abram and Sarai was some 800 miles away from his homeland in Haran ... a long, hard journey for a couple in their seventies. But that wasn't the end of it. Their journey took them to Egypt when famine struck Canaan, and then back again to Beth-El in Canaan where Abram had first pitched their tent.

Abram is told by God that his descendents will be as numerous as the stars in the night sky (Genesis 15:6), but he is nearly 100 years old before he sees this promise guaranteed by the birth of a son Isaac to him and Sarah.

However, God's difficult demands don't stop there. In Genesis 22:1-10 we read the troubling story of God's command that Abraham offer his son as a burnt offering:

> *After these things God tested Abraham. He said to him, "Abraham!" And he said, "Here I am." He said, "Take your son, your only son Isaac, whom you love, and go to the land of Moriah, and offer him there as a burnt offering on one of the mountains that I shall show you." So Abraham rose early in the morning, saddled his donkey, and took two of his young men with him, and his son Isaac; he cut the wood for the burnt offering, and set out and went to the place in the distance that God had shown him. On the third day Abraham looked up and saw the place far away. Then Abraham said to his young men, "Stay here with the donkey; the boy and I will go over there; we will worship, and then we will come back to you." Abraham took the wood of the burnt offering and laid it on his son Isaac, and he himself carried the fire and the knife. So the two of them walked on together. Isaac said to his father Abraham, "Father!" And he said, "Here I am, my son." He said, "The fire and the wood are here, but where is the lamb for a burnt offering?" Abraham said, "God himself will provide the lamb for a burnt offering, my son." So the two of them walked on together.*
>
> *When they came to the place that God had shown him, Abraham built an altar there and laid the wood in order. He bound his son Isaac, and laid him on the altar, on top of the wood. Then Abraham reached out his hand and took the knife to kill his son.*
>
> — Genesis 22:1-10

I cannot read this story without shuddering. I cannot imagine the pain that Abraham felt in his heart as he walked with his beloved son Isaac up that mountain path. I cannot conceive of the grief that Abraham felt as he bound his son and placed him on the wood arrayed upon the altar for sacrifice. And to imagine the fear that Isaac felt as he felt his father raise the knife over him to kill him — I can become physically ill thinking about it. Today, an act like this would be considered nothing less than extreme emotional abuse of a child!

If we know that much of the difficult demand that God issues to Abraham, we know that God intervenes through an angel to stop Abraham:

> *But the angel of the Lord called to him from heaven, and said, "Abraham, Abraham!" And he said, "Here I am." He said, "Do not lay your hand on the boy or do anything to him; for now I know that you fear God, since you have not withheld your son, your only son, from me." And Abraham looked up and saw a ram, caught in a thicket by its horns. Abraham went and took the ram and offered it up as a burnt offering instead of his son. So Abraham called that place "The Lord will provide"; as it is said to this day, "On the mount of the Lord it shall be provided."* — Genesis 22:11-14

Is there not some way for God to determine Abraham's fear and awe of God without putting him and Isaac through such a harrowing experience?

Isn't God capable of calling a wandering and faithless Israel back home to God without requiring Hosea to marry a faithless wife?

We are human, and we are going to ask questions like these of God, but at best, we may have to make peace with the reality that the answers may be well beyond our capacity to understand. Through the words of the prophet Isaiah we are reminded,

> *For my thoughts are not your thoughts, nor are your ways my ways, says the Lord. For as the heavens are higher than the earth, so are my ways higher than your ways and my thoughts than your thoughts.* — Isaiah 55:8-9

What we do know about God and Hosea is this: God is calling Hosea to be a prophet in about 745 BC. Hosea, a citizen of the northern kingdom of Israel, will speak the hard and gracious word of the Lord in a dire period in Israel's history. At Israel's northeastern border, Assyria is flexing its military muscle. And the timing of Assyria's growing strength couldn't be worse for Israel, who faces severe internal struggles of its own. In the period from 750 BC to the fall of Samaria in 722 BC, Israel will crown six kings, four of whom will be murdered by their successors while they are in office. This internal turmoil makes Israel a ready target for Assyria's aggression and a prime audience for the word of the Lord that Hosea is called to speak.

Hosea's word to the people of Israel, and to the people of Judah who are watching all of these events from a distance, is the word of the Lord to them: "You, my people, have been unfaithful to me. Like an adulterous wife to a faithful husband, you have spurned my love and provision for you and dishonored our relationship by worshiping the gods of your neighbors. Rather than looking to the God who has been faithful to deliver you from trouble, you have placed your trust in earthly kings who cannot protect you. And now you are in grave trouble because of your choices. They will lead to your destruction."

God believes that Hosea will be most effective in delivering this word of warning to God's people, if he himself experiences the pain of living with an unfaithful wife. This marriage imagery isn't new to Israel at this point in its life with God; the language of courting and wooing and marriage as characterizations of God's relationship with Israel goes back to the days when Moses led her ancestors on the forty-year wilderness journey to the promised land.

Israel's faithlessness will have its consequences. Samaria will fall in 722 BC and the remainder of the nation is seized in 718 BC. Judah will not be spared either, as it falls to Babylon in 587 BC. But God will preserve a faithful remnant while Judah is held in exile. During the forty years that the people of Judah are in exile, they begin to reconsider their faithlessness to God. The prophet Jeremiah, who goes with them into exile, speaks the word of the

Lord, offering hope for another chance to live as God's beloved, as "children of the living God" (Hosea 1:10).

The book of Hosea is not a long book, and I would encourage you to read it this week. Chapter 1 will introduce Hosea and Gomer and the three children Gomer bears. You may note, if you read carefully, that the first son is clearly identified as Hosea's child, but the author is vague about the parentage of the two other children. Each of the children is given a name that points to specific prophecies against Israel. Yet even before the first chapter is complete, God promises that Israel will be restored. Chapter 2 begins as a recounting of wife and mother Israel's sins and the judgment that will result from them. But the condemnation is transformed into a word of hope, a word of reconciliation — a promise that the Lord will once again woo his beloved people and win their love and faithfulness. Chapter 3 is brief, and scholars are unsure as to whether it repeats the idea of the first chapter, or is a sequel to it. Chapters 4 through 14 follow, detailing Israel's worship of Canaanite gods and her materialism. Exile is in Israel's future, says the Lord, and it parallels the isolation period that Hosea imposes on Gomer in chapter 3.

Ultimately, the message that Hosea speaks on behalf of the Lord is that the Lord is full of compassion and faithful to the promises made and cannot and will not let Israel go. It is a message of hope for Israel, Judah, and for all who hear this word — though we are unfaithful, God will forever be faithful.

We gather around this promise still today. We are unfaithful to God. Despite our intention to love God, our attention is drawn to the expensive, lovely, and coveted things of this world. We want them and they proceed to control us. Despite our professions of faith in God, we place our trust in human rulers. Despite our desire to serve God, we end up serving ourselves and hope that God will understand.

As we stray from God's beloved intent and holy purpose for us, it can seem as though we have become unworthy of God's mercy or pity. We may think that we have forfeited the privilege of being God's people. Unknowingly, we claim the names of Gomer's daughter and son born outside of her marriage bed with Hosea (whose name is a form of the Hebrew word for savior or deliverer). But God will not let those names and those ways shape our ultimate destiny. By the grace of God, we are called "children of the living God" (Hosea 1:10).

The *Lutheran Book of Worship* offers this introductory statement to the rite for marriage:

> *The Lord God in his goodness created us male and female, and by the gift of marriage founded human community in a joy that begins now and is brought to perfection in the life to come.*
>
> *Because of sin, our age-old rebellion, the gladness of marriage can be overcast, and the gift of the family can become a burden.*
>
> *But because God, who established marriage, continues still to bless it with his abundant and ever-present support, we can be sustained in our weariness and have our joy restored.*[1]

This is the good news — bad news — good news of life with God. It is the message that God commands Hosea to live with Gomer and their children, and the message God commands him to bring to Israel and to neighboring Judah, too. This is the good news — bad news — good news of our life with God today as well. May the good news that God calls us "beloved" despite our faithlessness, be a source of sustenance for us in times of weariness ... and may we, by the grace of God, know what it is to have our joy restored. Amen.

---

1. Lutheran Church in America, The American Lutheran Church, The Evangelical Lutheran Church in Canada, The Lutheran Church — Missouri Synod, *Lutheran Book of Worship* (Minneapolis: Augsburg Publishing House and Philadelphia: Board of Publication, Lutheran Church in America, 1978), p. 203.

Proper 13
Pentecost 11
Ordinary Time 18
Hosea 11:1-11

Parenting —
Not For The Faint Of Heart

Parenting is not, I repeat, *not* for the faint of heart. For many of us, it was easy enough to bring our sons and daughters into this world and to hold their tiny forms in our arms. We had no idea what was coming. The 4 a.m. feedings, the nights spent vainly trying to comfort a wailing child, watching as they took their first steps, the joys of toilet training, the "terrible twos" ... those moments are but distant memories now.

In the blink of an eye, our sons are teenagers, and as I am working on this text they are preparing for the final exams of their school year. The challenges that seemed so far off as we propped open our eyelids for those 4 a.m. feedings are upon my husband and me as we encourage our sons to study and do their best. Earlier today, as one of our sons and I spoke about the week ahead and its demands, I got that look that can send a parent around the block, so to speak — you know, the rolling of the eyes.

For a moment afterward, I remembered one of the first episodes of *The Cosby Show* — a situation comedy that ran from the mid-1980s to the early 1990s. The show featured Bill Cosby as Dr. "Cliff" Heathcliff Huxtable, an obstetrician-gynecologist; his wife, Claire, herself an accomplished attorney; and their five children, living in a brownstone in New York City. Although some argued that the show gave an inaccurate portrayal of African-American family life, most everyone agreed that it was a great vehicle for the comedic talents, wit, and wisdom of Bill Cosby. Cosby was quick to acknowledge that much of his material came from moments in his real-life family, especially the relationship with his TV son,

Theo. Cliff and Theo would go 'round and 'round about grades and other issues — and when things got a bit heated, Cliff would look his son straight into the eye and utter those immortal words, "Son, I brought you into this world, and I can take you out!"

Parenting — the kind of parenting that sacrifices to bring out the best in children and teens — is not for the faint of heart.

The lectionary introduced us to the prophet Hosea last week. In the early chapters of this Old Testament book, we hear of the prophet's unique prerequisite for being the mouthpiece of the Lord. Hosea is directed by God to marry a woman who is a prostitute, in order that he might experience in some small way the pain that God has known being pledged to an unfaithful people named Israel. Hosea marries Gomer, whom biblical scholars believe may have been a temple prostitute connected to the worship of Baal. We only read about the challenges of this marriage during the first three chapters of the book; the remainder of it, including today's reading from Hosea 11, are the oracles or prophetic messages that Hosea declares to the house of Israel.

The language of this oracle is the language of parenting. It is the language of delight in the tender moments of cradling and feeding little children, of helping them take their first steps. It is the language of deep frustration over preteens and teens who break curfew and defy your rules. Hosea bears and conveys God's deep love and devotion for Israel, as well as God's anguish and pain over Israel's rejection of God.

"When Israel was a child, I loved him, and out of Egypt I called my son" (Hosea 11:1.) The prophet's testimony begins like that of a parent delighting over the memory of a child, perhaps a child who has been adopted — delivered from suffering and death into joy and safety in God's house. It is as if God is leafing through a photo album, remembering the days of dandling a precious child on the knee. "The more I called them, the more they went from me; they kept sacrificing to the Baals, and offering incense to idols" (Hosea 11:2).

The time of joyful recollection is marred by grief over this child, and those who have joined him, as all of them have run away. They have left the joy and safety of the Father's house to chase after others who've promised them that their life was better, richer, more satisfying. These were the false promises that the community who worshiped the Baals used to entice Israel. "Worship our gods and your crops will yield greatly. Worship the Baals and you, too, will be fertile, and will welcome many sons and daughters into your home." And God's beloved children listened to their neighbors, rather than to the Lord. Israel forgot whose they were and who had delivered them, protected them, and provided for them. Israel forgot and turned to these carved god figures their Canaanite neighbors showed them. They prostrated themselves before these figures. They forgot the one who had given them life.

> *Yet it was I who taught Ephraim to walk, I took them up in my arms; but they did not know that I healed them. I led them with cords of loving kindness, with bands of love. I was to them like those who lift infants to their cheeks. I bent down to them and fed them.*
> — Hosea 11:3-4

Can you hear the anguish and pain the Lord feels? It is the pain felt by a loving parent whose provision has been forgotten, whose guidance has been rejected.

Some among us might be able to relate very keenly to this pain of which Hosea speaks. We have given the best we could to our children. Some of you have sacrificed your own dreams so that your children's lives might hold more promise than your own. All this seems to have been lost on your sons and daughters. They, like Israel, have gone their own way. You can see that the direction they are heading will land them in misery and despair.

When your children are very young, you can corral them with baby gates and fences around your yard. You can keep your eye on them nearly every moment of the day. But as they grow and head to school, you know that you will not be able to decide with whom they will play. You will not be able to single-handedly determine who will influence their decisions. As they begin to ride a bike and later to drive a car, you know that you will not be able to monitor their every move.

You do everything you can to teach them safety and how to choose friends who will be good for them. You impart your family's core values to them, your actions speaking much more loudly than your words. You pray with them and for them.

But what do you do when you realize that your children are headed toward disaster, and the baby gates and fences don't hold them anymore? What do you do when it appears that all that you have taught them has been rejected or, for the moment at least, forgotten?

We may be powerless to affect our grown children's choices, but our all-powerful God could intervene, right? God could simply put some obstacle in the way of those wayward Israelite children, preventing them from bowing down to the Baals. God could control them like puppets on a string, keeping them from straying.

God could, but God doesn't. When God created humanity, God's intent was that we would be stewards of creation. God's deepest desire was for a relationship with us. The first man and woman enjoyed the fullness of relationship with God. In Genesis 3, this relationship is characterized by God joining them in the garden at the time of the evening breeze. God created them to be partners for life with God. And partnership, although shaped and strengthened by boundaries, requires the commitment of all parties involved. You can't be coerced into true partnership, anymore than you can be forced to love someone.

God created us for relationship, for partnership, for love. That is why we are not and never will be puppets on strings controlled by God. God doesn't want robots who are wired and remote-controlled to love and serve. God desires men, women, and children filled with the Holy Spirit, the breath of God, the continuing presence of Jesus, who love God for who God is. God desires men, women, and children who serve God because we know that God created us for service. We know that we are most alive when we are loving God and serving God by loving and serving those around us.

Have you ever been away from your child for part of a day, or maybe more, and experienced the overpowering love that spills out of them when they see you again? "Mommy!" they cry. And then they leap into your arms. They wrap their arms around your neck. They tuck their heads in along your neck, nestled between your chin and shoulder. It is as if they are intent to lay every square inch of their skin next to your own. They can't get close enough! It is an amazing moment of oneness between a mother and child. There is nothing like it.

That is the deepest desire of God's heart for the Israelites, God's beloved and precious children. That is the deepest desire of God's heart for you, and for me, as well.

But Adam and Eve, and the Israelites, and we reject that amazing love. Adam and Eve chose wisdom for themselves, the opportunity to control their own destiny through pursuit of the knowledge of good and evil. The Israelites looked to their neighbors for wisdom about how to live in the land God had given to them and worshiped their gods, the Baals. We look to everything from the success of our kids in their endeavors to our investment strategies, from our spacious homes to national security to guide us. These become the things we worship, the things to which we bow. These become the things we love, and instead of loving us back, they take us captive.

> *They shall return to the land of Egypt, and Assyria shall be their king, because they have refused to return to me. The sword rages in their cities, it consumes their oracle priests and devours because of their schemes. My people are bent on turning away from me. To the Most High they call, but he does not raise them up at all.* — Hosea 11:5-7

God's grace is rejected as we selfishly go our own way. God knows and grieves over what happens to us when the stuff we love takes us captive. God's heart breaks when we choose slavery over freedom.

Judgment comes as the result of our self-centered ways. Sometimes the judgment is readily visible, as the exile experience will be for Israel and later for Judah. Sometimes it can be years or even generations before we reap what we have sown, before the consequences of our rejection of God's love comes home to roost in our lives. The gravest word of judgment is the word that God can utter to us. Remember Cliff Huxtable's words to his son Theo: "I brought you into this world, and I can take you out!" This is the word that God has every right to speak to all of us who have spurned God's love. This is the judgment that God can level against God's beloved. But God doesn't.

> *How can I give you up, Ephraim? How can I hand you over, O Israel? How can I make you like Admah? How can I treat you like Zeboiim? My heart recoils within me; my compassion grows warm and tender. I will not execute my fierce anger; I will not again destroy Ephraim; for I am God and no mortal, the Holy One in your midst, and I will not come in wrath.*
> — Hosea 11:8-9

God will not execute the anger and rage God feels over Israel's (and our) rejection. God is not a faint-hearted parent when it comes to the rebellion we sons and daughters raise. God is not like us. God is God, slow to anger and full of compassion. God will not reject us, even if we reject God.

No, instead God embraces us, taking on flesh and blood, revealing God's self to us in the person of Jesus. God comes to woo us, to call us back. God comes among us in Jesus to love us and to claim us from the forces that enslave and captivate us. God comes among us in Jesus to put those powers to death by his own death on the cross. God comes among us in the resurrected Jesus to embrace us, to offer peace and reconciliation, to join us to God's mission of drawing all creation into God's loving arms. God did bring us into this world, and God could certainly take us out! But instead, God takes us in and loves us forever. God delivers us from our captors and returns us to our home in the center of God's good and gracious will.

Parenting is not for the faint of heart. Thanks be to God — the one who gives us life and breath, whose heart never grows faint toward us. May you know the deep and abiding love God has for you, the holy and eternal purpose God has for you. May you find your true home in the center of God's love, and from that home extend that love to all who are still far from home. In the name of Jesus. Amen.

What God Expects From Worship

I heard it again at a meeting last week ... a comment about the length of the worship service. Somewhere along the way, people in our Christian tradition came up with the idea that worship should last about no more than sixty minutes.

The comment was innocent enough and was being made in reference to recommendations our ministry team would be making regarding the Sunday morning schedule of worship and learning. How much time should there be between the close of the first worship service and the learning hour? How much time should there be between the end of the learning hour and the next service? The comment that worship should be about an hour in length seems like a very practical consideration in the context of decisions like these.

Where do we develop these kinds of expectations about worship? Mass at the neighboring Roman Catholic parish never runs over fifty minutes and that includes communion. Services down the street at the Methodist church commence and dismiss within an hour's time. But our friends at the Apostolic church in town will worship for nearly two hours on any given Sunday, as will those in the multicultural congregation of our own denomination just a few miles away from us.

Was it the advent of the hour-long television show that served to cement our schedules into neat sixty-minute boxes on our calendars? Or was it the eight-hour workday that taught us to think of our days in hour-long increments? Although many of us look at our watches or cell phones several times an hour to gauge process

299

or progress, there are many places in the world where time is measured by daylight and starlight, sunrise and sunset, heat of the day and cool of the evening. In places like this, I have been told, Christian worship services might last several hours. There is no clock on the wall telling anyone to stop singing or preaching or praying. The people's worship begins when all are present, and it draws to a close when there is a sense that all are finished with the rites and prayers and songs.

What do we expect out of worship ... to be entertained? Do we expect to experience a sense of connection with the almighty? Are we expecting to gain wisdom for living or to feel better about ourselves?

Even more important is this question — what does God expect of us when we gather to worship? What does God desire of us when it comes to worship?

Our reading from the introductory verses of the book of Isaiah offers some rather blunt statements regarding what God won't tolerate when it comes to worship. The massive text ascribed to Isaiah doesn't begin with a story about his birth, childhood, or his call to prophetic ministry. The opening oracle appears to be a summary of the whole of Isaiah's work, spanning nearly forty years. This "word of the Lord" in chapter 1 is particularly hard on Jerusalem, the center of Judah's worship life. His words take close aim at the system of sacrifices maintained at the Jerusalem temple that were central to the worship of the Lord.

> *What to me is the multitude of your sacrifices? says the Lord; I have had enough of burnt offerings of rams and the fat of fed beasts; I do not delight in the blood of bulls, or of lambs, or of goats.* — Isaiah 1:11

By the middle of the eighth century BC when Isaiah began his prophetic work, the sacrificial system had been in place for several hundred years. We read about these offerings in detail in the book of Leviticus. Offerings of grain, turtle doves, pigeons, lambs, goats, and bulls all served specific purposes. Some, like the grain offering, were a witness to the Lord's gracious provision for the people.

Other offerings expressed gratitude and well-being, while still others served to remove the stain of people's sin from the Lord's sight. Aaron and his descendants were responsible for fulfilling these duties for the sake of the people.

These practices were meant to keep the righteousness and holiness of the Lord in the forefront of the people's minds and hearts. They were established to continually remind God's people of his ready provision and faithfulness. They were intended to remind the people of the Lord's passion for justice and care for the suffering. These sacrifices were meant to restore people to community when they sinned against one another and to reconcile them to the Lord when they forgot his purposes in favor of their own.

So why did the Lord no longer take delight in their prescribed offerings of bulls, lambs, and goats? By the time the prophet Isaiah was called to serve as God's mouthpiece, the priests' work of oversight for the sacrificial process had become corrupt with greed. The priests took advantage of those who brought offerings. They raced through prayers, festivals, and new moons, so that they could get on to more important things. They had developed a "git 'r done" attitude when it came to the worship of the Lord.

> *When you come to appear before me, who asked this from your hand? Trample my courts no more; bringing offerings is futile; incense is an abomination to me. New moon and sabbath and calling of convocation — I cannot endure solemn assemblies with iniquity. Your new moons and your appointed festivals my soul hates; they have become a burden to me, I am weary of bearing them.* — Isaiah 1:12-14

By Isaiah's time, the worship life of Judah had disintegrated into a series of rites meant to appease a God whom the people no longer seemed to know. They had lost touch with the God of their ancestors. They had ceased to respect God's core values of justice and mercy, especially toward those who were at risk in their society. Their many worship services and token religiosity were so far from what God intended that God was sickened by all of it.

Psalm 22:3 declares that God is enthroned upon the praises of Israel, but God isn't feeling the love. Worship that is devoid of devotion to God and commitment to God's ways is nothing more than a burden. And God turns away in disgust.

> *When you stretch out your hands, I will hide my eyes from you; even though you make many prayers, I will not listen; your hands are full of blood. Wash yourselves; make yourselves clean; remove the evil of your doings from before my eyes; cease to do evil, learn to do good; seek justice, rescue the oppressed, defend the orphan, plead for the widow.*   — Isaiah 1:15-17

God is so appalled by the actions of his people that when they raise their hands in prayer to him, God will not respond. God will not listen. Why? Because his people have hands bloodied by injustice and greed. Isaiah's words shed some light on the nature of their guilt. Their guilt lies in their relationships, especially with those on the fringes of society.

It's been said that the quality of a society is measured by its treatment of the helpless and poor. Here orphans and widows are code words for the poorest and most dependent people in Judah's society. And Judah doesn't fare too well when judged by that standard. Worshipers' hands are bloodied by their tolerance for and participation in oppression. Their indifference toward those who are orphaned angers God. Their failure to care for widows in their distress reveals just how self-absorbed and far from God his people really are.

Isaiah isn't the only prophet who denounces this downward spiral, this departure from the Lord's gracious intent. Amos preaches of justice being an identifying mark of God's people — and he mourns its absence in the northern kingdom of Israel. Hosea preaches a similar message, appealing to his listeners to live in love and walk with God, who like a gracious husband forgives their infidelities and welcomes relationship with them.

You see, when it comes to worship, God expects people to be transformed. God expects the love and trust they confess to really change the way they live. God expects people to be shaped by his love so that they love one another more and more. God expects that his ways of compassion and justice will be reflected in the people who have been created in God's image and delivered from slavery into freedom. God expects that people will become more deeply aware of God's generosity to them. God expects that they will be generous and gracious to one another, as God is with them. Then, as today, *God expects his people to love him and reflect his love in their relationships with others.* God is worshiped when God's people live in such a way that God's values shine through their words and deeds.

Isaiah 1:17 identifies some of the characteristics of the way of life and worship God expects. People who truly worship God will seek justice for all people. People who have been shaped by God's deliverance will commit themselves to rescue the oppressed. People whose lives have been defined by God's generosity will protect the orphaned and care for those who have been widowed. In short, people who live in a loving and worshipful relationship with God will do what God does. Their hearts will beat in time with God's heart. Their priorities as individuals, as households, as congregations, and as churches will be oriented toward whoever in their community is counterpart to Judah's widows and orphans — the homeless, racial and ethnic minorities, or families in crisis.

Instead, what God often finds in our congregations are people who are caught up in wars over the words and music of their worship life, and indifferent to the conflicts that rage in our world.

God finds people complaining about worship that takes more time than they want to give and oblivious to those who wonder if God has any time or love for them.

God finds beautiful sanctuaries and parlors, and people gathered in them who are void of compassion for the broken outside our doors.

Yet, in love and compassion, God invites us away from all that glitters and distracts us from real worship:

> *Come now, let us argue it out, says the Lord: though your sins are like scarlet, they shall be like snow; though*

they are red like crimson, they shall become like wool.
If you are willing and obedient, you shall eat the good
of the land; but if you refuse and rebel, you shall be
devoured by the sword; for the mouth of the Lord has
spoken.   — Isaiah 1:18-20

In imagery that prefigures our baptism into the life, death, and resurrection of Jesus, the guilt that bloodies our hands is washed away. We are reconciled to God. We are invited into God's presence and gifted with God's provision. Like the Israelites before us, we are offered a choice of life or death, of transforming worship or self-absorbed ignorance.

What did you come to worship today expecting? Did you expect to see friends? Did you expect to receive that peace that passes all understanding? Did you expect to go home with one or two life questions answered?

Or did you expect to be loved, forgiven, and refitted by God for the sake of the world? Do you think we might have time for that today? In the name of Jesus. Amen.

**Proper 15
Pentecost 13
Ordinary Time 20
Isaiah 5:1-7**

Garden Gone Bad

This summer I decided to take up some simple vegetable gardening. I knew it would happen someday. It's in my blood. My dad has planted and tended summer gardens of various sizes my whole life. For several years, our family's garden filled the whole half acre second lot behind our home. We had strawberries, melons, tomatoes, sweet corn, lettuce, onions, cucumbers, zucchini, acorn squash, and even pumpkins.

I don't remember much about Dad planting the garden each spring, but I suppose that is because planting wasn't my job. My job was weeding, and I absolutely hated it! Dad gave my brother and I the incentive of five cents for every two-quart bucket of weeds we pulled, which was a lot for seven- and nine-year-old children in the late 1960s, but he could have paid ten times that much, and I still would have hated it! Nonetheless, we picked the weeds and enjoyed the fresh berries and salad and corn throughout the summer.

When my husband and I bought our home, we gained a garden of similar size on our corner lot. But our children were very young, and we knew that the fenced-in yard would best serve our family as play space for the boys and for our dogs. We leveled the soil, planted grass, and built a swing set and fort there.

Now our boys are young men in high school. The fort and swing set have been passed on to another family with young children, and I have begun to think that it is time for our family to enjoy really fresh tomatoes. That's where I've begun — with cherry tomatoes and herbs in a container garden arrangement on our back

305

deck and Big Boy, Early Girl, and Beefsteak tomato plants along the fence in the side yard.

This all has seemed easy enough, until I discovered that the younger of our two dogs has found these staked tomato plants along the fence very interesting and very inviting. Maverick has begun tramping between the plants as if their stakes were agility weave poles. But even worse, he has been seen relieving himself on a few of them. All of which has required another trip to the garden shop to purchase some tomato cages to try to protect my precious plants.

Along with these concerns, I am learning to keep an eye on the amount of rain or lack of it and water accordingly. I have fertilized the plants and am weeding around them. I don't know how many tomatoes we'll end up with, but I am hopeful that our family will enjoy Caprese salad — sliced tomatoes with fresh mozzarella and basil and olive oil — very soon.

My efforts don't even begin to measure up to the work my dad does in his garden to this day, or even the weeding I so despised doing as a child. This little tomato project of mine has given me a new respect for the care that he had given his garden over the years.

> *Let me sing for my beloved my love-song concerning his vineyard: My beloved had a vineyard on a very fertile hill. He dug it and cleared it of stones, and planted it with choice vines; he built a watchtower in the midst of it, and hewed out a wine vat in it; he expected it to yield grapes, but it yielded wild grapes.*
> — Isaiah 5:1-2

As we hear the love song that Isaiah sings for his beloved and his vineyard, perhaps we feel a similar sense of awe and respect for this diligent gardener. It's obvious that he has put a great deal of effort into selecting rich soil and preparing space for a grapevine, planting the best vines, and then protecting and nurturing them to maturity and productivity. Can you imagine the dismay and frustration you would feel if after all that work you ended up with nothing more than wild grapes? (The Hebrew text for these wild grapes is most accurately translated "poison berries.") You can't get much more inedible or useless than that.

Friends, this is no ordinary love song; this is a sad song, a real tragedy. It is the kind of song that tugs at the heartstrings of its listeners, the kind that wins Country Music Song of the Year Awards hands down!

> *And now, inhabitants of Jerusalem, and people of Judah, judge between me and my vineyard. What more was there to do for my vineyard that I have not done in it? When I expected it to yield grapes, why did it yield wild grapes?* — Isaiah 5:3-4

Can you feel the frustration of Isaiah's beloved as he hears this dirge? He simply cannot remain silent any longer. So he interrupts Isaiah's heartbreaking song:

> *And now I will tell you what I will do to my vineyard. I will remove its hedge, and it shall be devoured; I will break down its wall, and it shall be trampled down. I will make it a waste; it shall not be pruned or hoed, and it shall be overgrown with briers and thorns; I will also command the clouds that they rain no rain upon it.* — Isaiah 5:5-6

Now whenever we hear a garden (or gardener) mentioned in the scriptures, a biblical interpretation principle called "first mention" is going to direct us to a very familiar place for people of the Jewish, Muslim, and Christian faiths. That place is Genesis 1 and 2. There in the opening narrative of God and humanity's story, we read that creation began with God and a garden, a thoughtfully planned and carefully cultivated place of life, beauty, harmony, and productivity. The Genesis narratives introduce us to a gardening God who is very invested in all of creation. But this gardener also has the power to wipe out any part of it that isn't full of life or beautiful. This gardener can destroy any planting that is not in harmony with the rest of the garden or doesn't produce.

God will take away this vineyard's protection and let it go. God will not give time or effort to it if it will not fulfill the purposes for which it has been created. Like a field that is plowed over and allowed to lay fallow, God will leave this land to grow over, hoping that in some future time, it may become useful for cultivation again someday.

> *For the vineyard of the Lord of hosts is the house of Israel, and the people of Judah are his pleasant planting; he expected justice, but saw bloodshed; righteousness, but heard a cry!* — Isaiah 5:7

Isaiah's poem ends with one more twist — the vineyard being lamented isn't just any place. This vineyard is God's people — Israel and Judah. Now we are getting to what is sometimes called the crowning glory of God's creation, aren't we? This unruly, unproductive vineyard is the whole of God's beloved people, who God created, declared to be stewards of God's creation, then later delivered from bondage, and finally planted in a fertile place where they could reflect God's image as readily as a good and well-tended vine bears tasty fruit. These people, created in God's image, were formed with the capacity to be righteous and do justice, as the one who planted them is righteous and just.

But when God came to the vineyard looking for justice, instead God found bloodshed. When God came looking for righteousness, instead God heard cries of distress. In the Hebrew this phrase is an excellent pun: God came looking for *mishpat,* and instead found *mispach*; for *tsedaqah*, but instead heard *tse'aqah*. It isn't quite as "punny" when rendered into English, but you might get the gist of it if I were to say that God looked for justice, but it was all a joke; God looked for righteousness, and found a load of rubbish.

As Isaiah sang in mournful tones, God will let his vineyard go. If it cannot (or will not) produce fruit, God will let it collapse in on itself, and begin again. Israel will be overtaken by Assyria, and Judah by Babylon. Each will be carried away from their homeland, transplanted as it were, in the territory of their conquerors. Righteousness and justice are not the ways of these conquerors, as a rule. And the people of Judah will sing mournful psalms in their captivity. However, forty years into their time in Babylon, God's righteousness will reach into their lives through King Cyrus, and the exiles will return home singing about the deliverance of their God. They will strive to be righteous and to do justice, to be the pleasant planting of the Lord.

And they will be, for a while. But the beloved gardener knows that it will take far more than planting and pruning and allowing fruitless vines to wither. At the right time, God will give everything he has for this garden, sinking his feet deep into the Judean soil in the person of Jesus. He'll teach about miraculous mustard seeds and enjoy the crunchy, nutty taste of grain freshly picked on a sabbath morning. He'll weave a telling story of sown seed and all its possibilities for growth or collapse, and curse a fig tree for its fruitlessness. Ultimately, he will die on a tree, and his blood will fertilize the earth, breathing new life and promise into all creation. Then after he has laid three days in the tomb, the risen, living Jesus will be mistaken for ... a gardener. But it is no mistake, for Jesus was with God in the beginning delighting in creation and promising to preserve, bless, cultivate, and enjoy it forever. It is a garden of righteousness and justice ... a garden where there is enough for all.

To quote the great hymn-writer, Fanny J. Crosby, "This is my story, this is my song" and it is your story and song, too. Grafted to Jesus through baptism into his death and resurrection, we have a song of hope and promise to sing, a song that invites all creation to delight in our beloved and trust his promises. It is a song that celebrates the value of all the living and pledges to preserve and bless it through righteousness and justice. It is a song each of us can sing, no matter how weak or strong our voices may be, or how perfect or out-of-tune our pitch.

Friends, may your lives sing a song for your beloved God — a song celebrating this wondrous creation and the gift of our lives. May your lives point to Jesus — and sing of the life we have through his life, death, and resurrection. May your lives and your voices be Spirit-breathed and empowered — and may the song you sing invite others to join in the song. Amen.

Proper 16
Pentecost 14
Ordinary Time 21
Jeremiah 1:4-10

When God Calls

Today, and for the next several weeks, the Revised Common Lectionary devotes attention to one of the most intriguing figures in all of the Old Testament — the prophet Jeremiah. Jeremiah began his work as the bearer of God's word to the nation of Judah during the time of King Josiah's reign in 627 BC. His prophesying continued even as Judah's brightest and best were forced to leave their homeland for exile in Babylon in approximately 586 BC.

Jeremiah is sometimes called "the weeping prophet" because, as the message of prophets goes, he had some of the worst news to deliver to his listeners. Jeremiah has also been called the "prophet of the midnight hour," because the message he is given to preach comes just as his countrymen and women are experiencing the horrors of which he preaches. The time to listen to the prophets' words, to repent and return to the Lord has come and gone, and God's people have made no real effort toward reconciliation. Jeremiah is the one called by God to let Judah know that the jig is up. God's judgment on Judah's sin is going to come upon them, and they will not be able to escape it.

Our reading from Jeremiah 1 introduces us to this young man, the son of a priest from Anathoth in the land of Benjamin. As Jeremiah tells it, God initiates the conversation, seemingly from out of the blue.

> *Now the word of the Lord came to me saying, "Before I*
> *formed you in the womb I knew you, and before you*

311

were born I consecrated you; I appointed you a prophet
to the nations." — Jeremiah 1:4-5

There was a time when at least one son in a family was determined to be the one to assume the family business. In many Roman Catholic families, it was common practice in early times to strongly urge at least one son into the priesthood, and/or one daughter to enter a religious order in service to the church. Today our sons and daughters would not be too keen on the idea of their occupation in life being determined for them. But according to God, Jeremiah's vocation was determined even before he was born.

I was not reared in the Wesleyan tradition, but I know that there is a phrase that describes the way God works with Jeremiah. It is called *prevenient grace.* Prevenient grace is grace that comes before — before anything you or I can do or even think about doing. Before Jeremiah even knows that there is such a being as God, God already knows Jeremiah personally. By the way, the apostle Paul testifies to this same prenatal knowledge and appointment by God as he describes his own call:

> *But when God, who had set me apart before I was born*
> *and called me through his grace, was pleased to reveal*
> *his Son to me, so that I might proclaim him among the*
> *Gentiles, I did not confer with any human being, nor*
> *did I go up to Jerusalem to those who were already*
> *apostles before me, but I went away at once into Arabia,*
> *and afterwards I returned to Damascus.*
> — Galatians 1:15-17

Before Jeremiah can even ask the question, "What am I going to be when I grow up, Daddy?" God takes steps to equip and prepare him for the ministry of prophecy that he will be called to fulfill. God grants Jeremiah great insight into the human condition. God equips Jeremiah with great tenacity. God gifts Jeremiah with deep compassion — a willingness to truly suffer with God's people as they enter into the painful experience of exile. And God even puts the words Jeremiah is to say into his mouth for him. The prevenient nature of God's grace is one of the things that makes God's grace so amazing.

> Then I said, "Ah, Lord God! Truly I do not know how
> to speak, for I am only a boy." — Jeremiah 1:6

God also is quite *persistent* when it comes to calling Jeremiah to ministry. When God calls Jeremiah, there is none of the "Here I am, Lord; send me!" enthusiasm that Isaiah expresses in response to his call. In fact, Jeremiah's response mirrors those of the great prophet/leader Moses and the prophet/judge Gideon. Jeremiah is initially quite resistant to the idea of being God's mouthpiece to the people of Judah. He protests that he is too young, too immature to be able to carry out this call. But God is persistent, and although we hear no acceptance speech from Jeremiah, he apparently agrees to serve.

Consider what aspects of your own sense of call might illustrate God's persistence. When I entered Trinity Luther Seminary in the early 1980s, I was a young woman, barely 21 years old. My sense of call had developed slowly and almost imperceptibly as I became involved with campus ministry during college. In fact, having grown up as a Roman Catholic, I was not even fully aware that women were being ordained in the denomination that I had begun to call home while at college. In conversation with our campus pastors and a seminary senior who had been very active in the campus ministry, I began to explore the idea of a seminary degree but was still somewhat reticent about the idea of being a pastor.

At the opening convocation, the president of the seminary, Dr. Fred Meuser, addressed the student body. I remember thinking, "I am sure that this address will help to guide me toward embracing ordained ministry." So you can imagine how Dr. Meuser confounded me when he said very emphatically, "If there is any other career you think you would be happy doing, you really should leave now and try that out. Then, after you have tried out those other vocations, if you still have a call to be a pastor, we will welcome you back. There will be a place here for you."

313

Those words sound quite different from the words God spoke to Jeremiah — but Dr. Meuser commended them to us because he knew that God is persistent. He knew that no matter how far or wide we might wander, or how many different types of employment we might attempt, if we are called by God to be pastors or associates in ministry, God will ultimately guide us to that type of service. In fact, my graduating class was one of the first in which nearly half of the men and women were second-career students. They had, knowingly or unknowingly, done exactly what Dr. Meuser had directed, and the persistence of God's call had ultimately brought them to seminary in preparation for service as ordained and lay ministers of the gospel of Jesus Christ.

When God calls people into ministry, it is a very *personal* call. God's call is not to a one-size-fits-all, cookie-cutter type of ministry. Nor is the call God issues always specifically directed toward maintaining the programs or projects of a specific congregation. Frederick Buechner, in his book, *Wishful Thinking: A Theological ABC* writes:

> *The kind of work God usually calls you to is the kind of work (a) that you need most to do and (b) that the world most needs to have done.... The place God calls you to is the place where your deep gladness and the world's deep hunger meet.*[1]

Earlier today, I shared this quote with a couple who are members of the congregation I serve. In the thirteen years that I have been with this congregation, I have been blessed with the privilege of walking with them through good times and at least one very sorrowful one — the untimely death of their adult daughter. The grief one feels at a child's death is like no other — no matter how old that child may be. We simply are not prepared to bury our children. But God has held these two people in his promises and provided strength and healing for them over the years. And one of the ways that God has ministered to them and then prepared them for a very personal ministry is through two very high-spirited Portuguese Water Dogs that they now have as members of their household.

Bill discovered his call to ministry in companionship with their dogs rather quickly. Another lover of the breed and member of our congregation invited Bill to train their "Murphy" to be a therapy dog. Bill, retired from a career in human resources, was a natural in training Murphy to be patient and attentive to the needs of others, and soon he and Murphy were certified for therapy visits with hospitalized children and elderly residents of nursing centers. As Bill was discovering this very personal calling, I could see a joy return to his grieving heart. He and Murphy are a team — there is a deep gladness that emanates from them as they visit with sick and lonely people who have a deep hunger for connection and joy.

Judy, Bill's wife, was not drawn to this ministry. She is energetic and had especially enjoyed learning how to lead the dogs through agility exercises that included running, jumping, and making their way through a series of weave poles. As you might guess, this kind of energetic dog handling doesn't work in hospitals or libraries or senior residences.

Yesterday, Judy received a call from a friend with Portuguese Water Dogs who had injured her back and needed someone to take her and her dog's place at a very new kind of ministry. For about a month, several dogs and their owners have been visiting with a group of autistic children and showing them how dogs can run an agility course. Judy was hesitant at first, but she knew that she was needed and agreed to go. Although she and her dog had not run an agility course for several months, both of them knew exactly what to do. Judy watched in amazement as the children responded to the dogs and even attempted in some cases to run the agility course set up in the backyard with them. As Judy told me this story, I could hear the joy in her heart, as she, too, has discovered where her deep gladness and the deep hunger of parents with autistic children are meeting.

When God calls us, it is a very personal calling for the sake of a person or a community or a world in need. It is a Spirit-breathed opportunity where our skills, interests and, in many cases, our experience are just what is needed to bless and enliven a life or minister to a specific situation. And as the situation we are ministering

315

to changes or our lives change, the nature or shape of our call will change, too.

Jeremiah will experience this as his prophetic ministry with the people of Judah proceeds. In the beginning he will implore God's people to repent of their idolatry and corruption. In graphic detail, he will describe the invasion of Babylon and the drought through which they will suffer. Intermittently he will plead with the Lord to be patient and gentle with the nation, and he will join his people in mourning the righteous judgment they are enduring. Jeremiah will suffer for his testimony, as the priests in Jerusalem try to silence his prophecies of doom and gloom. In his suffering, he will even rail at God for seducing him into prophetic ministry. He will point to a day when God will deliver Judah from its suffering, when they will return from exile to be re-established in the land of their ancestors. In all of it, he will not be a distant bystander, pointing to these things, but he will live them. In so doing, he points those of us who are joined to God's people through the new covenant, to Jesus, the founder of that new covenant. For Jesus also fulfills God's call with his whole person, with his whole life, and also with his death on the cross, and his descent to the dead. Just as God's promise to deliver the exiled people of Judah to their home, so too Jesus is raised to life as a pledge of the promise that all who trust him will know the joy of life with God. Both Jeremiah and Jesus carry out a very personal ministry, putting their bodies where their (and God's) hearts are.

In an entry of her blog on preaching, Dr. Mary Hinkle Shore, a professor at Luther Seminary in St. Paul, Minnesota, writes:

> *Putting our bodies where our hearts are is more than the old "ministry of presence." It is offering a physical, visual account of the hope that is in us. A friend of mine commented in a sermon once that he noticed as his parishioners served a meal at a homeless shelter an "invisible line." The homeless men stayed on one side of the table, and the church workers stayed on the other side. "What would it be like if we mixed that up?" my friend wondered out loud. What message — what word of God, even — might we be embodying if we*

walked around the table to the other side, or if we stood together on the serving side with men who lived at the shelter? Jeremiah will do this sort of embodiment throughout his career. Jesus will too.[2]

May you hear the call of God in your life — a call that is grounded in prevenient grace, persistently spoken, and personally issued to you for the sake of a world in need. And may your faith, breathed into your heart by the Holy Spirit, guide you to answer that call in the name of Jesus. Amen.

———————

1. Frederick Buechner, *Wishful Thinking: A Theological ABC* (New York: Harper and Row, 1973), p. 75.

2. Mary Hinkle Shore, *Pilgrim Preaching* (http://maryhinkle.typepad.com/pilgrim_preaching/2004/01/the_embodied_wo.html).

Proper 17
Pentecost 15
Ordinary Time 22
Jeremiah 2:4-13

Finding Fault With God

It is never a pleasant prospect to deal with someone who has a complaint with you. As a new pastor, and a very young one at that, one of the things I struggled with most was the experience of conflict with members. I remember as if it were yesterday a significant misunderstanding that developed between the congregation's "matriarch" and me very early in my time there. I prayed about the difficulty we were having, and I knew that I needed to go to her home and ask for the opportunity to talk things out. I will never forget the look on her face as she opened the door and saw me standing there (shuddering inside, I may add). She looked at me and said, "I didn't think you had it in you to come here and meet with me about this face-to-face." Then, after a long pause, and the slightest nod of her head, she added, "Come on in." In those moments, a new sense of respect grew that served both of us well throughout my ministry there.

Finding fault with someone is easy — getting to the bottom of it can be much more difficult. Sometimes you know instinctively what the stumbling block in the relationship is, and other times, you wrack your brain wondering about it. I've sat with many heartbroken spouses and puzzled with them over what could have made their partner break their commitment with them so suddenly. "What fault did he find in me that made him leave?" I've cried with many parents who have tried to make sense of their son or daughter's complete and utter repudiation of them and their family life. "What did I not do for her?"

Sadly, there are many reasons why a person might find fault with a friend, a family member, a boss, or a coworker. Sometimes we don't listen well, or we refuse to see an alternative possibility or perspective on reality. Sometimes the person rejecting us feels that we have not been honest with them or respectful of them.

In our reading, the prophet Jeremiah gives voice to God's anguish over Israel's departure from the covenantal relationship.

> *Hear the word of the Lord, O house of Jacob, and all the families of the house of Israel.* ***Thus says the Lord: What wrong did your ancestors find in me that they went far from me,*** *and went after worthless things, and became worthless themselves?*
> — Jeremiah 2:4-5 (emphasis mine)

Truth is, some people do feel God has been in the wrong where their lives are concerned. Some people have judged God and have found God to be been unfair, less than gracious, and even spiteful.

One of the most unusual and highly public examples of a person finding fault with God is that of then Nebraska State Senator, Ernie Chambers. To be fair, Chambers was generally thought of as a hothead. He had a long history of taking controversial stands on issues. In response to a lawsuit filed in federal court that he considered frivolous, Chambers set out to prove that anyone can sue anyone at anytime.

To prove his point, he got himself a lawyer and proceeded to sue God.

His lawsuit, filed in September 2007, accused God of making and continuing to make terrorist threats of grave harm to innumerable persons, including constituents of his jurisdiction. In addition, "God has caused fearsome floods, egregious earthquakes, horrendous hurricanes, terrifying tornadoes, pestilential plagues, ferocious famines, devastating droughts, genocidal wars, birth defects, and the like as well as calamitous catastrophes resulting in the widespread death, destruction, and terrorization of millions upon millions of the earth's inhabitants including innocent babes, infants, children, the aged, and infirm without mercy or distinction."

Now, Chambers' efforts were little more than political grandstanding, but the senator is certainly not alone in his accusations. Perhaps one or two of you here have friends or family members who have judged God ... and found God lacking. Perhaps you yourself question some of God's ways.

Comedian George Carlin died in June 2008, and with his death came many formal retrospectives and millions of views of some of his recorded routines on YouTube. I was a young, inquisitive teen when Carlin broke onto the national comedy scene with "Seven Words You Can't Say on Television," and I still remember watching him guest-host the very first episode of *Saturday Night Live* in 1975. One of the routines with which I was less familiar was his routine on the value of religion. In it, Carlin comes down quite hard on God and the Christian church:

> *Religion has actually convinced people that there's an invisible man living in the sky who watches everything you do, every minute of every day. And the invisible man has a special list of ten things he does not want you to do. And if you do any of these ten things, he has a special place, full of fire and smoke and burning and torture and anguish, where he will send you to live and suffer and burn and choke and scream and cry forever and ever 'til the end of time! But he loves you! He loves you!*
>
> *... But I want you to know something, this is sincere, I want you to know, when it comes to believing in God, I really tried. I really, really tried. I tried to believe that there is a God, who created each of us in his own image and likeness, loves us very much, and keeps a close eye on things. I really tried to believe that, but I gotta tell you, the longer you live, the more you look around, the more you realize, something is f***ed up.*
>
> *Something is wrong here. War, disease, death, destruction, hunger, filth, poverty, torture, crime, corruption, and the Ice Capades. Something is definitely wrong. This is not good work. If this is the best God can do, I am not impressed. Results like these do not belong on the résumé of a Supreme Being.*[1]

Some might be offended by any reference to George Carlin in a Christian assembly, since he was an avowed atheist. But it is safe to say that his perspective on God is held by many people today. They are people with whom you work and go to school and sit down alongside at family dinners. Chances are, they are not here among us in worship to speak to all the "whys" and "wherefores" that have led to their rejection of God. Chances are, their rejection of God has been fueled by negative experiences they had in Christian congregations or with Christian leaders. That fact should give every one of us pause to think.

It used to be, when I would hear someone finding fault with God, my hackles would be raised. My interest would be piqued. I would often have jumped right into a conversation with that someone, because I wanted to introduce them to the God of grace and love who has captured my heart in Jesus Christ. Frankly, it was all about me, hoping to be convincing enough to be part of God's winning another soul away from doubt or rejection.

Today, I find myself listening to their questions ... hearing their doubts ... and when I do speak, honestly acknowledging that there are portions of God's story that cause me to question as well.

One of those portions is the story of God's command to Abraham that he sacrifice his beloved son Isaac at Mount Moriah (Genesis 22:1-14). It is a skillfully told story, to be sure, but it is also one of the most disturbing things about God that I will ever read in scripture. I know the theological explanations about God's repudiation of child sacrifice. And this is but one of the portions of scripture where God's people are tested by God or with God's permission. However, the idea that God would even think of commanding Abraham to slay his son is quite hard to explain to someone who has been a victim of abuse.

How does one reconcile God's command that the Israelites kill every living creature they encounter as they enter into the promised land? (Joshua 6:21). Many people of deep faith find it a real challenge to accept this kind of destruction as God's will.

As a pastor, I have had many talks with parishioners, neighbors, and community members who somewhere along the way in life have found fault with God. Some of these people are exceedingly bright — their reasoning abilities boggle my mind. And there is little or no room for a supreme being in their view of the world. Like Carlin, they expect that a truly all-powerful God would intervene to stop atrocities before they ever started. A divine being who truly valued life would reveal that commitment to life by standing in opposition to the forces that threaten it.

For others, the fault they find with God is deeply rooted in personal suffering and loss. Whether it has been the death of a precious child, or of a lifelong dream, or of their own innocence, they have come to the conclusion that if there is a God at all, that God does not care about them. These are the conversations that call for heartfelt, compassionate listening. These are the conversations that call for the deepest respect we can offer.

When people have judged God and found fault, God does not need you or me to make a case for his supremacy, his divinity, or his all-surpassing wisdom. God's authority will not stand or fall based on our skillful debating or witty repartee or heartwarming stories of God's provision. If we are to be God's instruments for reconciliation in a person's life, it will be because the *love* of Christ compels us (2 Corinthians 5:14). If we are to be God's instruments to renew or establish faith in a person's heart, it may well be because they have seen faith and hope and love at work in our lives, especially at times when we have endured painful times of loss or doubt. That is the proof, isn't it? Any of us can talk until we're blue in the face about our love, joy, peace, and all the other fruit of the Holy Spirit. But those who are wondering if any of this stuff we talk about could possibly be true are watching to see if our walk matches our talk.

Perhaps the greatest witness we can offer to those who wonder if there really is a God who could love them, who could withstand their doubts and rage, and still embrace them is by loving them and listening to their doubts and pain. If we view skeptics, agnostics, and atheists as worthless, then we become worthless as far as being witnesses for God is concerned. If, on the other hand, we see these in light of God's economy of grace — as precious ones, created in the image of God, for whom Jesus willingly laid down his life, then we may be allowed to journey alongside them from despair to hope. We may be given the opportunity to love them as they are and where they are and watch as God does the transformational work in their lives in God's time.

You see, it is often in asking the hard questions that faith is restored or received. It is in facing conflict directly and working through it that true maturity is developed. It is in embracing the ambiguities and suffering we endure that deep and satisfying peace is given us.

So may this community of faith be a place where it is acceptable to ask hard questions. May this gathering of God's people learn to acknowledge and work through conflict, rather than avoid it or vilify it. And may you receive and point others to the peace that God gives in the midst of challenging times. In the name of Jesus. Amen.

---

1. George Carlin, "Religion" recorded on the album, *You Are All Diseased*, under the label Laugh.com. Release date May 18, 1999.

Proper 18
Pentecost 16
Ordinary Time 23
Jeremiah 18:1-11

In The Potter's Hands

I am not a potter, and I do not play one on television! However, as a student of the scriptures and the life and times of the people in the biblical narrative, I can say with some certainty that crafting pottery is one of the world's oldest professions. Alongside bone and bricks, fragments of earthenware or pottery have long been gathered and studied by archeologists to understand something of the ancient inhabitants of the Middle East and nearly every other ancient culture throughout the world.

Few of us can remember when there was no such thing as plastic for bottles or melamine for dishware; most of us can't remember a time without cardboard boxes! But for thousands of years, various forms of pottery, hollowed-out gourds, and animal hides were all that people had with which to transport water from one place to another, prepare meals, or secure precious documents. Additionally, clay figurines were shaped by hand to serve as earthly representations or reminders of the "gods" that were worshiped by the Canaanites and other peoples of the region.

Archaeologists tell us that in the time of the prophet Jeremiah, pottery was used for storing foods and ointments, for carrying water, for standard measurements of all kinds of items, and for washing clothing. Oil lamps of various sizes were also crafted from clay and fired in ovens. Every community would likely have had at least one potter who could supply the various needs of its residents. Because pottery was quite easily broken, there would always be a strong demand for his or her wares. It was a common fact of life that some of a household's water jars would be dropped or otherwise broken in transit, in much the same way that drinking glasses and pitchers are broken in our own homes.

When Jeremiah is directed to go down to the potter's house, it is likely a very familiar place to him. God's intent in this section of Jeremiah is to provide a highly recognizable visual aid to make his case for his anger with the house of Israel. As Jeremiah watches the potter, he finds that the vessel upon which the artisan is working is not measuring up to his plan for it. It is not going to be the vessel he intends. And as many of us have done countless times with play-dough or modeling clay, the potter abandons the form he has been creating by folding the partially formed vessel in on itself. He shapes it once again into a simple lump of clay so that he can attempt to rework it into a vessel with which he will be pleased.

Because I am not a potter, I do not know how common an occurrence this is, but it seems that every time I have watched a potter throw a pot, as it's called, I have seen them "go back to square one" with clay at least one or two times. Because there are so many factors that go into the shaping of a useful and beautiful piece of pottery, it seems that the starts and restarts serve to get the temperature of the clay, the amount of water added to it, and the vision in the mind of the potter to become one.

When the word of the Lord comes to Jeremiah, we discover that God identifies very closely with this potter. And for the prophet and those who would hear him speak the word of the Lord, this would not be a foreign idea. Not only are clay vessels and figures an integral part of daily life in Jeremiah's time, the image of humanity as clay in God's hands is a very familiar one as well. In Job 10:8-9 Job refers to himself as having been formed by God and fashioned like clay:

> Your hands fashioned and made me; and now you turn
> and destroy me. Remember that you fashioned me like
> clay; and will you turn me to dust again?
> — Job 10:8-9

Job, even in the in the midst of great suffering, acknowledges his maker's right to destroy him whom he has made.

And in the later writings of the prophet Isaiah, God's people make this confession:

Yet, O Lord, you are our Father; we are the clay, and you are our potter; we are all the work of your hand.
— Isaiah 64:8

This imagery characterizing a fragile humanity and its maker may be inspired by the second account of creation:

Then the Lord God formed man from the dust of the ground, and breathed into his nostrils the breath of life; and the man became a living being. — Genesis 2:7

Here is narrative that would inspire any artist, as lifeless clay is shaped by God and lives when God breathes into it. The relationship between artist and art, between creator and creature is very clear. The power the artist holds to create or destroy is implicit in this scene from creation.

So much has changed since the day the Lord God created the man and woman and planted a garden in Eden. No sooner than had that garden been planted, it seems that the creatures forgot that they were creatures in the hands of a gracious creator. When offered the opportunity to become like their creator, the creatures "bit," and the beauty and order of God's artistry became flawed.

This first sin, creatures rejecting their identity as God's creatures, is at the core of all sin and brokenness. Isaiah quotes the Lord God who names this core sin for what it is:

You turn things upside down! Shall the potter be regarded as the clay? Shall the thing made say of its maker, "He did not make me"; or the thing formed say of the one who formed it, "He has no understanding"?
— Isaiah 29:16

Yes, you and I turn things upside down. We believe that we ourselves are the final authority on the way we should live and how we should give. We choose to act selfishly toward others and

327

with contempt toward God, as if to say, "He did not make me!" We make this life all about ourselves — what we need, what we want, and how we will get it, because we somehow think "He [God] has no understanding."

What is it that we think God does not understand? Is it our desire to be in control? Is it our search for meaning, for purpose? God does understand these things about us ... because we have been created in God's image. It is because we stray from God's image of grace and generosity, of love and service, that we struggle with issues like control and the quest for meaning and purpose.

It is because the house of Israel has strayed from the God who created them that the Lord says to Jeremiah,

> *Can I not do with you, O house of Israel, just as this potter has done? says the Lord. Just like the clay in the potter's hand, so are you in my hand, O house of Israel. At one moment I may declare concerning a nation or a kingdom, that I will pluck up and break down and destroy it, but if that nation, concerning which I have spoken, turns from its evil, I will change my mind about the disaster that I intended to bring on it. And at another moment I may declare concerning a nation or a kingdom that I will build and plant it, but if it does evil in my sight, not listening to my voice, then I will change my mind about the good that I had intended to do to it.*
> — Jeremiah 18:6-10

God's people have become something other than God created them to be. Like the spoiled vessel on the potter's wheel, we do not resemble the vision God had for us when the idea of us formed in the mind of God. And so, like the potter, God has the right, and as an artisan, the responsibility to collapse the spoiled vessel, add more water, and work with it once again to achieve the desired result. God will not throw out the clay, for it is valuable and holds the promise of something beautiful within. But to release its beauty and purpose, the clay will need to be reformed in the potter's hand.

The people of Jeremiah's day were not prepared for the nature of that reform. As Israel was defeated by Assyria and led to live in the land of their enemies, so too Judah would face defeat at the hands of Babylon, and its artisans and leaders and their households would be forcibly relocated to Babylon. The forty years they spend there are a time of grief and loss, but those years also serve to reform them into a people more responsive to God. Those who return to Judah are deeply committed to serving God in their generation and preparing the way for future generations to acknowledge God, as well. Through the experience of exile, the clay that is God's people Judah, is reshaped by God's promises into a people more closely resembling God's original intent for them.

Even the experience of exile and return could not *fully* form God's people for life with God. So in the fullness of time, a child is born who is God's perfect plan in every way. This child, born in Bethlehem of Judah and named Jesus, is truly the Son of God and the Savior of the world. Jesus reveals the will of his Father as he takes clay into his hands and places it on the eyes of the blind man, restoring his sight. In everything he does, he reflects God's values of life, wholeness, justice, and compassion. But this broken creation cannot see God's ideal in Jesus — they see only judgment and threat to their way of being. So they kill him, nailing his hands and feet to the tree of a cross.

However, God's hands are not tied by humanity's rejection of his Son. Though they believe themselves to be in control (as we still do today), God rolls away the stone that seals Jesus' lifeless body inside. He raises Jesus from death to life and declares Jesus' reign over all creation. Saint Paul writes:

> He [Jesus] is the image of the invisible God, the first-born of all creation. — Colossians 1:15

Jesus shows us God, and he shows us what God has created and intends us to be, as well.

Although we fall short of that intention, although we "turn things upside down" in our hunger for control and our misguided ideas about meaning and purpose, God in grace places us in Jesus' hands, as we in baptism are joined to Jesus' death and the power of his life. Again, Paul writing to the Corinthians, declares:

329

But we have this treasure in clay jars, so that it may be made clear that this extraordinary power belongs to God and does not come from us. We are afflicted in every way, but not crushed; perplexed, but not driven to despair; persecuted, but not forsaken; struck down, but not destroyed; always carrying in the body the death of Jesus, so that the life of Jesus may also be made visible in our bodies.   — 2 Corinthians 4:7-10*

The treasure in fragile clay jars is our lives, formed by the hand of God according to God's plan for all creation. God's light shines through the cracks and flaws that define our human existence.

I am not a potter, and I do not play one on television. But I do have two priceless pieces of pottery. They are not absolutely perfect in shape, nor are their glazed surfaces vibrant or particularly distinctive. They are precious to me because they are the handiwork of our two sons, crafted when they were students in elementary school.

God looks at us crackpots that way, too. Each of us is unique — no two of us alike. God loves each and every one of us as if there were only one of us. And God loves us just as we are, but too much to let us stay that way.

We will be remolded and reshaped by God, sometimes in dramatic ways, sometimes in subtle, almost imperceptible ways. But no matter what, God's purpose in reshaping us is always the same: that we might more faithfully reflect God to the world around us.

So let us trust life in the potter's hands, making the words of Adelaide A. Pollard our daily prayer and song:

Have thine own way, Lord! Have thine own way!
Thou art the potter; I am the clay.
Mold me and make me after thy will,
While I am waiting, yielded and still.[1]

In the name of Jesus. Amen.

1. "Have Thine Own Way, Lord," words by Adelaide A. Pollard, 1902. In the public domain.

Proper 19
Pentecost 17
Ordinary Time 24
Jeremiah 4:11-12, 22-28

From Life To Death To ...

How many of you remember the movie *Duck and Cover*? It really wasn't a movie but more of a "short" — just over nine minutes in length. But don't sell it short — it featured a great leading role, Bert the Turtle, and a very catchy theme song:

> *There was a turtle by the name of Bert*
> *and Bert the turtle was very alert;*
> *when danger threatened him he never got hurt*
> *he knew just what to do ...*
> *He ducked!*
> *And covered!*
> *Ducked!*
> *And covered! He did what we all must learn to do*
> *You and you and you and you!*
> *Duck, and cover!*[1]

In what looks like a dramatized cartoon, Bert the Turtle follows the "duck and cover" rule when a monkey dangles a firecracker over his head and survives the blast. But then the movie takes a more serious tone as live footage of a nuclear blast is run, and viewers are assured that the way to survive such a blast is to "duck and cover."

Duck and Cover was produced by the United States Civil Defense Administration in 1951, about two years after Russia detonated its first nuclear device. As the Cold War between the United States and Russia grew, Civil Defense began designating

333

fallout shelters and devising other means for protection from nuclear attack.

Other films addressed the threat of nuclear attack. *On the Beach* in 1959 and *The Day After* in 1984 imprinted terrifying images of the complete destruction and desolation that would occur after a nuclear holocaust. Those of us who came of age in the 1970s and 1980s seriously questioned whether we would live to see forty years of age. We seriously feared the total annihilation of the world, the undoing of God's good creation. It wasn't until later in the 1980s that concentrated efforts toward peace between the United States and Russia eased the fears of nuclear destruction of our nations, and ultimately our planet.

When I read this passage in Jeremiah, I cannot help but see the terrifying images of *The Day After* and the films I viewed when I visited Hiroshima and Nagasaki, Japan, as a high school exchange student in 1976-77. In Japan, the only nation to have been attacked with nuclear bombs during World War II, the memorials to those who died and those who survived are surrounded by pictures taken as the bombs detonated and in their aftermath. A burning hot wind ignited fire upon anything that remained standing after the massive blast. Entire neighborhoods were laid waste, all structures destroyed. The cities lay in ruins and the fruitful foothills looked like a desert.

As I walked through the halls of the memorials in Hiroshima and Nagasaki, there was nothing to be said. There was only a deep, deep silence as we viewed the black and white photographs completely absent of human or any other visible life.

The verses of Jeremiah 4 are some of the bleakest images in all of the Old Testament. This is not the kind of text most pastors will choose as fodder for preaching. The nation of Israel had been duly warned of their continuing sin against God and the judgment facing them. God had pleaded with them to repent and return to God, but to no avail.

Jeremiah may have believed that Judah would choose repentance after watching its neighbor to the north fall to Assyria. He may have hoped that all he would need to do would be to remind

Judah of the fall of Israel and their choice would be clear. They would choose God and choose life.

But Judah will not choose life, and Jeremiah laments their ignorance:

> *For my people are foolish, they do not know me; they are stupid children, they have no understanding. They are skilled in doing evil, but do not know how to do good.* — Jeremiah 4:22

Had I never visited Hiroshima or Nagasaki, or toured the concentration camp in Dachau, Germany, I am not sure that I would hear this text in the same way. Because I have no fears regarding adequate food or safe water for my household and my community, I am not sure that, today, I can begin to grasp the gravity of destruction and desolation in this text.

The tragedy of this text today is that despite the fact that millions of people claim faith in God, are readers of the Holy Bible, and are baptized into the life, death, and resurrection of Jesus Christ, there are still places around the world where this kind of destruction and desolation are the norm. There are millions who are dying of starvation and disease. Most, if not all of this starvation and suffering could be alleviated and prevented if we were all committed to living in harmony with God's will for creation.

As stewards of God's creation, we are entrusted with the care of the environment. We are charged with the responsibility of fair distribution of its resources. We are called to provide for those who are at greatest risk — the "widows and orphans" of our world and our day.

But as Adam and Eve, and the people of Israel and Judah before us, we choose to tend to our own needs and wants first. We have bought into the ungodly premise that "God helps those who help themselves." Trust me, you can look all you want for this modern, North American Christian commandment in the Holy Bible, but you will not find it. It is not there. What you will find are commandments like these:

335

Be fruitful and multiply, and fill the earth and subdue it, and have dominion over the fish of the sea and over the birds of the air and over every living thing that moves upon the earth. — Genesis 1:28

He has told you, O mortal, what is good; and what does the Lord require of you but to do justice, and to love kindness, and to walk humbly with your God? — Micah 6:8

Religion that is pure and undefiled before God the Father, is this: to care for orphans and widows in their distress, and to keep oneself unstained by the world. — James 1:27

In his public ministry, Jesus also shows clear preferential treatment for the poor, the suffering, the disenfranchised, and the outcasts. In his storytelling and in his encounters, he readily embraces those whom the rest of his society would prefer to forget. His teaching in the sermon on the plain pronounces blessing on those who are poor, promising them nothing less than the kingdom of heaven (Luke 7:20). The parables of the lost sheep and the lost coin in Luke 15:1-10 clearly communicate Jesus' intent that no one be excluded from God's banquet table. The story of Lazarus and the rich man in Luke 16:19-31 paints a tragic picture of a man who has the means to deliver another from poverty and death, but cannot be bothered to do so. When he later finds himself in torment, and sees Lazarus at peace at Abraham's side, the rich man pleads for mercy for himself. When the barrier between them cannot be traversed, the rich man begs that a warning might be given to his brothers about the afterlife they may face.

Abraham replied, "They have Moses and the prophets; they should listen to them." He [the rich man] said, "No, father Abraham; but if someone goes to them from the dead, they will repent." He [Abraham] said to him, "If they do not listen to Moses and the prophets, neither will they be convinced even if someone rises from the dead." — Luke 16:29-31

336

Brothers and sisters in Christ, we worship and are disciples of someone who has risen from the dead — Jesus of Nazareth, Son of God, and Savior of the world! Are we convinced? Are we willing to trust this one who has given his life for us and to us? Will our hearts beat with his? Will we align our values with his? Having been made right with God through his cross, will we dare to confess our selfishness and offer to others the love and mercy God has shown to us?

Even in the determined decree of God in Jeremiah 4:22-28, God utters a mere breath of mercy:

> *For thus says the Lord, "The whole land shall be a desolation; yet I will not make a full end."*
> — Jeremiah 4:27

God breathes a word of mercy in the midst of the harsh, hot heat of his anger. God pledges that humanity will not be utterly destroyed. God suggests that there is breath and space to turn around, to take our attention off ourselves and onto the broken in body and spirit, in the desolate places of our world.

We need not duck and cover from God as Adam and Eve did after their sin. Let us return to God. Let us trust God with our needs and the needs of those around us and dedicate ourselves to the care and redemption of all whom God has made.

In the name of Jesus. Amen.

---

1. Archer Productions, Inc., *Duck and Cover* (Distributed by the United States Federal Civil Defense Administration, 1951).

Proper 20
Pentecost 18
Ordinary Time 25
Jeremiah 8:18—9:1

When There's Nothing
Left To Do But Mourn

When a person is diagnosed with a serious disorder, one that threatens their very existence, life as we know it is turned upside down. There is research to conduct about traditional and alternative treatments. There are specialists with whom to consult. Sometimes there are changes in lifestyle and in priorities to be considered, as Tim McGraw sang in his 2004 hit, "Live Like You Were Dying."

I have watched this process in many parishioners over the years. Quite often everyone, including the person with the terminal diagnosis, is amazed when they outlive their prognosis by months and sometimes even years. Medical science and mental attitude can do amazing things to sustain and extend the quality of life and the number of months a person has to live.

But there comes a point, when treatments can no longer fend off the threat ... or the prospect of death becomes more tolerable than the treatment of the disease. At this point, hospice organizations can be a tremendous resource to a terminally ill person and their family. Hospice care encompasses nearly every aspect of a dying patient's needs so that she and her loved ones can simply be with one another. Hospice's ability to manage pain is a great blessing that enables loved ones to be as present with one another as possible until the end.

It is at this point in a terminally ill person's journey that he and his family often truly begin to mourn. There has been grief work going on since the moment the words of the diagnosis fell upon the ears of those in the physician's office, but the stage of grief that Dr. Elisabeth Kübler-Ross calls "acceptance" is the stage when there's nothing left to do but keep watch and mourn.

From the moment God called Jeremiah to be a prophet to Judah, Jeremiah began to accompany an entire people diagnosed with a serious disorder. No sooner had God pledged to put the words in Jeremiah's mouth, God warned of the grave trouble that was coming:

> *The word of the Lord came to me, saying, "Jeremiah, what do you see?" And I said, "I see a branch of an almond tree." Then the Lord said to me, "You have seen well, for I am watching over my word to perform it." The word of the Lord came to me a second time, saying, "What do you see?" And I said, "I see a boiling pot, tilted away from the north." Then the Lord said to me: Out of the north disaster shall break out on all the inhabitants of the land. For now I am calling all the tribes of the kingdoms of the north, says the Lord; and they shall come and all of them shall set their thrones at the entrance of the gates of Jerusalem, against all its surrounding walls and against all the cities of Judah. And I will utter my judgments against them, for all their wickedness in forsaking me; they have made offerings to other gods, and worshiped the works of their own hands.* — Jeremiah 1:11-16

With these words, Jeremiah's life is turned upside down. He knows that he has been called to accompany a rebellious people whose days of freedom and leisure are numbered. As the people of Judah are confronted with their faithless ways, God offers them the remedy that will prolong their days:

> *If you return, O Israel, says the Lord, if you return to me, if you remove your abominations from my presence, and do not waver, and if you swear, "As the Lord lives!" in truth, in justice, and in uprightness, then nations shall be blessed by him, and by him they shall boast.*

For thus says the Lord to the people of Judah and to the inhabitants of Jerusalem: Break up your fallow ground, and do not sow among thorns. Circumcise yourselves to the Lord, remove the foreskin of your hearts, O people of Judah and inhabitants of Jerusalem, or else my wrath will go forth like fire, and burn with no one to quench it, because of the evil of your doings.

— Jeremiah 4:1-4

Here is the remedy for your ills, Judah — repent of your worship of idols. Give up your useless covenants and treaties with other nations, and you will be blessed and celebrated as a hale and hearty nation once more.

But as Israel before her, Judah chooses not to adjust her lifestyle, and ignores her sin-sickness. No matter what Jeremiah will say or do as God's mouthpiece, Judah will deny that anything is wrong with her. And her ills will become even more pronounced.

Run to and fro through the streets of Jerusalem, look around and take note! Search its squares and see if you can find one person who acts justly and seeks truth — so that I may pardon Jerusalem. Although they say, "As the Lord lives," yet they swear falsely. O Lord, do your eyes not look for truth? You have struck them, but they felt no anguish; you have consumed them, but they refused to take correction. They have made their faces harder than rock; they have refused to turn back. Then I said, "These are only the poor, they have no sense; for they do not know the way of the Lord, the law of their God. Let me go to the rich and speak to them; surely they know the way of the Lord, the law of their God." But they all alike had broken the yoke, they had burst the bonds. Therefore a lion from the forest shall kill them, a wolf from the desert shall destroy them. A leopard is watching against their cities; everyone who goes out of them shall be torn in pieces — because their transgressions are many, their apostasies are great.

— Jeremiah 5:1-6

341

God looks for every opportunity possible to offer Judah healing, but the proud nation would neither acknowledge her need nor willingly accept the cure. The physician is ready, but the patient is not willing, The patient is relying on her name and the prestige of her possessions to protect her. And so, once more, God and Jeremiah urge Judah to give up her illusions and face the facts of her illness.

> *The word that came to Jeremiah from the Lord: Stand in the gate of the Lord's house, and proclaim there this word, and say, Hear the word of the Lord, all you people of Judah, you that enter these gates to worship the Lord. Thus says the Lord of hosts, the God of Israel: Amend your ways and your doings, and let me dwell with you in this place. Do not trust in these deceptive words: "This is the temple of the Lord, the temple of the Lord, the temple of the Lord." For if you truly amend your ways and your doings, if you truly act justly one with another, if you do not oppress the alien, the orphan, and the widow, or shed innocent blood in this place, and if you do not go after other gods to your own hurt, then I will dwell with you in this place, in the land that I gave of old to your ancestors forever and ever.*
> — Jeremiah 7:1-7

And now, for the first time, the prophet Jeremiah acknowledges that there is nothing left for him to do but mourn. Although his ministry with the people of Judah will continue on for several years, he knows that no matter what he says or what he does, Judah will not listen. Judah will not own up to her condition. Judah will not seek healing. No, Judah will be destroyed, or at the very least, she will be severely debilitated. She will eventually fall to the forces of Babylon. The treaties previously forged with neighboring nations will do her no good. Even her claim of holiness as the place that is home to the temple of the Lord will mean nothing to the Lord. The Lord can raise up another temple in three days.

All of this is not to say that Jeremiah won't continue to warn the people of Judah, won't continue to call them to repent. Jeremiah will continue to serve God's purposes, even as it causes him pain and anguish and grief to do so. His life will be threatened. He will forego the joys of marriage and family. He will face ridicule and despair, but Jeremiah has been called of God, called to a ministry for which he would never have asked. And he cannot help but fulfill it.

> *O Lord, you have enticed me, and I was enticed; you have overpowered me, and you have prevailed. I have become a laughingstock all day long; everyone mocks me. For whenever I speak, I must cry out, I must shout, "Violence and destruction!" For the word of the Lord has become for me a reproach and derision all day long. If I say, "I will not mention him, or speak any more in his name," then within me there is something like a burning fire shut up in my bones; I am weary with holding it in, and I cannot.* — Jeremiah 20:7-9

We are getting ahead of ourselves in the amazing story that is Jeremiah's life and ministry. In today's reading from chapter 8, we hear the anguish and the grief of a man of God who truly loves his people. That's one of the most important things we pastors are called to do — to love you. It's not about becoming friends with you, enjoying "a cold one" in your backyard, or writing letters of reference for your children. Ours is a call to love you as the people entrusted to our care — to love you through thick and thin — to love you with "tough love" when you get out a bit ahead of your "high-beams," so to speak, and to love you with compassion when you stumble and fall.

Can you hear Jeremiah's pain for the people of Judah? Can you hear his pleading for something by which they might be restored?

> *Is there no balm in Gilead? Is there no physician there? Why then has the health of my poor people not been restored? O that my head were a spring of water, and my eyes a fountain of tears, so that I might weep day and night for the slain of my poor people!* — Jeremiah 8:22—9:1

343

The balm of Gilead for which Jeremiah pleads is the healing salve carefully extracted and refined from the resin of balsam trees of the territory of Gad. This balm was revered far and wide for its healing powers. The balm of Gilead is first mentioned in Genesis 37, as the cargo being carried by the caravan of Ishmaelites who bought Joseph from his brothers. Then Joseph became like that healing balm for the sake of the line of Abraham who may have been snuffed out by famine, had Joseph not attained a position of authority in Egypt and resettled them there.

When there is nothing left but to grieve, what do we do? We love those who are suffering; we keep vigil with them. And we pray for their complete healing. It is a healing that comes from beyond exile, from beyond the grave. It is a healing that is born in the very heart of God. A beloved African-American spiritual sings of this healing:

> *Refrain*
> *There is a balm in Gilead*
> *to make the wounded whole;*
> *there is a balm in Gilead*
> *to heal the sin-sick soul.*
>
> *Sometimes I feel discouraged,*
> *and think my work's in vain,*
> *but then the Holy Spirit*
> *revives my soul again. Refrain*
>
> *If you can't preach like Peter,*
> *if you can't pray like Paul,*
> *just tell the love of Jesus,*
> *and say He died for all. Refrain*[1]

The true balm of Gilead that would deliver Judah and all God's people flows from the heart of God. It is the precious blood of Jesus, God's Son. As Jeremiah walks through the valley of the shadow of death with his "poor people," he points them toward God and promises them that they will not suffer forever. He testifies that God will be compassionate and will lead them back home in time.

344

When there is nothing left but to grieve, as Christians our call is to accompany the suffering through their grief. We love them through their journey and grieve with them — but we grieve as a people who have hope. We grieve as a people who know that there is "a balm in Gilead" to make us all whole. We know that the Holy Spirit has the power to revive our discouraged souls. We know that the love of God shown us in the death and resurrection of Jesus will carry us through — through suffering and even through death to life and to peace.

In the name of Jesus. Amen.

---

1. "There Is A Balm In Gilead," words from an African-American spiritual. Words in the public domain.

Proper 21
Pentecost 19
Ordinary Time 26
Jeremiah 32:1-3a, 6-15

Sold!

As we conclude several weeks of readings in the book of the prophet Jeremiah and next week look at the companion text from the book of Lamentations, a common thread begins to emerge. It is the thread of grief. Jeremiah has been called by God to a truly thankless job — that of accompanying the people of his homeland into a time of loss and grief. Because of decades of idolatry and treaties with neighboring nations, the people of Judah will lose the land God once graciously gave to their ancestors. The events in today's reading take place around 588 BC as the Babylonian army is laying siege to Jerusalem.

Let me set the stage with some history here. Jeremiah began prophesying while Josiah was king over Judah in about 627 BC. Although Josiah's efforts to put an end to idol worship and to shape the nation's values and practices around the Deuteronomic law were only moderately successful, he died while trying to keep Egypt from teaming with Assyria against Babylon. Judah became a vassal nation in 609 BC. As a series of kings ruled and were overthrown or assassinated in Jerusalem, a power shift resulted in Assyria taking control of Judah's destiny in about 605 BC. Jeremiah's visit to the potter and his expressed grief over Judah likely took place at about this time.

Jehoiakim ruled in Judah for several years providing some internal stability, but Babylon was quietly gaining strength. In 598 Jehoiakim died, and while his son, Jehoiachin, was still acclimating to the role, King Nebuchadrezzer of Babylon invaded Jerusalem. Nebuchadrezzer looted the temple and treasury, and took

Jehoiachin and the queen mother into custody, but did not destroy the temple or the city at that time. Zedekiah (the uncle of Jehoiachin) was left to rule Judah as a puppet king, whose strings were orchestrated by Babylon.

Jeremiah began to preach more intentionally about the fall of Judah, warning that the Judeans would live in exile for seventy years. Because Jeremiah continued to call the people of Judah to faithfully serve and worship Yahweh, it appears that King Josiah's reforms were not sustained after his death. Despite so many of his prophecies coming to pass, Jeremiah's message is not received well or embraced. Zedekiah has Jeremiah imprisoned in the palace jail. After all, the great prophet Isaiah, speaking more than 100 years before, had promised that that the temple and the city of Jerusalem would remain and not fall into the hands of the enemy. When King Zedekiah begins to trust that word more than Jeremiah's, he becomes restless and tries to lead an overthrow of Babylon.

As a result of the king's attempted coup, the Babylonian army is knocking at the door. Jeremiah, confined in the palace, and King Zedekiah is questioning Jeremiah's loyalty because of his prophecies of doom.

> *Jeremiah said, The word of the Lord came to me: Hanamel son of your uncle Shallum is going to come to you and say, "Buy my field that is at Anathoth, for the right of redemption by purchase is yours." Then my cousin Hanamel came to me in the court of the guard, in accordance with the word of the Lord, and said to me, "Buy my field that is at Anathoth in the land of Benjamin, for the right of possession and redemption is yours; buy it for yourself." Then I knew that this was the word of the Lord.* — Jeremiah 32:6-8

As the city is about to be destroyed and Jeremiah apparently will be spirited away to relative safety in Egypt, he does something amazing. He buys a field in his hometown of Anathoth in the land of Benjamin, just south of Jerusalem. Jeremiah buys the field in order to keep its possession in the family.

Jeremiah's very public action of buying this property, knowing that he will not step foot on it for many years, demonstrates the continual rhythm of loss and restoration that characterizes Jeremiah's prophecies at this point in Judah's history. Where prior to this, Jeremiah's message was almost totally one of gloom and doom, now he speaks of exile, but weaves into this dire prophecy the promise that someday, Judah will return to their homeland. Jeremiah is so sure of it that he puts his money where his mouth is! His prophesying has begun to morph into a message of consolation. He does not backpedal from the grievous period ahead that Judah faces. In fact, he has already written to the people of Judah now living in exile to Babylon, urging them to put down roots there:

> *Thus says the Lord of hosts, the God of Israel, to all the exiles whom I have sent into exile from Jerusalem to Babylon: Build houses and live in them; plant gardens and eat what they produce. Take wives and have sons and daughters; take wives for your sons, and give your daughters in marriage, that they may bear sons and daughters; multiply there, and do not decrease. But seek the welfare of the city where I have sent you into exile, and pray to the Lord on its behalf, for in its welfare you will find your welfare.* — Jeremiah 29:4-7

Can you hear the consolation in these words? God is saying to God's people, "I have not forgotten you; I am still watching out for you. I will bless your sons and daughters with wives and husbands and children. And I will hear you when you pray for this place that is your home right now — as I bless it, you will be blessed."

Perhaps you can hear God's pledge of faithfulness even more clearly in these words:

> *For surely I know the plans I have for you, says the Lord, plans for your welfare and not for harm, to give you a future with hope. Then when you call upon me and come and pray to me, I will hear you. When you search for me, you will find me; if you seek me with all*

your heart, I will let you find me, says the Lord, and I
will restore your fortunes and gather you from all the
nations and all the places where I have driven you, says
the Lord, and I will bring you back to the place from
which I sent you into exile. — Jeremiah 29:11-14

Although God's people have given their worship to idols rather than to God, although they have put their trust in treaties with enemies rather than in the Lord of hosts, although they have for all intents and purposes abandoned God, God has not abandoned them. And when the hours and days and years are darkest, the word of the Lord that comes to prophets like Jeremiah and Ezekiel and others is a word of consolation. The word these prophets are given by God to speak is a word of hope. Jeremiah demonstrates his trust in this promise of hope by buying land and securing its deed in an earthenware jar that will keep it safe over the years until he or other family members return to reclaim it.

These words are not merely Jeremiah's attempt to appease King Zedekiah! In chapter 32 alone, the phrases, "The word that came to Jeremiah from the Lord" and "Thus says the Lord" are recorded no less than seven times in a mere fifteen verses (Jeremiah 32:1-15). These are the prophet's way of indicating that this word surely comes from the Lord. As surely as the people of God now grieve and suffer loss, they will someday know joy again.

Last week, Jeremiah's heartfelt lament gave us pause to think about how we deal with grief, how we accompany those who face the valley of the shadow of death as David called it in Psalm 23. People need time to be in grief; they cannot and should not be rushed out of it. There is a time in the process of grief work when people must be allowed to sit with their pain, acknowledge it, and own it. To try to rush someone around or over grief will simply leave those emotions unresolved or buried, to resurface unexpectedly and painfully. Like the old camp chant about the bear hunt goes, when we're coming to short grass, or tall grass, or woods, or a river, "You can't go over it, you can't go under it, you can't go around it, you've got to go through it."

In the midst of our grieving over any loss, small or large, God will minister to us, offering us consolation, filling us with hope, reminding us that ours is a God who conquers death and promises life. Some people I know have been encouraged by signs in nature — a bird or a butterfly that is not where it should be. At a wedding I conducted several years ago, the bride and groom released monarch butterflies as a symbol of life. One of the butterflies, once freed, never left the bride's side. In fact, when all the others had flown away, it remained on her bouquet for nearly the whole reception. She and her mother saw in that butterfly the presence of the bride's father who had died in an accident years before.

In Jeremiah's case, the symbol of life comes in the unusual yet quite demonstrative command — "buy your cousin's field." Isn't it ironic that today, most recently widowed women and men are counseled against selling or buying property for at least a year after their spouse's death?

As we accompany others through times of loss and grief, God may guide to specific actions that can convey godly consolation. God will prompt us to speak words that offer hope God gives us the privilege of "buying a field in Anathoth" the response-ability of speaking the words and carrying out the actions that point hurting hearts to the promises of God.

Suffering is a reality of human existence. But God promises that our suffering will not be in vain. God also promises that we will not be alone in our suffering. Jesus, the very presence of God, has made suffering a holy and redemptive path through his willingness to embrace the cross. In raising Jesus from death, God promises that all who are joined to him in baptism will pass from death to life as well. We who trust these promises live as people who can venture, who can risk, who can "buy a field in Anathoth" for the sake of the brokenhearted.

I would encourage those preaching on this text to describe some specific ways that the people of their own faith community are witnessing to God's faithfulness by "buying a field in Anathoth" in their neighborhoods, workplaces, schools, towns, and cities.

May you discover the opportunities into which God leads you where you can accompany grieving, hurting people on their journey to hope and health. And may you discern well the privilege God will give you to "buy a field in Anathoth" ... and not hesitate to do it.

In the name of Jesus. Amen.

The ABC's Of Grief

Grief is one of the universal experiences of humankind. Its characteristics are recognizable across time and space. Because humanity is finite by nature, there will be a time to laugh and a time to cry for every man, woman, and child on earth.

We have been exploring the period in Old Testament history leading up to the Babylonian exile. The prophet Jeremiah has been our guide for the last six weeks. If it seems that we have been hopping and skipping through Jeremiah, you are right. It would appear that somewhere between the original scribing of Jeremiah and the rendering of those texts into a book of the Bible, some juggling took place. Those who designed the lectionary, the schedule of weekly readings that millions of Christians join in reading in worship, explored Jeremiah carefully for signs of a cohesive chronology from the reign of King Josiah until the destruction of Jerusalem. The order of our readings from Jeremiah, though a bit convoluted, have served to chronicle the story of once-mighty Judah's fall.

Today we depart from Jeremiah for a week to explore a text from Lamentations about the condition of the city of Jerusalem. There were some who formerly believed that Lamentations was also written by Jeremiah, but detailed study of the text shows few, if any, parallels in style or vocabulary with the book of Jeremiah.

It may be that Lamentations was a communal effort, a collection of poetry attempting to console the anguish of a people and their beloved city. The year is 586 BC. The siege is over, the enemy nation Babylon has conquered and destroyed Jerusalem. All the "brightest and best" of Judah's population have been marched off to exile in Babylon. The city is a ghost town, and the beloved temple lay in ruins.

Lamentations is written in an ancient form of lament called a "qina." The "qina" of Lamentations is distinctive because it is written in acrostic form — that is to say, the first stanza begins with a word beginning with the letter *aleph*, the second stanza begins with the second letter of the Hebrew alphabet, *bet*. Each new stanza begins with the next letter of the Hebrew alphabet. This may have made the lament easier to remember, or it may have been intended as a showcase for the poet's writing skill.

So in a very real sense, we have here the ABC's of grief. As I meditated on these first six verses of Lamentations 1, an English A, B, and C emerge as well. Perhaps they can give us a window into the world of a grieving person and guidance into how we might walk with them through it.

A Is For Abandoned

*How lonely sits the city that once was full of people!
How like a widow she has become, she that was great
among the nations. She that was a princess among the
provinces has become a vassal.* — Lamentations 1:1

It must be an utterly strange and haunting experience to walk through the empty streets of a city that had once been bustling with people and teeming with life. We see these images in movies from time to time, but most of us have no idea of what it would be like to be conquered, forced to leave our homeland, or perhaps even worse, to be among those who are left behind to pick up the pieces. I am not sure if there could be anything lonelier than to have been in Jerusalem in the days and weeks after the exile.

Abandonment is one of the keenest pains a grieving person feels. A widow or widower feels as though she or he has been left behind. And even though their spouse had absolutely no control over the time or nature of their death, it is not unusual for the person still living to feel anger at their loved one for abandoning them.

354

As friends of ours have grieved the death of their parents, nearly all of them at some time or another have used the word "orphaned" to describe their feelings. Generally, the death of our parents leaves us as the patriarchs and matriarchs of our families, and this can be a very lonely and uncomfortable feeling.

The most bitter grief we can bear is the death of a child. Words cannot begin to describe the sense of loneliness and abandonment parents experience when a son or daughter dies. No matter how old we are as parents, I am not sure that anything prepares us for this kind of grief. When a child dies, our dreams for that child's future and the life we would share with them dies, as well.

When a grieving person verbalizes their loneliness, there is a tendency among us to comfort them in their pain by assuring them that they are not alone. Although our hearts are in the right place as we say this, we really aren't comforting them at all. We are telling them that what they are feeling is not valid. We are telling them not to trust what they are feeling. We are signaling to them that we are not comfortable with their pain and anguish.

There is an ancient rite of grief in Jewish tradition called "sitting shiva." To "sit shiva" is to visit with a person who is mourning and generally it is to do so in silence or with only a few words spoken. The mourner is free to express their pain, their anger, their feelings of abandonment, and no one tries to convince them otherwise. They simply sit and listen and share food and grief.

When we visit with those who grieve, the most important thing we can do for them is to be there. We don't need to offer pearls of wisdom or lofty prayers. They just need us to listen — in the days immediately following their loved one's death and especially weeks and months later, when they may feel as though their loved one and they have been forgotten, abandoned.

B Is For Broken In Spirit

She weeps bitterly in the night with tears on her cheeks; among all her lovers she has no one to comfort her; all her friends have dealt treacherously with her, they have become her enemies.

355

*Judah has gone into exile with suffering and hard
servitude; she lives now among the nations and finds
no resting place; her pursuers have all overtaken her
in the midst of her distress.*

*The roads to Zion mourn, for no one comes to the
festivals; all her gates are desolate, her priests groan;
her young girls grieve, and her lot is bitter.*

*Her foes have become her masters, her enemies
prosper, because the Lord has made her suffer for the
multitude of her transgressions; her children have gone
away, captives before the foe.*

— Lamentations 1:2-5

Those who grieve experience brokenness in spirit and a sense of defeat. This is different than the sense of abandonment. It is more a sense of anger with oneself, sometimes combined with feelings of regret. "If only ..." becomes part of the lament at this time; "if only I had insisted she see a doctor sooner" or "If only I had been more careful, more thoughtful, more loving."

The broken in spirit assume some amount of blame and guilt for the loss they are experiencing. In the case of Judah's lament, there is an acknowledgment that "the multitude of her transgressions" have led to her suffering. God is included in the equation, as the one who makes her suffer, but ultimately the onus falls on faithless Judah.

How do we care for someone who is broken in spirit? When a person comes face-to-face with their transgressions, confession of sins is good for their soul. Any Christian can hear the confession of another person and remind them of God's forgiveness, compassion, and love. It may be that you can guide this person toward pastoral care by an ordained minister if he or she would prefer to speak confidentially.

It takes time to heal one's spirit. It takes time to regain trust. You can help a friend or loved one by taking cues from them. There will be baby steps, stumbling blocks, and major milestones ahead. Make time to embrace them and celebrate them with him or her.

C Is For Cry

To even speak a word of lament is an act of faith. Even though this poetry expresses disappointment with God for allowing this tragedy to happen, the fact that the poetry speaks of God at all presupposes that God is listening. Lamentations exists because those who grieved Judah's fall trusted that there was still someone beyond them who cared and possibly even someone who would come to their aid. The same is true for anyone who grieves today. We dare to cry out, to reach out, because we believe that someone will hear us.

During the Second World War, in England, there were many infants who were placed in over-crowded hospital wards with few caregivers. Tragically, the caregivers were simply unable to give all the children the attention, let alone the love, they needed. Within a few weeks, the caregivers began to realize that some of the babies were crying less and some had stopped crying all together. Because their cries had gone unheeded for so long, the infants ceased to trust that their cries would bring someone to them, and so they stopped.

We cry because we believe someone will hear us. We reach out in our grief because we want someone to join us. Our lament may be an expectation that someone can or should fix our situation. Have you ever had a day that just begged to be unpacked, processed, talked through, so that you might be able to put the events into perspective and move on? Early in our marriage, when I would come home having had a day like that, I would begin to talk it through with my husband. He would set his wonderful logical engineer's mind to work solving my problems.

It took a while, but together we discovered that what I was really looking for was someone to listen, someone to care, someone who would simply be there for me with unconditional love ... and an occasional insight or two!

Perhaps a person cries out to God, wanting ready relief from suffering and pain. Or she cries out, knowing full well that there is no simple delivery from the mess in which she finds herself. No matter what motivates us to cry out to God, there is something deep inside of us that longs to know that we do not grieve alone. It is that God-shaped space in us that only God can fill. As we are shaped for God to dwell in us, and share life with us, God shares grief and sorrow with us as well. Throughout the prophets' writings we have heard the laments God has cried for God's people. As surely as the people of Judah felt abandonment and broken in spirit, God also felt their pain. In fact, it was God's pain even before it was theirs. They are not alone — God weeps with them. And God looks to the day when mourning will turn to dancing, and sorrow will be transformed into joy.

Our God is deeply and fully acquainted with grief. God's own heart broke when his Son Jesus suffered and died upon the cross at Calvary. But ultimately God is a God of life, whose love and compassion conquer the grave and grant new and eternal life.

May you and those with whom you share the joys and sorrows of life know the peace of a God who promises relationship where there has been abandonment and healing for broken spirits. And may you know with certainty that your cries will always be heard.

In the name of Jesus. Amen.

Sermons On The First Readings

For Sundays
After Pentecost
(Last Third)

Restoring
God's Activity

R. Kevin Mohr

Introduction

In the last third of the season after Pentecost virtually all of the first reading lessons begin to focus on promises having to do with a future saving or restoring activity of God. All of the readings but one are from the prophetic books of the Babylonian exile and the period of restoration shortly after the remnant returned to Judah and Jerusalem. The contexts addressed by those lessons were uniformly depressing and disappointing. To each of those situations, however, God, through the prophet, tries to get the people to see the bigger picture; to look beyond a depressing past and a disappointing present to the future with God. The prophetic refrain, over and over again, is that God has not given up and will not give up on his people ever; that the God who forgives the disobedience of the past and who holds the future is with his people in the struggles of the present. Just hold on! Those are good words for God's people of every time and context to hear.

— R. Kevin Mohr

Proper 23
Pentecost 21
Ordinary Time 28
Jeremiah 29:1, 4-7

Making Ourselves At Home

In a scene from the romantic comedy, *While You Were Sleeping*, "Ox" Callaghan is waxing eloquent at the breakfast table one morning about those rare moments in life when everything seems to be going just right and falling into place. "In that one minute," he says, "you have peace." But his son, Jack, who is Ox's partner in the family business, has finally decided it is time to break the news to his dad that he wants out to start his own business, and so he bursts his father's bubble, saying, "Pop, this isn't that minute."[1]

The Jewish people in the sixth century BC really didn't need anyone to tell them that they were not in one of those good times. On the contrary, God's chosen people were going through one of the darkest periods in their history, one that would, perhaps, only be superseded in sorrow by the destruction of Jerusalem in 70 AD and then the holocaust of World War II.

After being a vassal state of the Assyrian empire for nearly 100 years, the country had been completely overrun by Assyria's archenemy, Babylon. The political leaders in Judah had consistently made poor choices, often backing or counting on the wrong horse in the geopolitical race of the ancient Middle East, as Assyria, Egypt, and then Babylon jockeyed for position and power. The temple had been ransacked and stripped, and the vast majority of the political, financial, religious, and social leaders had either been killed or carried off, along with all of the wealth of the nation, into exile in Babylon.

And now, a letter comes from the prophet Jeremiah. He was among the remnant of those who were out of the Judean power loop before and, therefore, were allowed to remain in Judah and Jerusalem by the occupying power. Jeremiah had been out of favor with the royal court in Judah because he had not toed the party line, but had warned that the salvation of the people would not come through political alliances. More to the point, Jeremiah had urged the people and their leaders to accept the punishment of God through the Babylonians and not resist the occupying power.

No doubt, Jeremiah was probably the last person the exiles wanted to hear from at that moment because it was almost inconceivable he would not say a smug, "I told you so!" But as much as Jeremiah may have wanted to rub it in, the message God actually sent via his letter was even more surprising than his not gloating. The Lord said:

> *Build houses and live in them; plant gardens and eat what they produce. Take wives and have sons and daughters; take wives for your sons, and give your daughters in marriage, that they may bear sons and daughters; multiply there, and do not decrease. But seek the welfare of the city where I have sent you into exile, and pray to the Lord on its behalf, for in its welfare you will find your welfare.* — Jeremiah 29:5-7

God, through Jeremiah, basically tells the people, "make yourselves at home" — even in exile in a foreign land! On an emotional level, the people of Judah in Babylon could have identified with Dorothy, from *The Wizard of Oz*, chanting over and over again in their minds, if not out loud, "There's no place like home! There's no place like home!" The whole identity of the Jews as the people of God was intimately tied up with the land given to them by God, and their worship of God had become — perhaps? — obsessively focused on the temple in Jerusalem. Resign themselves to life in exile? No way! Their attitude then could be summed up in the words of one of the psalms of lament written during the exile:

> *By the rivers of Babylon — there we sat down and there we wept when we remembered Zion. On the willows there we hung up our harps. For there our captors asked*

us for songs, and our tormentors asked for mirth, say-
ing, "Sing us one of the songs of Zion!" How could we
sing the Lord's song in a foreign land?
                                        — Psalm 137:1-4

Devastating things can happen that dislocate us physically, emotionally, spiritually. Life becomes totally out of joint because the old, familiar orientation points are gone or are at least no longer visible. There is an unreal quality to everything. One of the names given to that experience for those who have moved from one country to another is "culture shock." As a former missionary who has lived in five different countries, I know that culture shock *is* all that and more, even when you prepare for the change and actually choose it.

For example: Immediately following language study in Malagasy back in the early 1980s, my wife, Debbie, and I were assigned to do rural evangelism work among the Bara people of southern Madagascar. After a fourteen-hour trip on a terrible road we arrived at our destination, Betroka, a dusty town that looked almost like something out of a Hollywood western. Tired, thirsty, exhausted, and nervous, we stepped out of the Land Rover only to find that the local church women were not expecting us yet and so had not cleaned up the old missionary residence that had been vacant for five years. Debbie almost immediately descended into culture shock that manifested itself in an obsessive desire to get the house clean, starting with the bathroom. For four days, she could do virtually nothing other than clean and scrub that bathroom and sleep whenever possible. All of our barrels and boxes of possessions were strewn throughout the house, unopened because "the house wasn't clean yet."

On the fifth day, I firmly but gently announced to Debbie that we were going to begin opening our barrels and put our things up so that we could make the old place start to feel like home. I unlocked and removed the steel wring from the first barrel and started pulling things out. Debbie scowled at me and cried at first, but within minutes, she was helping me unpack (*and* telling me where to put things!) and the crisis was over.

365

As hard as our experience of culture shock was, the emotional and psychological damage that would result from a forced, violent deportation and exile in a foreign land — as the people of Judah went through in the sixth century BC — must have been extremely traumatizing indeed. God's word via Jeremiah to the exiles, however, turns out to be remarkably similar to what we discovered was the key to dragging ourselves out of culture shock in Madagascar. God tells the people, in effect, to start "opening up their barrels," to get on with living, and to make themselves at home in exile. The alternative was for them to stay traumatized zombies, to remain casualties, and allow a victim mentality to hold them back from the blessings of God and from being a blessing to others.

While we were wrestling with our culture shock and sitting in that dusty building in Betroka, we could neither experience the blessings God wanted to share with us through the people of the town, nor could we fulfill the mission to which we had been called. The disorientation we were experiencing threatened our role in God's blessing to the Bara people by sharing with them the good news of Jesus Christ. In a similar way, though the people of Israel were in exile, their basic calling and identity had not changed. They were still God's people, and they were still heirs to the same mission of promise given to Abraham and Sarah so long ago: "... in you all the families of the earth shall be blessed" (Genesis 12:3b).

The exiles were called to be a blessing even in what appeared to be a supposedly accursed situation. But they could only be that blessing and in the process be blessed themselves if they got on with living and made themselves at home. I cannot help but wonder if God's advice to the people was not meant to be a subtle reminder of the earlier sojourn in a foreign land by their ancestors who were being oppressed by their Egyptian overlords. In spite of that difficult prior situation, the children of Israel grew in numbers and thrived and were eventually led miraculously out of slavery in Egypt by God. The unexpected message of Jeremiah's letter acknowledges the reality of God's punishment of his people by the hands of the Babylonians, but in its parallel to the Egyptian experience it points ahead to the wonderful words of verses 10-14 that promise the exiles a "future with hope."

Jeremiah's letter also speaks to us. The message from God is not just a pious platitude encouraging us to make the best out of bad situations. It is a reminder to us that God is not limited even when we believe our lives have been restricted and then cut-off from all that is familiar and known. It is a reminder for us as followers of Jesus Christ of what we now know because of the cross and resurrection: that God is at work even in the most difficult of situations and experiences. If God could work in and through the oppression of Egypt, if God could work through the depressing shock of exile in Babylon, if God could work, hidden, in the suffering of the cross, then God's people can live in the present and be at home anywhere. God in Christ pitched his tent, opened the barrels of God's blessings, and made himself at home among us even though it meant going to the cross and back. Therefore, anywhere God takes, leads, or puts us is a place of blessing for us and through us for those among whom we live and make our home. Amen.

---

1. *While You Were Sleeping*, produced by Joe Roth & Roger Birnbaum, directed by John Turtletaub, 103 minutes, Hollywood and Caravan Pictures, 1995.

Proper 24
Pentecost 22
Ordinary Time 29
Jeremiah 31:27-34

Not Another Rerun!

Not another rerun!

Many of us probably expressed that sentiment at some point during the past summer when we sat down in front of the television for an hour or so of relaxation after a hard day's work. Disappointment then set in as we surfed our favorite channels only to discover that overly hyped unreal "reality" shows and reruns of programs we had already seen were all that was being shown. By the time fall came around we were eager for something new.

Our desire for something new extends to more significant areas of life as well. For example, politics. There is little doubt that the possibility of something new fueled a great part of the interest in the 2008 presidential campaign with our first African-American candidate in one of the major parties and one of the first female vice-presidential candidates in the other. The desire for something new, especially in the political arena, is first of all a recognition that things are not going well and that a change needs to be made.

The exiles in Babylon and the remnant left behind to eke out an existence in the devastated land of Judah were certainly looking and hoping for a change in their social, political, and economic situation. They were bitter and searching for someone — the previous generations or even God — to blame for their misfortune, as evidenced by the proverb referred to in verses 29 and 30. The people knew from hard personal and communal experience that the original covenant had not worked out too well — the Babylonian exile was all the proof anyone needed. They were tasting the bitter fruit of poor choices made by earlier generations, and it just didn't seem to be fair! Something obviously needed to change.

Chapters 30 and 31 in the book of Jeremiah (often given the title of "the book of consolation") address that hope for change in the form of the promise of a new covenant between God and his people. Before the message moves directly to talk of the new covenant, there is a mini-rerun of or, perhaps, more correctly speaking, a flashback to Jeremiah's call in chapter 1:10. In a direct echo of Jeremiah's commissioning as a prophet to the people and the nations, God uses essentially the same verbs of activity to preview the new thing God is about to do: to pluck up and break down, to overthrow, destroy, and bring evil, and to build and to plant.

Now, even though verses 38 and following will later speak of rebuilding the walls and the buildings of the city, the metaphor here seems to be more pastoral or agricultural. The imagery is one of God as a concerned and involved farmer who has watched over the land. The language used here reminds me of my best friend, Maurice.

Maurice is a third generation wheat and barley farmer from Australia, and while I was attending boarding school in Adelaide, South Australia, during my high school years, I would often go home with Maurice to his family's farm on weekends. As a person with no farmers in my own family tree, it was quite amazing for me to see how close he and his father were to the land. They didn't just work the land, but they had a relationship to it. Even when they were physically off of their property for an extended length of time (which rarely happened), they were thinking about the land and worrying about the weather, or actually talking about what they needed to do for the next crop. They were watching over and working the land all the time so that it could be fruitful. That is how God's concern for and involvement with his people is presented by Jeremiah.

God, the prophet says, is planning to re-sow the land and make it alive and fruitful again. That necessarily involves clearing and preparing the land for planting. While the clearing of the land is by nature destructive of what was there before, the real goal is something constructive, positive, and life-giving. The punishment of defeat and exile, therefore, was not really proof of God's departure or absence, but of his tending of his people. Continuing the agricultural metaphor, partially cleared land is useless, so God through Jeremiah is trying to help the exiles and the remnant see that the punishment for the people's unfaithfulness in the past must run its full course because it is an integral part of God's restoration.[1]

As caring as the image of the concerned farmer is, when the new covenant is actually spoken of directly in verse 31 and following, the metaphor changes again. It becomes even more intimate. Now, God's self-presentation is as a suitor/parent/husband who, in the past tenderly led the people by hand out of the land of Egypt. Even though treated unfaithfully throughout the history of his people since then, God comes back again, but not just with a rerun of what didn't work before. God comes back with a new covenant.

What is it, though, that makes this covenant in some way new?

The newness does not consist in a radical discontinuity with the content and structure of the old covenants. The covenant at Sinai in particular also emphasized the initiative of God and an intimate relationship between God and his people (Exodus 19:1-6). The point is that God's character remains constant and trustworthy; what changes is humanity and its desire to keep the law and the covenant. That change is represented in the words, "I will put my law within them, and I will write it on their hearts; and I will be their God, and they shall be my people" (Jeremiah 31:33).

The covenant at Sinai had been written on tablets of stone. The stipulations of that covenant were quite literally spelled out and were to be memorized and studied. However, what was meant to be a living relationship all too easily became a "head thing" with external criteria and a checklist of what to do or not do. The temptation for people is always to try to turn the living reality of faith into an object that we think can be controlled or managed. By the time of Jesus, for example, the covenant at Sinai had been so objectified that the scribes and the Pharisees had constructed a huge "hedge" of lesser laws as a protection around the centerpiece of the Ten Commandments. For Protestant Christians especially, the temptation is to insist on doctrinal purity to the point that even people from the same faith tradition sometimes cannot pray together! The relationship to God and to God's people becomes primarily a matter of the head and not of the heart.

But let's not jump to a hasty conclusion! When we borrow the phrase, "written on the heart" from Jeremiah, we often misunderstand what God, through the prophet, was saying. Upon hearing that phrase we immediately think in terms of emotions because, for us, the heart is used as a metaphor for the seat of our emotions. However, in the Hebraic thought system the bowels or the stomach were considered the center of human emotions, not the heart. The heart was the center of intellect and will and for making decisions. So, to say that the law would be written on people's hearts means that the new covenant would not be based on something as transitory and volatile as our emotions. Instead, God declares, it would be "put within" us. To use computer language, it would be embedded in us where it most matters, in the same way that an embedded computer system is not just an added-on peripheral, but is something that has become integral to how the computer functions and makes decisions.

The new covenant, similarly, is no longer something external to us, but functions within us. God gives us "the capacity to be faithful and obedient."[2] As a result, the covenant relationship to God can become all that it was originally intended to be: "a warm delight to the people, not a cold prescription."[3]

The foundation for the newness of the covenant is introduced by the preposition "for" in verse 34: "for I will forgive their iniquity, and remember their sin no more." God's selective memory loss is the key to God's most important communication with us, as the following story illustrates:

A bishop went to visit with a woman of his diocese who claimed to have direct verbal communication with the Lord. After meeting with her, the bishop was still skeptical of her claims. In order to put them to the test, he asked the woman to find out from God what sins the bishop would confess in the next week. Later, the woman came to the bishop to make her report. The bishop inquired, "So, what did God say were the sins I confessed this past week?" "Well," the woman replied, "the Lord said, 'I don't remember anymore.' "

372

The fresh start the new covenant promises is possible because while we may hold grudges against earlier generations and even against our creator, God does not. In fact, for our sake God suffers from intentional selective memory loss when it comes to our sins and unfaithfulness. The knowledge of God's merciful and forgiving character works an internal change in us and engraves God's law, that is God's will and character, on our hearts and embeds it deep within our core. God's selective memory loss means that God doesn't give up on us. The people in exile were tempted to believe that God had given up on them. The prophet tried to help them see the big picture, one that even had room for the hardships of life in exile as being part of God's plan for restoration and renewal, in the same way that a farmer must first do the hard work of clearing the land before it can become fruitful.

The land cannot prepare itself for planting; the farmer has to do it. Similarly, the future of God's people did not hang on Judah's self-restoration, but on a new act by God. Our fate does not hang on our self-restoration but on the new covenant that finds its ultimate fulfillment in what God has done in Christ Jesus. That means we do not have to keep reliving the same old reruns of our lives. God is not a cold-hearted judge, keeping score, but is like an attentive spouse who leads us into a deeper relationship or like a watchful farmer who plants something new and living deep within us so that we can become all that God wants us to be. Amen.

---

1. D. A. Carson, R. T. France, J. A. Motyer, G. J. Wenham, editors, *New Bible Commentary: 21st Century Edition*, 4th Edition (Downers Grove, Illinois: InterVarsity Press, 1994), p. 694.

2. Gene M. Tucker, *Preaching the New Common Lectionary: Year C Lent, Holy Week, Easter* (Nashville: Abingdon Press, 1985), p. 106.

3. *Op cit*, Carson, et al, p. 696.

Earth, Wind, And Fire

While serving as a missionary to Madagascar with my family in the 1980s and 90s, I witnessed at least two locust swarms. On one level I was fascinated by the spectacle of a good portion of the sky suddenly becoming black with a thick cloud of locusts. There was something eerily beautiful about the shimmering light that managed to pass through the swarm to the ground as the insects passed overhead. Even a small swarm may cover several square miles of sky and weigh thousands of tons. Locusts eat the equivalent of their own weight in a day, and, driven by the winds, a swarm can travel some 300 plus miles a day during the late afternoon and evening. The largest swarm on record covered 400 square miles, consisting of approximately forty billion locusts!

However, I knew that my detached, academic wonder could not be shared by my Malagasy students, coworkers, and friends at the regional seminary where I taught for eight years. At the first sight of a swarm, the alarm would be given and the whole town would gather with shouts and whoops and the flailing of arms holding brightly colored cloth in an attempt to keep the swarm from landing in the area. The Malagasy knew all too well that the arrival of the locusts was a devastating life-and-death situation. This is so because locust swarms almost always occur in those marginal semi-arid regions of the world often subject to frequent droughts as well; places where there is little margin for error when it comes to agricultural production.

Once the locust swarm moves on after having destroyed the young crop, there is the anxious wait to see if more rains will come.

That precipitation is needed for a replacement crop or even for next year's planting. One crop failure is bad enough, but two in a row could spell disaster for an area. Verse 23 of Joel chapter 2 perfectly captures the level of joy that accompanies the arrival of that desperately needed and looked-for rain in areas impacted by locust swarms.

God's message through the prophet Joel acknowledges the harsh reality the people continued to experience in the land of Judah after the return from exile and even after the temple of Jerusalem had been rebuilt. Drought, as is often the case, had followed a devastating locust swarm that, God admits, had been sent against the people as punishment. What the prophet proclaims here is nothing new. The faith and theology of Israel was essentially a land-based theology, tied integrally to the promise of a land for the children of Israel. It goes all the way back to the story of the fall in Genesis, where the creator announces to the first humans that the affects of human sin will be manifested in the earth:

> *Cursed is the ground because of you; in toil you shall*
> *eat of it all the days of your life; thorns and thistles it*
> *shall bring forth for you.*   — Genesis 3:17b-18

Therefore, it is not surprising to find that, for Joel, "the land is the barometer of Israel's relationship with Yahweh."[1] The apostle Paul picks up on this divine ecology when he speaks in Romans, chapter 8, of the whole creation waiting and longing and groaning for the redemption of God's children (Romans 8:19-23). While today we may not be able to make the direct one-to-one association between our disobedience and specific events in the natural world as Joel did, the church has recently begun to recognize and acknowledge in a new way that the overall condition of our fragile planet is related to human sin. We have not been the faithful stewards of creation we were meant to be.

However, as important as our imprint on the land is, the focus of this text lies elsewhere. God, through the prophet Joel, uses the imagery of a restored and fruitful land as a barometer for showing the character and restoring activity of God. It is God's imprint on the land and on the people that matters in the ultimate sense, which will bring about the changes that are needed, changes that will help to heal the people of the psychological damage they have suffered. A change is in the wind.

After having consumed so much grain, locusts are not able to fly long distances on their own but wait for the late afternoon breezes to rise up, take flight, and spread their destruction. It is also the wind that signals the end to a drought. A fresh breeze comes up with the hint of moisture and freshness in it; the wind no longer has a dry, baked, dusty smell. A change, we say, is in the wind, and soon, that wind does bring the early and the later rains, the first, to soften the cracked and parched earth and make it ready for planting; the later rains to nourish and grow the crop. Those rains, borne on the wind, will mark the land as renewed in the immediate time of the original hearers of Joel's message. But those wind-borne rains also bring to mind for the prophet a future spiritual wind of change.

That change will be brought about by the outpouring of the Spirit of God. Perhaps not coincidentally, the Hebrew word for wind and spirit is the same, *ruach*. While the wind-borne rains signal a change in the physical living conditions of the people, the gift of God's Spirit ushers in a radical new stage in their life together; a stage that is far more inclusive and expansive. The Spirit will be poured out on "all flesh" — not just a few spiritual leaders as in the past — and there will be no barriers based on age, sex, or social status. The renewal of the land was one sign of God's presence; now the outpouring of the Spirit is an even stronger indication of God's life-giving and restorative presence. Whereas the people before were dependent upon political and spiritual leaders who, more often than not, lacked vision and discernment and led the people away from God's will, a change is in the wind. God promises a new day when the spiritual gifts will be so prevalent among the people that they will never again be put to shame because they will all have equal access to God's revelation.

Twice in these verses we are told that God is acting so that the people will not "again be put to shame" (vv. 26- 27). Shame is far more significant than just embarrassment. Embarrassment is a temporary emotional response to a specific situation. Shame is a condition that can become chronic, a state of being that affects our ability to function in the world because it eats away at who we understand ourselves to be. Shame can take a deep hold on us when we come to realize that we are not living up to whom we think we should be. Mistakes are embarrassing; chronic failures, that are the result of weaknesses of character or because we have allowed ourselves to be led astray by others when we should have known better, are extremely shameful.

The people who had returned from exile in Babylon knew they had not simply made a few mistakes. They had failed to live up to the expectations of their covenant relationship with God. Therefore, they had not just been embarrassed, but had been put to shame, and that shame made their future look bleak.

God addressed that shame with the surprising good news that though they had been punished and suffered greatly, God was still with them and would continue to bless them in and through creation. Salvation would be both a "now" and "then" experience: now through physical renewal of the land; later through a spiritual renewal of all flesh in the outpouring of the Spirit of God. The promise of God's presence, however, looks beyond the present and the future to the final consummation of "the great and terrible day of the Lord" (v. 31), a day of "fire and columns of smoke" (v. 30) as well. Only with the removal of their shame by God's promise of continuing presence could the people begin to face the future with hope.

It is the same for us. We are included in the message of hope, because the Spirit will be poured out on "all flesh." And in the suffering, death, and resurrection of Jesus Christ we know that our shame has been dealt with once and for all. Jesus took our shame upon himself and it was crucified on the cross with him. God in Christ took the greatest emblem of shame — the cross — and used it to break the power of shame over our lives through the resurrection (Colossians 2:12-15).

Contrary to what Satan would have us believe, our shame does not mean that sin and the fear of death have the final say over our lives; God's loving and restoring presence does. Therefore, God's people can be glad and rejoice because on that great and terrible, final day of fire, everyone who calls upon the name of the Lord will be saved. Amen.

---

1. D. A. Carson, R. T. France, J. A. Motyer, G. J. Wenham, editors, *New Bible Commentary: 21st Century Edition*, 4th Edition (Downers Grove, Illinois: InterVarsity Press, 1994), p. 788.

Put Within Us

Note: This text was also dealt with earlier in the exposition of the first reading for Proper 24.

In the years immediately prior to 1517, Martin Luther was slowly but surely killing himself physically, emotionally, and spiritually. As penance for his sins he would flog himself and sleep naked in his cell. His confession sessions sometimes lasted hours as he tried to ensure that every sin, no matter how minor, had been confessed. Luther believed what scripture and the church said about the seriousness of sin and the righteousness of God. Therefore, he was at an impasse, caught between the righteous nature of God and the sinful nature of his humanity. How was a relationship between the two possible? The demands of this righteous God were so great and impossible for sinful humanity to fulfill that Luther later admitted, "I was myself more than once driven to the very abyss of despair so that I wished I had never been created. Love God? I hated him!"[1]

What Luther realized later through his study of scripture and his resultant rediscovery of the gospel, was that for there to be the possibility of a loving relationship with God the whole nature of humanity needs to be changed. That change is what God promises to accomplish through the new covenant, first proclaimed by the prophet Jeremiah.

After years of political maneuvering, time had run out for Judah. The Babylonians had come in 598 BC and would come again in 586 to destroy the country and the city of Jerusalem totally after an abortive, futile, and ill-advised rebellion by the puppet king, Zedekiah, whom Babylon had installed on the throne. Chapters 30 and 31 are set between the two Babylonian invasions when tensions were extremely high and time was terribly short for Judah. All human options had been exhausted. Was the impending doom God's final word to his chosen people? Was the covenant ended?

The covenant first established at Sinai was certainly broken. The emphasis here, though, is not specifically on transgressions of the law and the breaking of covenant stipulations as handed down through Moses at Sinai, but on a failed relationship. In poignant words of sadness, God speaks as a distressed parent and a hurt husband in verse 32: "I took them by the hand ... though I was their husband." What had been disrupted was the basic relationship that gave purpose, meaning, and life to God's people. In that sense, the old covenant was ended, and it could not be saved by acting as if nothing had happened. Above all, the relationship could not be restored by those who had broken it in the first place.

We know the reality of that principle from daily life. If I say or do something that hurts my wife and damages our relationship, there really is nothing I, as the offender, can do or say to restore the relationship. Ultimately the offended party, my wife, is the only one who can resurrect our relationship. She must take the initiative.

God declared through Jeremiah that he would take the initiative to "make a new covenant." The word "make" is literally "cut." The use of this word is probably intentional in order to make the first hearers and readers think beyond the Sinai covenant back to the one made with Abraham in Genesis, chapter 15. To "cut" a covenant refers to the widespread ancient practice of cutting sacrificial animals in two, laying each half over against the other in two opposing lines, and then having the two parties in the covenant walk between the split carcasses, with the spoken or implied self-condemnatory oath that "may the same be done to me if I break this covenant."

As a missionary child in Papua New Guinea in the late 1970s, I actually witnessed a covenant-cutting ceremony between two warring tribal groups. The ceremony was virtually identical to that practiced in the ancient Middle East of Bible times. However, I was too young to fully understand the significance of what I had seen that day until my parents later explained that the tribal leader of the group that had been attacked first, refused to walk between the carcass halves, thereby dooming the two groups to another round of senseless payback killings.

In God's covenant with Abraham (still known as Abram then), though the carcass halves were laid out, only the presence of God passed between the pieces. The first covenant with the primal ancestor of God's chosen people, then, was unilateral. The new covenant with God's people will also be unilateral. God will take the initiative and restore and renew the relationship. Since a failed relationship was the root cause of the broken covenant, what was truly needed was not more or better laws but a change of heart that would allow God's people to be faithful. That is exactly what God promises to do.

"I will put my law within them, and I will write it on their hearts," God says in verse 33. The stipulations of the Sinai covenant were inscribed on tablets of stone and later written down in documents, something external to the people of the covenant. God will now ensure faithfulness by making the covenant something radically internalized and a part of who and what the people of God are. What goes on at the cellular level gives us a physical illustration of this significant spiritual change God announces.

As science and technology have allowed us to delve deeper and deeper into the wonder of the living cell, the DNA molecule, with its now-famous double-helix structure, continues to astound us with its complexity and significance for all life. So much DNA is packed into the nucleus of a cell, for example, that if it were stretched out it would measure roughly three miles long! Even more amazing is what DNA, the genetic molecule of all living things, is able to do. DNA is the information-bearing molecule that determines everything about the physical make-up of each living thing. The basic code or language for this information is the same for all life, but the combination, location on the double helix, and the length of the molecule makes all the difference in the world between species and individuals.

Significantly, because the code or language and the base structure are the same, individual or collections of genes on one molecule can be moved between and within species. Genetic information can be spliced in and combined with the original material, creating new effects. That is how some very important medical advances have occurred, including, for example, the treatment of diabetes through the creation of human insulin and growth hormones.

The genetic changes produced through gene splicing and manipulation sound a lot like the fundamental spiritual change in humanity God wants to bring about by putting the law within his people and writing it on their hearts. God, in effect, intends to write himself into his people, into their "spiritual DNA" at the core of their being. New "spiritual code" will be spliced in so that it becomes a part of who the people are and what they are able to do in terms of keeping the covenant. No longer will the covenant relationship be something that is just "worn on the sleeve," so to speak; or in the language of the old covenant, worn as a phylactery on the forehead or attached to the wrist (Deuteronomy 6:8-9). Changing the metaphor, all those who are in relationship to God will be just like the computers and electronic equipment that bear the white and blue "Intel Inside!" brand stamp. The covenant relationship will be so internalized that God's people will, in effect, bear the stamp, "God Inside!" on their hearts. Because that stamp is written on their hearts — in Hebrew thought, the seat of intellect, decision, and will, *not* emotions — it will be manifested in obedient faithfulness to the covenant relationship with God. The law, written on the heart, is not really a legal matter. All of the laws, in fact, have always been nothing other than a description of what it means to be in relationship to God and others. Now the law can be summarized down to its core as follows, " 'I am yours, and you are mine,' says the Lord. That is the language of love and faithfulness."[2]

For us as followers of Jesus Christ, we understand God's new covenant as having been inaugurated in Jesus and made available to all people through faith in his life, death, and resurrection. The Reformation is often understood and interpreted as a time in which great theological doctrines were formulated and explained clearly

384

for the masses. But that way of viewing the events of the sixteenth century misses the main point. Luther, in his despair, did not need new doctrines; he needed a way to be in relationship to God. In Jesus Christ that is what he found and was so eager to share with others.

In Jesus Christ we truly see "God inside" and "God with us" who is not against us but forgives our sins radically (v. 31). In Christ, we see the new covenant — we see the "language of love and faithfulness" — in the flesh and in action. In him we see what it means to be in relationship to God and God's people, and through him we are invited into that relationship in a new way. Through the faith relationship with Christ Jesus it is no longer we who live, but Christ who lives in us (Galatians 2:20). Therefore, the apostle Paul could write, "If anyone is in Christ, there is a new creation" (2 Corinthians 5:17). There, the language of love and faithfulness — the language of the new covenant — is spoken and lived from deep within because we have been stamped with the love of God. Amen.

---

1. Roland H. Bainton, *Here I Stand: A Life of Martin Luther* (New York: Mentor Books, 1950), p. 44.

2. Gene M. Tucker, *Preaching the New Common Lectionary, Year C, Lent, Holy Week, Easter* (Nashville: Abingdon Press, 1984), p. 68.

Oh, By The Way ...

The book of Daniel presents us with the words and visions of the prophet Daniel, who lived and worked in the Babylonian empire during the exile of the Jewish people there in the sixth and fifth centuries BC. Obviously, that was a difficult time for God's people, but, *oh, by the way*, the book of Daniel itself was probably put in its final form perhaps 300 years later during the persecution of the Jewish people under Antiochus IV Epiphanes circa 165 BC. So the book is probably best understood to be addressing the trying times and the context of the Jewish people in the second century BC.

This is the only time we get to read from Daniel in the whole three-year lectionary cycle, but we have a very chopped-up reading that skips eleven verses. In this truncated and disjointed form the passage is admittedly hard to understand at first. A big part of the problem — beyond skipping eleven verses! — is that we, in our day and age, simply don't really "get" apocalyptic literature, which is the form or genre of the book of Daniel. Part of the problem in understanding apocalyptic writings is that scholars are not in total agreement about what constitutes the genre, and some dispute that the genre even exists! A very tentative bare-bones definition for our purpose here is that an "apocalypse" is a *revelation* given by God through a *mediator* to a *seer* concerning *future events*.[1]

Another main reason we don't understand apocalyptic literature is that we have been conditioned by certain popular theologians of the late 1960s and 1970s, and by some television evangelists still on the air today, to think of apocalyptic writings as blueprints for the end times. That lens for understanding this type of literature results in a frenzy of speculation about a timetable for the last days. The result is that while we become focused on trying to understand the details literally, the main point, the central message, becomes obscured and lost.

The main point also gets obscured and lost sometimes in our All Saints Day/Sunday celebrations. We often focus on the stories of the great ancient martyrs of the faith or turn the celebration into a memorial service for those loved ones who became glorified saints through death in the past year. But *oh, by the way*, the day is called *all* Saints, so we, the *living* saints, are also included. In fact, this day is meant for our encouragement and comfort in much the same way that Daniel's message and story was originally meant to inspire the people who were alive in the second century BC when it was first written down in its final form. So the focus of All Saints is on our situation.

Back to the text, such as it is: Daniel sees a terrifying vision of four of beasts coming up out of what is suggestive of the primordial chaos when God first began creating (vv. 2-3; compare that with Genesis 1:1-2). The verses left out of our reading give all of the gory details (vv. 4-8), which is probably just as good, because then we would be tempted to try to figure out what each detail means and signifies. We would quickly lose the basic message. The fact that some of us even try to figure out all of the specific details of a passage like this is the height of hubris, given that Daniel himself professes to have no clue as to the significance of the beasts. He is simply terrified and troubled by the visions he has been given. Therefore, still in the depths of his trance, Daniel approaches one of the heavenly attendants for consolation and interpretation. In verse 17 he is informed that the four beasts each represent a distinct king or kingdom that will reign on earth. And then, almost as an afterthought — *oh, by the way* — the attendant continues, "But the holy ones of the Most High shall receive the kingdom and possess the kingdom forever — forever and ever" (v. 18).

This almost parenthetical afterthought is very typical of biblical apocalyptic writing. What is amazing about this genre is that the main point of the literature is usually revealed in the "*oh, by the way*...." We see that literary device all throughout the one apocalyptic document of the New Testament: the book of Revelation. Revelation is filled with fantastical scenes describing through metaphor and symbolic language the hardship of life on earth for God's people, but those scenes are juxtaposed with alternating scenes of the Lamb sitting on the throne. These parenthetical *oh, by the way*s are the real message: No matter what happens here on earth, God's reign is not in jeopardy; evil will be defeated and destroyed, and God has a plan and a glorious future for his saints.

That, too, is the basic message of Daniel, chapter 7. In verse 9-14, that were left out of the reading, we hear of both the power of the ancient one (or the ancient of days) over the four beasts, and the everlasting glory and dominion given to the Son of Man. No matter what powers might threaten, whether in 400 BC in exile in Babylon or under Antiochus IV Epiphanes or even today, God rules, and his holy ones' future is secure.

Now, kings and queens and presidents have magnificent tombs and memorials raised up for them after death. In Ohio, we claim seven or eight former presidents as native Ohioans. Within a couple hours' drive of my home I can visit four impressive presidential memorials. But, *oh, by the way*, the fact of the tombs of the kings and queens buried in Westminster Abbey in London, the fact of the pyramids and the Valley of the Kings in Egypt — the fact of all those tombs and memorials proves that the power and dominion of earthly rulers does not last.

There is only one who will always be on the throne — the ancient of days, and those who are his faithful servants will be part of his kingdom forever — and just in case we are uncertain if eternity is really meant here, the attendant adds on another "forever and ever" for emphasis. That promise given to Daniel has been verified by the resurrection of Jesus Christ. He is that Son of Man who received glory and dominion over all peoples, nations, and languages. Because Christ is risen — he is risen indeed! — the events of human history, no matter how great and terrifying, cannot touch the destiny of God's holy ones. And therefore, as the apostle Paul writes in Ephesians, we, the saints now living on earth, can live to the praise of his glory (Ephesians 1:6, 14). Amen.

1. Paul D. Hanson, *Old Testament Apocalyptic* (Nashville: Abingdon Press, 1987), p. 32.

Help From Habakkuk?

It can be really depressing to listen to the news anymore. It doesn't matter which network you watch, everywhere you turn it's the same old bad news: natural and manmade disasters, the continuing conflicts in the Middle East and in Iraq and Afghanistan, medical miscues, entertainers gone wild and self-destructive, sports heroes disappointing us. Then there's a federal government that often seems to be, at best, incompetent or, at worst, corrupt. What makes it even more depressing is that at least 51% of us voted those currently in the White House and on Capitol Hill into office! We have no one to blame but ourselves. We seem to have lost our way.

What do we do? Where can we turn?

Almost 500 years ago a monk in Germany was faced with a similar state of affairs. All of society in his day was built around the institution of the church. However, that monk found institutional corruption all around him, supported by a theology that was essentially bankrupt and could not adequately deal with the question of evil in this world and the power of sin in a person's life. In his struggle and search for an answer that monk found it in a most unlikely place. Martin Luther found help from Habakkuk.

Help from Habakkuk? Habakkuk? Most of us probably can't find it in our Bibles — hint, it's between Nahum and Zephaniah (as if that's any help!) — nor can we figure out how to pronounce it: is it Ha-BAK-kuk or HA-ba-KKUK?

While biblical names have always figured prominently on lists of children's names, I would bet that when the young couples today start working on a list of names for their future children, Habakkuk is *not* going to be on that list. Habakkuk as a name or as a book of the Bible, seems to get short shrift.

This is the only passage from Habakkuk that appears in the three-year cycle of readings for worship, so you aren't going to hear many sermons based on this short book of only three chapters either. In fact, in 25 years of ministry, with a conservative estimate of about 1,000 sermons given, I believe this is the first one I've preached from Habakkuk!

Back to that German monk: In Luther's search for meaning and help he stumbled upon Habakkuk as he was studying Paul's letter to the Romans. When he read Paul's quoting of the last phrase from the reading in Habakkuk, "the righteous live by their faith" (2:4), at that moment, the good news of Jesus Christ finally broke through and grabbed hold of the heart, mind, and soul of that fearful, angry, and confused young man — and the world has not been the same since.[1] If you are a Protestant Christian, then, in a very real sense you are in church today because Luther found help from Habakkuk. Maybe, just maybe, then, Habakkuk can speak to us and be of help to us, too!

The situation Habakkuk describes in his first two chapters could be right out of one of our nightly newscasts. As the prophet looks around him he sees only injustice, violence, and destruction. He even asks the questions that we ask: "Where is God in all of this?" "Is God listening to us?" "Is God with us?" "Are we being punished?"

The response God gave to Habakkuk is the same response we are given. In the midst of everything that is frightening and challenging, God reminds us that the perpetrators of violence and injustice in this world are sowing the seed of their own eventual destruction, but that the seed for life has already been planted in the righteous.

God promises that the righteous will live — that is, they will endure — by faith. This is not obnoxious Christian triumphalism or unrealistic cockiness. This does not mean that everything will go our way and turn out how we want it. It is not a matter of having a bigger, which we believe means a better, faith, but faith through patience, serving, giving, and forgiving without expecting anything in return.

We have to admit, however, that's not natural for us. We think like the disciples — when things are going tough, or when Christian discipleship turns out to be more radical and demanding than we expected, we ask, "Lord, increase our faith!" (Luke 17:5). The assumption is that if I just had more faith, then everything would be okay in my life, in my family, in my church, in this country, and even in the world.

But when we say, "amen," to the disciples' request we betray a basic misunderstanding of faith as a commodity we possess or as a personal achievement. Jesus' parable of the mustard seed illustrates our mistake in thinking (Luke 13:18-19; 17:5-6). In that story Jesus is saying that the level of faith really isn't the issue. What matters is in whom you put your trust — the quality not the quantity is the issue. When we think of faith as a commodity or as an achievement we end up trusting in our trust — we end up making faith a work. But that doesn't free us; it just enslaves us to doubt and fear about whether we can ever be sure we have done enough.

Again, what matters is the one in whom we trust — not ourselves, not even our faith, but the love of God, through Jesus Christ, crucified and risen. That is our treasure to guard. That is what Luther rediscovered and what set him free. That is what will set us free to grow in faith.

It's interesting that when the disciples were sent out to do the more spectacular stuff, like casting out demons, healing, and preaching, they didn't ask for more faith. But when Jesus started talking about resisting temptation and not leading others into temptation, about confronting fellow believers with their sin, and then forgiving them when they sinned, well, then the disciples realized this discipleship thing wasn't really about fame and glory.

Faith is all fine and good, and we claim to want more of it, if it will help us get healing for ourselves or a loved one. Faith is "cool" if it will help us pass a test or meet a deadline. But we don't want it to cramp our style or our lifestyle. The truth of the matter is that many people only want an inoculation of Christianity — just enough of it to protect them from catching the real thing. However, the faith Jesus calls us to, and the sort of faith that endures and leads to life — real life, a life worth living — is one that will make us more Christ-like in sacrificial living, giving, loving, and forgiving.

In one scene in the movie *Evan Almighty*, Morgan Freeman, who plays God, is incognito as a waiter in a restaurant. He has a conversation with the wife of the lead character, Evan Baxter, a first-year US Congressman, who believes God has told him to build an ark. In some lines of great wisdom and spiritual insight, the waiter/God says:

> *If someone asks for patience, do you think God gives that person more patience, or does he give him more opportunities to be patient? If he prays for courage does God give him courage or opportunities for him to be courageous? If someone prayed for the family to be closer, do you think God zaps them with warm, fuzzy feelings, or does he give them more opportunities to love each other?*[2]

That's how it is with faith. Faith, like a muscle, can only grow through exercise and daily, vigorous use. That is how the quality of our faith increases — by putting it into practice on a daily basis right where God has planted us, even in the midst of a world that seems to be falling apart at the seams.

God, the Father, has given us more than what we need to cope with this world through the life, death, and resurrection of the Son and his continuing presence with us through the power of the Holy Spirit. Our hope is secure because death, violence, oppression, and injustice do not have the final word in our lives or in the world.

Therefore, as the psalmist says, we can commit our way to the Lord, trusting that God will act (Psalm 37:). And as HaBAKkuk (or HAbaKKUK) reminds us, we can endure the struggles of the present with patience and hope with joy because of the promised future God has planned for us. Amen.

1. Roland H. Bainton, *Here I Stand: A Life of Martin Luther* (New York: Mentor Books, 1950), pp. 49-50.

2. *Evan Almighty*, produced by Barber, Birnbaum, and Bostick, directed by Tom Shadyac, ninety minutes, Universal Pictures and Spyglass Entertainment, 2007.

Making Something Out Of Nothing

Making something out of nothing. We often use that phrase in a negative sense. For example, when we believe someone is reading way too much into a situation or when someone is overreacting and jumping to conclusions that aren't merited by the actual situation or facts, we dismiss the person's comments by saying, "You're making something out of nothing," or "You're just making a mountain out of a molehill!" The Jewish people who had returned out of exile in Babylon to Judah and Jerusalem during the reign of Darius/Cyrus of Persia were pretty down about the situation facing them. After seventy years in exile under the Babylonians, those who wished to had been allowed to return to their homeland. However, what may have begun in great excitement with high expectations quickly settled into a hard struggle for existence. The return had turned into a huge disappointment; what originally looked like small molehills in the first blush of effort, soon began to look like insurmountable mountains as the returnees struggled to survive under difficult conditions.

What made the situation worse was the memory of how things used to be. Though the final 100 years of Judah as a state had been played out under pressures from the surrounding empires, the communal memory viewed the time before the exile through rose-tinted glasses. The hardships that came from being kicked around as a political soccer ball by Egypt, Assyria, and then Babylon, were conveniently forgotten. All that was remembered was how good things supposedly had once been, and especially how grand the temple in Jerusalem had been before.

The Jewish people had a history of experiencing selective memory loss when it came to looking back on their past. Many centuries earlier the children of Israel, fresh after having been led out of Egypt, began to favorably compare their condition as oppressed slaves in Egypt with the initial challenges of freedom on the road with God. After only a few days of hardship in the wilderness they were ready to return to slavery in Egypt! Faced with the challenge of relative freedom again, their descendants who had returned from Babylon in the sixth century BC were also suddenly afflicted with a faulty memory of their recent past. We should not be too quick to criticize, though, because those discouraged people in Jerusalem did not have a monopoly on that particular character flaw. Humanity in general seems to be afflicted with the same spiritual "genetic" defect in terms of memory.

When the real world does not match up to our oftentimes unrealistic expectations, we tend to elevate the not too distant past to the status of a golden age. What was not long ago thought of as the "bad old days" and the source of our current troubles, suddenly is transformed into the "good old days." The revisionist memory of those "good old days" can be a heavy burden that sabotages the present and potentially robs us of the future God has in mind for us. The warm memory of a fuzzy, golden age of the past can paralyze us from working in the reality of the present. That happens at all levels of human interaction, but especially in times of crisis when a nation or a family or even a church has to deal with change. That's what happened to the people who returned to Jerusalem; they couldn't reconcile their memory of a supposed "golden age" and the grandeur of the temple before with the crude new beginning they were making.

The words of the prophet Haggai, then, were words meant for a depressed and discouraged people who had been paralyzed by their memory of the past and how the present did not seem to match up. They had discovered that it is easier to just give in to the disappointment than it is to make the effort at something new. They had given up and so they had no energy for the effort that was needed.

Haggai makes the case that, in spite of the slow and difficult start to the work of rebuilding, in spite of the setbacks, and in spite of the apparent futility of it all, God was going to make something out of nothing. The prophet proclaimed that the people were making too much out of the difficulties of the return from captivity and exile, and, instead, should have been focusing on the promise of the presence of God with them.

Now this message shouldn't have been surprising to God's people then, and it shouldn't be surprising to us now. Making something out of nothing seems to be God's preferred *modus operandi* — God's normal method of operation. "In the beginning" scripture informs us, God quite literally made all matter out of nothing other than God's own thought and plan and spoke it all into existence. Later, God started a nation out of two senior citizens, Abraham and Sarah, whom, we are told by the apostle Paul, were so advanced in age that they were as good as dead (Romans 4:10). When the descendants of Abraham and Sarah were in danger of being eliminated by the ancient Egyptians, God led the slaves out of bondage to freedom and nationhood. Later, an insignificant shepherd boy would be anointed king and become the ideal for all the future rulers of God's chosen people.

Making something out of nothing — that's how God works. Haggai was certain of it and proclaimed in his message to the people that God was going to do it again. It bears repeating, that shouldn't have been and shouldn't now be a surprise for God's people. Therefore, God says through Haggai, "... work, for I am with you, says the Lord of hosts, according to the promise that I made you when you came out of Egypt. My spirit abides among you; do not fear" (Haggai 2:4c-5). Take note of the language and the tense of the verbs here: "I *am* with you ... my Spirit *abides* among you." While the people were focused on the past presence of God in the temple with his people, God proclaimed in the present tense that he was still with the people in their then-present, difficult situation and that God's Spirit had not departed, but was still among the people.

The good news is that God meets us where we are, not where we want or would prefer to be. Former President George W. Bush learned the hard way the value and importance of meeting people where they are when, in the opinion of many, he made the mistake of not going into the Hurricane Katrina disaster area quickly enough after that event. Apparently the Chinese leadership learned from President Bush's mistake; after the 2008 massive earthquake, they were almost immediately on the ground in the affected area. The God revealed in the Bible is not a God just for the happy, easy, and peaceful times, but meets us where we are in all of the messiness of life where the needs are greatest, "even and especially in downsized circumstances like a rebuilt temple in a ravaged Jerusalem."[1]

Seventy years earlier than Haggai's time, the Jewish people were surprised by the prophet Jeremiah's message that God would be with them even in exile. Then, in the midst of the depressing reality of their return to what they had hoped would be the dawning of a new golden age, they were reminded that God was still with them in the difficulties of the rebuilding phase. Significantly, they were reminded that God's presence with them was not dependent upon the grandeur of the temple building made with their own hands. In other words, they could not "make" God be present with them, but God's presence was a promise given to them.

As long as we are under the mistaken impression that our efforts can somehow cause God's presence and favor to be with us, we condemn ourselves to disappointment and become slaves to the paralyzing fear of failure. However, once we receive the promise of the presence of God as pure gift, then we are freed to work for God in the present with courage and joy without fear. The present reality, no matter how difficult it may appear, does not give us the full, big picture. What we see going on around us can be deceiving. All of the biblical prophets, but especially those of the exile and return, were always trying to get the people of God to see the bigger picture and thereby have hope. Without that hope nothing of lasting significance will ever even be begun. The reformer, Martin Luther, once said, "Everything that is done in the world is done by the hopeful." It was the gift of hope that made it possible for those who had returned to Jerusalem to "take the promises of God in hand, along with an ax, and go into the mountains to chop down trees for the Temple."[2]

Haggai's basic message for God's people then and now is that because of the promise of God's presence with us we no longer need to be in the negative business of making something out of nothing through worry and disappointment, which only leads us into depression. Instead, we are to let God, in the positive sense, make something out of our nothings. Our failures, our weaknesses, our difficulties are not a barrier for God. After all, "for God all things are possible" (Matthew 19:26). In fact, *nothing*, in the hands of God, always becomes *something*. Those of us who live after Easter have the greatest sign of God's ability to make something — a new creation — even out of the nothingness of the cross of Christ. Therefore, we have hope. We can take courage. We can both pray and work, knowing that God holds the future. Amen.

------

1. "In the Dust and the Dirt: Greater Glory in Lesser Circumstances," *The Journey with Jesus: Notes to Myself*, Daniel B. Clendenin, June 8, 2007. Accessed May 29, 2008. http://www.journeywithjesus.net/Essays/20071105JJ.shtml.

2. "24th Sunday After Pentecost, November 11, 2007," Dennis Bratcher, copyright © 2007, Dennis Bratcher. CRI / Voice, Institute. Last modified: October 24, 2007. Accessed May 28, 2008. http://www.cresourcei.org/lectionary/YearC/Cproper27ot.html.

A New Beginning

I am a lousy typist. My keyboard skills are rudimentary and functional, at best. I blame it all on the fact that I grew up before the computer age and went to a small boarding school in Australia for my high school years, one that didn't offer a typing class to those students on the academic track. The end result is that I suffer from a lot of stray finger movements and poor positioning when I type, especially on the smaller keyboard of my laptop computer. That can be disastrous when an imprecise and inadvertent little finger movement brushes the insert or delete key right in the middle of the final editing of a sermon. One moment, I am blissfully — if slowly — inserting new insights and additions; the next, I discover — when I finally look up at the screen — that the three most important paragraphs of my message have just been delete/typed over. Thank God (and I mean that sincerely) for the Ctrl + Z "undo" command!

Using the metaphor of typing input, most of the messages of the prophet Isaiah could be understood as insertions that more or less flow on from what came before. However, on a few occasions, Isaiah seems to have purposefully hit the delete key. In chapters 42 and 43 of Isaiah, for example, God speaks through the prophet announcing a "new thing" God is about to do (Isaiah 42:9; 43:18 ff). That "new thing" then was the return of the people from exile in Babylon. The first reading for this Sunday is perhaps the most emphatic and dramatic announcement of all. God is planning an even newer "new thing," something so new that mere editing will no longer suffice. What God has in mind is not just a restoration or a return to the status quo before the exile; it is such a new thing that it demands the verb only used of God in the Hebrew scriptures. In fact, it is the very first verb of the Bible and describes the primary activity of God — to create. This new creative act of God is so novel that the former things will no longer be remembered or come to mind.

What are those "former things"? Now it is possible that God is saying the new creative work about to be accomplished is so novel that the mighty acts of God from the past will be overshadowed by this new thing. Possible, but unlikely, I think. Given the context of this passage it is more probable the former things that will not be remembered are the "former troubles" — that is, the defeat by Babylon, the exile and its aftermath, referred to in verse 16 immediately before our reading (Isaiah 65:16b; 64:20-22).

There have been times in the past when I was working on a sermon and it just simply wouldn't work out right. No matter how many times I manipulated the theme I was working with, moving words and phrases and even whole paragraphs or sections around, I couldn't get it right. My disappointment in the process would eventually lead me to begin to lose interest in the sermon and despair of ever getting it done in time for Sunday — a pastor's nightmare! What I really needed was to start all over again from the foundation of the text. I needed fresh, new insights from God's word.

The people to whom Isaiah chapter 65 was originally addressed were living through a long nightmare. Though God's people had been allowed to return from exile in Babylon, few had actually chosen to do so after 538 BC. Twenty or more years later the returnees still faced nearly insurmountable economic and social obstacles that made survival a day-to-day struggle. As time went on with little or no improvement in conditions, the people were faced with a theological crisis. The prophets had all promised, hadn't they, a new day and a glorious future after exile? Where was the expected restored Davidic kingdom? The city of Jerusalem was still in ruins, the temple, if already rebuilt, was a pale shadow of its former glory, and the people were on the verge of despair. They were disappointed in their situation, in their ability to get beyond survival mode to reconstruction, and, most significant of all, there was disappointment with God.

To start talking about disappointment with God is problematic for us. It is a problem for us because so many of the most visible and apparently "successful" ministries in modern American religious life are intentionally and relentlessly upbeat and positive with a strong emphasis on the triumphs of Christian living. This popular version/corruption of the Christian faith is not helpful because, as Phillip Yancey points out in his book, *Disappointment With God*, when the promised and expected dramatic evidence of God working in our lives does not materialize, it inevitably leads to feelings of "disappointment, betrayal, and often guilt."[1] When actual experiences do not live up to our expectations over a long period of time we start to give up on ourselves, others, and even God. Those feelings of disappointment with God probably occur far more frequently than we are willing to publicly — or even privately — admit.

The advice to "just try harder" simply won't do it for us. An edited, more upbeat version of our lives isn't what is needed. Since the disappointment is with God, only an act of God can remedy the situation. What is required is a new thing, and only God can do that for us because only God can create. Therefore, any genuine newness that could and would come for the returnees in Judah, would not be their own doing, no matter how righteous they might have tried to be. The evidence of their own history weighed heavily against their succeeding in that effort. It is the same for us. The evidence of history also weighs heavily against our efforts at self-editing. No, any newness that emerges in the community of faith's future will always be God's creation. It is a gift.

God announces just such a gift: A new heavens and a new earth in which the failures and punishments of the past will no longer be remembered, disaster will be replaced with realized potential, and joy, not disappointment, will mark the relationship between God and his people. All of the negative former things will be no more, as if they had been typed right over. The language and imagery used does not only address the situation of the exile and restoration,

405

but also the curses of the fall and the blessings of the original creation. Verse 17 immediately calls to mind the first verse of Genesis, "In the beginning when God created the heavens and the earth ..." (Genesis 1:1). The curse of work and the struggle of agriculture will be reversed (vv. 21-23a), sickness and death will begin to be undone (vv. 19-20), and the first blessing of creation, to be fruitful and multiply, will be renewed for God's people (v. 23). This new thing God is about to do is almost a matter of going "back to the future."

In other words, this is not just hopeful, wishful thinking, pie-in-the-sky stuff. The Hebrew verb "create" in verses 17 and 18 is not a pure future tense. It can be translated as "I am beginning to create." Therefore, the new heavens and the earth, though not yet fully manifested, have already begun to appear. There is continuity and discontinuity with present reality; what God does always has an "already but not yet" quality to it from a human perspective locked in time. But the prophet is able to see time and space from God's perspective, which is not chronological and episodic. Past, present, and future are all held by God, and from God's perspective are not isolated events in time but are part of a whole with a plan and a purpose.

So, while the tone of the message is apocalyptic and futuristic, the promised future echoes the purity of God's beginning for the world, and the message is meant for the here and now, real-life situation of God's people in the present. God's new creation begins now and is expressed in down-to-earth images that are familiar: Jerusalem, agriculture, work, and birth.

The slate is wiped clean — the former things will not be remembered — and so God's people can move ahead into the future planned for them by going "back" to God's new beginning with a fresh start. This text is an appropriate one for us liturgically as we come to the end of the church year. It leads us to reflect upon God's fulfillment of his plan and purpose for all of creation in terms of realized potential. The whole disaster of the exile was proclaimed by the true prophets from the seventh through fifth centuries BC as being the direct result of the failure of God's people and its religious and political leaders to realize their full potential as the people

406

of God. God's solution to humanity's self-inflicted wounds, however, is not to leave us to our own devices. A bit of self-editing will not do the job. God does not even wait for us to come to our senses and ask for help, but "before they call I will answer, while they are yet speaking I will hear" (v. 24).

God takes full initiative. That is our only hope. Only God's initiative could redeem the mess God's people had made of their history and its effects on their present and future. God still takes full initiative. Only he can type over the mess we have made of our lives through disobedience and give us a fresh start through forgiveness. For Christians, we understand that a new beginning is made available and is realized in our lives through faith in the life, death, and resurrection of Jesus Christ. In his ministry of healing, freeing, and restoration we see the firstfruits of the new creation God has begun. His death for us "Xs" out or deletes all of those "former things" that leave us in bondage to fear and disappointment. In him we become God's new creation. In Christ, the firstborn of all creation, we have fullness of joy. In him we can again be a delight to God, living and working toward the full potential of God's future for this world God loves so much. Amen.

---

1. Phillip Yancey, *Disappointment With God* (Grand Rapids: Zondervan, 1988), p. 9.

Christ The King
Proper 29
Jeremiah 23:1-6

Shepherds Who Will Shepherd

A few years ago, Michael Crichton, of *Jurassic Park* and the television series *ER* fame, wrote a novel called *State of Fear*.[1] Crichton's book wasn't just for entertainment, though; it had an agenda, evidenced by the presence of footnotes, a 31-page bibliography, two appendices, and an addendum, titled "Author's Message." One of the basic messages of the book is that governments and special interest groups try to control society through maintaining a constant "state of fear" by manipulating and even creating the information made available to the public on social issues and world events.

While a person might question many of the conclusions Crichton suggests, his basic premise resonates with God's verdict against the religious and political rulers of God's people in the days of Jeremiah, the prophet. Those leaders were supposed to help the people become all that God had meant for them to be. They had failed miserably in their divinely appointed role of giving direction and support to the people and in aiding them to serve and love the Lord their God with all their heart, soul, and mind (Deuteronomy 6:5).

The religious and political leaders — court prophets, priests, and kings — had conspired together to control information — they oppressed and tried to shut up those contrary voices, like that of Jeremiah (Jeremiah 20:1-2; 26:10-11). They tried to make God's spiritual whistle blowers, the prophets, into the scapegoats, a tactic still used today. One other modern deplorable political tactic is perhaps hinted at in the reference to sheep "missing" from the flock

(v. 4). The phrase seems eerily similar to the sinister practice of making political prisoners and opponents or whole racial and tribal groups go "missing" through torture or genocide. Political manipulation and control of that kind certainly produces a "state of fear" that has a devastating affect on those who are being led.

God's message through the prophet Jeremiah is, first of all, a biting satirical condemnation of improper and failed leadership. The condemnation relies heavily on word plays and associations in the Hebrew language. The leaders, including especially the kings of Judah following the death of Josiah in 609 BC, were not being the shepherds they were supposed to be but instead were destroying the sheep and the flock, bringing evil on the people. The words for shepherd and for evil (v. 2) are very close in Hebrew: *ra 'ah* (shepherd) and *roa'* (evil). In written form the only difference between the two is that of one less root character for "evil." This wordplay suggests that when shepherds are less than they were meant to be, the people under their care experience evil — they are destroyed, scattered, go missing, and are filled with fear and dismay.

Therefore, because they had not attended to God's flock in the positive sense of caring for them, God will, in the negative sense, attend to the leadership (v. 2). At this point the biting satirical condemnation changes to a promise of what the true shepherd of God's people will do. All that God plans to do will be a reversal of what the failed leadership had done in the past: God intends to gather the remnant of his flock, bring them back to their fold, and will raise up for them shepherds in God's stead who will shepherd (vv. 3-4). Even the fact of the people having been driven away into other lands takes on a positive sense as having been part of God's ultimate plan for his restoration of the people. This restoration harks back to creation with the blessing to "be fruitful and multiply" (v. 3) and will result in the removal of fear and dismay from among God's people (v. 4; Genesis 1:28). All of this will occur because God will raise up leaders who will fulfill their God-given ministry as shepherds.

Isn't it interesting that powerful animal images have been used to represent most countries or kingdoms in human history? The lion for England, the bear for Russia, and for the United States, not the turkey (as suggested by Benjamin Franklin, believe it or not!), but the bald eagle. For God's people, though, the most cherished and meaningful image was that of the shepherd, a rich combination of both power and gentle care. The metaphor of the shepherd was rooted in the nomadic past of God's people as well as in God's choice of Moses — himself a herder when he received the call — to lead the children of Israel out of Egypt and through the wilderness for forty years. Given that established pattern, it is no wonder that God later anointed a shepherd boy, David, as king over God's people. In other words, the model of the Messiah, the anointed shepherd of Israel, was not really based *on* David, but the other way around: Leadership in Israel was a matter of growing into the ideal of God as the peoples' true shepherd.

Therefore, Zedekiah, though technically in the royal line, was not a "righteous [or legitimate] branch" (v. 5). He was not a shepherd "after God's own heart" (1 Samuel 13:14), but a puppet of the Babylonians. In fact, his reign was so antithetical to God's intent that his name is ridiculed in a final wordplay. The puppet king's name meant, "the righteousness of the Lord," which is in the reverse order of the name by which the future king out of David's line will be called: "the Lord is our righteousness." In other words, Zedekiah was the opposite in wisdom, justice, and righteousness of what a true shepherd of God's people should be.

Zedekiah and all the last kings of Judah suffered from a failure of conscience that was disastrous for the people and the nation. Jewish and Roman leadership in the time of Jesus was also marked by the same failure, which resulted in an attempt at deicide (god-killing) when Jesus was crucified and put to death. The same has been true all through human history, even that of our nation. Haven't we been at our weakest when our leaders have shown a failure of conscience and done or allowed things to happen that violate at least the spirit if not the letter of our "covenant" — the US Constitution? Isn't that true in the church or the family as well when we cave in to societal pressures or slavishly adhere to tradition and how things have always been done or put our own needs and wants before those whom we are supposed to be shepherding?

411

The failure of Zedekiah and those shepherds immediately prior to him is a precautionary word for all who would lead God's people — pastors, teachers, mentors, and parents. If you think about that list for a moment, you'll realize that no follower of Jesus Christ is excluded. Over the course of a lifetime each of us will be called to at least one of those shepherding roles. Whether as a pastor or teacher or council member or as an adult Christian simply trying to daily live out the faith as a model for younger believers, we all have a bit of the shepherd's ministry.

Our model is that "righteous branch" whom God did raise up: Jesus, who enfleshed the ideal of God's shepherding of his people. Jesus, the good shepherd, the true shepherd-king, was not born in a palace, but in a stable with simple shepherds in attendance, making up his first audience. He was not carried about in a chariot or by palanquin above the dust of life, but walked in it with the people. He was robed in the towel of servanthood. He was crowned with the thorns of suffering, and raised up, not on an ornate throne, but on a rough, wooden cross. The true shepherd-king would gather God's flock from every nation, tribe, and race, and by his death and resurrection would free all from Satan's fearmongering. The true shepherd-king would not let even a convicted criminal hanging on a cross next to his own go missing, but would graciously usher him into the kingdom and into the presence of God.

That is our model. Leadership in the church and in the family isn't about manipulation, control, and dominance. It is all about sacrifice and service that removes fear and dismay and gathers in the lost, the missing, and the scattered. It is all about following Jesus, in word and deed. Only in him and in his way do we receive the great joy and responsibility of fulfilling our God-given ministry as shepherds for the flock that God loves so much. Amen.

---

1. Michael Crichton, *State of Fear* (New York: Avon Books, 2004).

Thanksgiving Is
Nine-Tenths Of Possession

In law I believe there is a basic legal principle that goes something to the effect that "possession is nine-tenths of the law." In other words, in a property or land dispute, the onus is really on the person who claims the other has his or her possession. It is a corollary, I suppose, to "innocent until proven guilty." Therefore, the person who has possession of the disputed property does not have to prove ownership, the plaintiff does.

It seems to me that the first reading for Thanksgiving Day suggests a similar theological principle: that thanksgiving is nine-tenths of possession. While we may be able to get our heads around the legal principle about possession being nine-tenths of the law, the theological principle may not immediately be as clear and obvious. What *do* I mean by the phrase, "thanksgiving is nine-tenths of possession"? Let's take a close look at the reading.

The lesson from Deuteronomy 26 looks ahead to the future when the people of Israel will have been in the land promised to them by God long enough to have planted their first crops. By the basic legal principle of "possession is nine-tenths of the law" they will by then have already possessed the land. However, on the theological level there would still be something missing from the equation.

What is missing? An important element we've all seen before. How many times did we, as children, receive a gift from some family member at Christmas or for a birthday and become so caught up in the excitement of the gift that our parents had to stop us and remind us of an important part of receiving a gift? Children of every generation have heard their parents ask that same leading question, tinged with a bit of embarrassment on the parents' part, "Honey, what do you say...?" The words the parents want to hear, of course, are "thank you." Sometimes, if the child is so wound up that he or she refuses to say those two magic words, the gift might have to be taken away for a while, until the child has calmed down enough to be verbally appreciative. The level of appreciation for a gift is often revealed in the tone of the thanks spoken by the recipient. That tone can be quite instructive of how much the person likes and will — or will not — use and, therefore, "have" or possess the gift. There's no question about it: Some of the most basic human interactions show how thanksgiving for, and possession of, a gift are very closely intertwined.

So, though the people had been in the land at least long enough to prepare the fields, plant, grow, and begin to harvest a crop, their possession of the land wasn't truly complete. There was still one final element to the equation, and that element was thanksgiving to God. It was not until the people took the firstfruit of the ground and laid it before God that they were truly able to declare that they had come into the land that God had sworn to give to their ancestors (vv. 1-3). The deep theological principle here is that we don't really possess the gifts of God until we give thanks for them. Thanksgiving *is* nine-tenths of possession.

Our lesson for today reveals that biblical thanksgiving has a shape and a structure to it that can be summed up as follows: Thanksgiving is intentional, sacrificial, liturgical, and communal.

First, thanksgiving is an intentional act of the will. It is not just a transitory, spontaneous emotional response (v. 3). It is part of the joyful duty of being in covenant relationship to God. As such, it is something that can be planned for in advance and, to a certain degree, scheduled so as not to be forgotten. Perhaps, you too, have experienced the shame of a "thank you" that was forgotten and thereby put a close relationship under some strain. The opposite of that is the fun involved in planning out a surprise thank you to someone who has been a blessing to you or to your congregation.

Next, biblical thanksgiving usually involves surrender and sacrifice. There is a certain amount of risk in offering up the firstfruits of the ground. Those firstfruits are sometimes the best of the crop; they are certainly a sure thing. There is no guarantee the rest of the crop will come in; the land may flood, locusts swarms, or wildfires may destroy the crop, or sickness and injury may prevent the owner from getting the harvest in on time. The offering up of the firstfruits is an intentional and sacrificial act of faith in the continuing blessings of God (vv. 2, 4, 10). The amazing thing that people of faith have discovered down through the ages is that sacrificial giving back to God in thanksgiving doesn't really leave you poorer. Martin Luther's experience speaks for them all. He said, "I have held many things in my hands, and I have lost them all; but whatever I have placed in God's hands, that I still possess."

Thanksgiving, according to Deuteronomy 26 is also liturgical and, therefore, public in nature. It involves a proclamation, a recital of who and whose we are, where we are from and where we are headed, because of what God has done for us. The act of thanksgiving recognizes that it is God who actually owns everything. One offertory prayer beautifully captures that reality:

> *Merciful Father, we offer with joy and thanksgiving what you have first given us — our selves, our time, and our possessions, signs of your gracious love. Receive them for the sake of him who offered himself for us, Jesus Christ our Lord. Amen.*[1]

The liturgical recital acknowledges that our very identity as God's people and as stewards of God's creation is closely tied to thanksgiving (vv. 5-9). To be a steward *is* to be thankful.

Finally, biblical thanksgiving is not simply a private spiritual transaction between God and me witnessed by a religious professional, but thanksgiving to God is not complete until it has been shared with others. We are used to thinking of Thanksgiving Day as primarily family time. However, the original Thanksgiving celebration at Plymouth and Deuteronomy 26 encourage us to enlarge our vision.

The Pilgrims' feast significantly included not just all social strata of the colonists but also the local Native-American tribe. I seriously doubt that we would still be celebrating the memory of that day if the Native Americans had not been invited to be an integral part of the event. Similarly, the children of Israel were to include the resident aliens who lived among them in their thanksgiving event. This provision is significant because the people of God had themselves been resident aliens in Egypt. To exclude the aliens among them would have been to deny their own history and identity and to betray what God had done for them in giving them a land. In the words of Jesus, they were to do unto others as they would have others do unto them — and *not* as the Egyptians had treated them. Thanksgiving means to break with old, oppressive patterns. The celebration itself is a protest against those old exclusivist and prejudiced patterns of acting and thinking.

The gifts of God, chief among them being the gift of God's love in Christ Jesus, really aren't ours in the fullest sense until we have thanked God by sharing them with others. When that happens the thanksgiving grows and grows — and with it, the blessing of the gift.

Thanksgiving *is* nine-tenths of possession. Amen.

---

1. Lutheran Church in America, The American Lutheran Church, The Evangelical Lutheran Church of Canada, and The Lutheran Church — Missouri Synod, *Lutheran Book of Worship* (Minneapolis: Augsburg, 1978), p. 67.

Lectionary Preaching After Pentecost

The following index will aid the user of this book in matching the correct Sunday with the appropriate text during Pentecost. All texts in this book are from the series for the first readings, Revised Common Lectionary. (Note that the ELCA division of Lutheranism is now following the Revised Common Lectionary.) The Lutheran designations indicate days comparable to Sundays on which Revised Common Lectionary Propers or Ordinary Time designations are used.

(Fixed dates do not pertain to Lutheran Lectionary)

Fixed Date Lectionaries *Revised Common (including ELCA)* *and Roman Catholic*	Lutheran Lectionary *Lutheran*
The Day Of Pentecost	The Day Of Pentecost
The Holy Trinity	The Holy Trinity
May 29-June 4 — Proper 4, Ordinary Time 9	Pentecost 2
June 5-11 — Proper 5, Ordinary Time 10	Pentecost 3
June 12-18 — Proper 6, Ordinary Time 11	Pentecost 4
June 19-25 — Proper 7, Ordinary Time 12	Pentecost 5
June 26-July 2 — Proper 8, Ordinary Time 13	Pentecost 6
July 3-9 — Proper 9, Ordinary Time 14	Pentecost 7
July 10-16 — Proper 10, Ordinary Time 15	Pentecost 8
July 17-23 — Proper 11, Ordinary Time 16	Pentecost 9
July 24-30 — Proper 12, Ordinary Time 17	Pentecost 10
July 31-Aug. 6 — Proper 13, Ordinary Time 18	Pentecost 11
Aug. 7-13 — Proper 14, Ordinary Time 19	Pentecost 12
Aug. 14-20 — Proper 15, Ordinary Time 20	Pentecost 13
Aug. 21-27 — Proper 16, Ordinary Time 21	Pentecost 14
Aug. 28-Sept. 3 — Proper 17, Ordinary Time 22	Pentecost 15
Sept. 4-10 — Proper 18, Ordinary Time 23	Pentecost 16
Sept. 11-17 — Proper 19, Ordinary Time 24	Pentecost 17
Sept. 18-24 — Proper 20, Ordinary Time 25	Pentecost 18

417

Sept. 25-Oct. 1 — Proper 21, Ordinary Time 26	Pentecost 19
Oct. 2-8 — Proper 22, Ordinary Time 27	Pentecost 20
Oct. 9-15 — Proper 23, Ordinary Time 28	Pentecost 21
Oct. 16-22 — Proper 24, Ordinary Time 29	Pentecost 22
Oct. 23-29 — Proper 25, Ordinary Time 30	Pentecost 23
Oct. 30-Nov. 5 — Proper 26, Ordinary Time 31	Pentecost 24
Nov. 6-12 — Proper 27, Ordinary Time 32	Pentecost 25
Nov. 13-19 — Proper 28, Ordinary Time 33	Pentecost 26
	Pentecost 27
Nov. 20-26 — Christ The King	Christ The King

Reformation Day (or last Sunday in October) is October 31 (Revised Common, Lutheran)

All Saints (or first Sunday in November) is November 1 (Revised Common, Lutheran, Roman Catholic)

US/Canadian Lectionary Comparison

The following index shows the correlation between the Sundays and special days of the church year as they are titled or labeled in the Revised Common Lectionary published by the Consultation On Common Texts and used in the United States (the reference used for this book) and the Sundays and special days of the church year as they are titled or labeled in the Revised Common Lectionary used in Canada.

Revised Common Lectionary	Canadian Revised Common Lectionary
Advent 1	Advent 1
Advent 2	Advent 2
Advent 3	Advent 3
Advent 4	Advent 4
Christmas Eve	Christmas Eve
The Nativity Of Our Lord/ Christmas Day	The Nativity Of Our Lord
Christmas 1	Christmas 1
January 1/New Year's Day	January 1/The Name Of Jesus
Christmas 2	Christmas 2
The Epiphany Of Our Lord	The Epiphany Of Our Lord
The Baptism Of Our Lord/ Epiphany 1	The Baptism Of Our Lord/ Proper 1
Epiphany 2/Ordinary Time 2	Epiphany 2/Proper 2
Epiphany 3/Ordinary Time 3	Epiphany 3/Proper 3
Epiphany 4/Ordinary Time 4	Epiphany 4/Proper 4
Epiphany 5/Ordinary Time 5	Epiphany 5/Proper 5
Epiphany 6/Ordinary Time 6	Epiphany 6/Proper 6
Epiphany 7/Ordinary Time 7	Epiphany 7/Proper 7
Epiphany 8/Ordinary Time 8	Epiphany 8/Proper 8
The Transfiguration Of Our Lord/ Last Sunday After Epiphany	The Transfiguration Of Our Lord/ Last Sunday After Epiphany
Ash Wednesday	Ash Wednesday
Lent 1	Lent 1
Lent 2	Lent 2
Lent 3	Lent 3
Lent 4	Lent 4
Lent 5	Lent 5
Passion/Palm Sunday	Passion/Palm Sunday
Maundy Thursday	Holy/Maundy Thursday
Good Friday	Good Friday

Easter Day	The Resurrection Of Our Lord
Easter 2	Easter 2
Easter 3	Easter 3
Easter 4	Easter 4
Easter 5	Easter 5
Easter 6	Easter 6
The Ascension Of Our Lord	The Ascension Of Our Lord
Easter 7	Easter 7
The Day Of Pentecost	The Day Of Pentecost
The Holy Trinity	The Holy Trinity
Proper 4/Pentecost 2/O T 9*	Proper 9
Proper 5/Pent 3/O T 10	Proper 10
Proper 6/Pent 4/O T 11	Proper 11
Proper 7/Pent 5/O T 12	Proper 12
Proper 8/Pent 6/O T 13	Proper 13
Proper 9/Pent 7/O T 14	Proper 14
Proper 10/Pent 8/O T 15	Proper 15
Proper 11/Pent 9/O T 16	Proper 16
Proper 12/Pent 10/O T 17	Proper 17
Proper 13/Pent 11/O T 18	Proper 18
Proper 14/Pent 12/O T 19	Proper 19
Proper 15/Pent 13/O T 20	Proper 20
Proper 16/Pent 14/O T 21	Proper 21
Proper 17/Pent 15/O T 22	Proper 22
Proper 18/Pent 16/O T 23	Proper 23
Proper 19/Pent 17/O T 24	Proper 24
Proper 20/Pent 18/O T 25	Proper 25
Proper 21/Pent 19/O T 26	Proper 26
Proper 22/Pent 20/O T 27	Proper 27
Proper 23/Pent 21/O T 28	Proper 28
Proper 24/Pent 22/O T 29	Proper 29
Proper 25/Pent 23/O T 30	Proper 30
Proper 26/Pent 24/O T 31	Proper 31
Proper 27/Pent 25/O T 32	Proper 32
Proper 28/Pent 26/O T 33	Proper 33
Christ The King (Proper 29/O T 34)	Proper 34/Christ The King/ Reign Of Christ
Reformation Day (October 31)	Reformation Day (October 31)
All Saints (November 1 or 1st Sunday in November)	All Saints' Day (November 1)
Thanksgiving Day (4th Thursday of November)	Thanksgiving Day (2nd Monday of October)

*O T = Ordinary Time

420

About The Authors

Derl G. Keefer is the Adult Developmental Ministries Coordinator with the Adult Department of Sunday School and Discipleship International Ministries for the International Church of the Nazarene, located in Kansas City, Missouri. He has served in that position since 2001, following nearly three decades as the pastor of Nazarene congregations in Michigan, Indiana, and Illinois. Keefer is the author of *Open Doors for Teaching, Preaching, and Public Speaking, Let's Get Committed*, and four volumes of sermon outlines for Nazarene Publishing House; he is also the co-author of *Wedding Sermons & Marriage Ceremonies*, and the editor of two volumes of *The Wesleyan Preaching Annual*. His articles, devotions, and sermons have appeared in numerous publications, including *Preaching* magazine and *The Abingdon Preaching Annual*. He is a graduate of Southern Nazarene University and Nazarene Theological Seminary.

David J. Kalas is the pastor of First United Methodist Church in Whitewater, Wisconsin. He previously was the pastor of Emmanuel United Methodist Church in Appleton, Wisconsin. Prior to moving to Wisconsin in 1996, Kalas served for fifteen years in youth and pastoral ministries in Virginia and Ohio. He is a contributing writer for the preaching journal *Emphasis* (www.sermonsuite.com), and he is a coauthor of *Sermons on the First Readings* (Series II, Cycle A). Kalas is a graduate of the University of Virginia and Union Theological Seminary of Virginia.

Stephen P. McCutchan is a retired Presbyterian pastor who served congregations in Maryland, Pennsylvania, and North Carolina. McCutchan edits a quarterly newsletter for the Presbytery Pastoral Network, and he is a contributing writer for the online service *The Immediate Word* (www.sermonsuite.com). He is also the author of three volumes of lectionary devotions for CSS: *Water from the Rock*, *Streams of Living Water*, and *Water from the Well*; as well as *Good News for a Fractured Society* and *Experiencing the Psalms: Weaving the Psalms into Your Ministry and Faith* (Smyth & Helwys), which won the 2001 Angell Award from the Presbyterian Writers Guild. McCutchan collaborated on a CD titled *Deep Well for the Pastor* with singer David Bailey, available through the Presbyterian Distribution Service. He is a graduate of Muskingum College and Union Theological Seminary in New York City. For more information or to read McCutchan's blog, visit his website at www.smccutchan.com.

Chrysanne Timm has served as the pastor of Lutheran congregations in the Toledo, Ohio, area since 1985, and she is now the senior pastor of Olivet Lutheran Church (ELCA) in Sylvania, Ohio. She has been a member of the Board for Ministry of the Northwestern Ohio Synod, and currently serves on the synod's Mutual Ministry Committee for the Bishop. Timm is a graduate of Ohio State University (where she majored in Japanese language and literature) and Trinity Lutheran Seminary.

R. Kevin Mohr has served since 1999 as the pastor at English Evangelical Lutheran Church in Bluffton, Ohio. Prior to his current position, he and his wife Deborah were foreign missionaries of the ELCA in Madagascar for seventeen years, working with the Malagasy Lutheran Church. Mohr is a member of the Northwestern Ohio Synod's ethnic diversity taskforce, and he has served on the synod's Global Mission Board and its Companion Synod Committee. He is a graduate of Heidelberg College and Trinity Lutheran Seminary.